WITHDRAWN

CANEVILLE

CANEVILLE

THE SOCIAL STRUCTURE OF

A SOUTH AFRICAN TOWN

by Pierre L. van den Berghe
with the assistance of Edna Miller

WESLEYAN UNIVERSITY PRESS
Middletown, Connecticut

Library of Congress Catalog Card Number: 63-17796
Manufactured in the United States of America
FIRST EDITION

To Gordon W. Allport

"Of all vulgar modes of escaping from the consideration of the effect of the social and moral influences on the human mind, the most vulgar is that of attributing the diversities of conduct and character to inherent natural differences."

—JOHN STUART MILL

CONTENTS

Acknowledgments   ix

Chapter I.   The Aims, Scope, and Method of the Study   3

        II.   Caneville in Place and Time   15

       III.   The Cultural System   31

        IV.   The Power System   65

         V.   The Economic System   123

        VI.   The Status System   151

       VII.   Race Relations   197

      VIII.   Caneville in Transition   241

        IX.   Conclusions   254

Bibliography   261

Index   265

MAPS

South Africa showing location of the Sugar Belt   14

Township of Caneville   26

ACKNOWLEDGMENTS

Throughout my period of field work in Caneville my collaborator Edna Miller and I have encountered kindness, friendship, co-operation, and warm hospitality from a great many people. To name them would be an invidious task and would reveal the identity of the town. All local proper names used here, whether of places, persons, or organizations, are ficticious. I should however like to mention collectively the teachers of the various schools, the employees of the Caneville Sugar Company and the Town Council, and a number of businessmen, religious leaders, independent professionals, and members of voluntary associations. The sugar company in particular extended its full co-operation with the clear understanding that I would remain completely independent from it. Doing field work in Caneville has proven an enriching and rewarding experience for Edna Miller and me. We both grew very fond of the town and made many friends. We want to express our sincerest thanks to the people of Caneville for all they have given us.

To Gordon W. Allport, to whom this study is dedicated, I owe not only great intellectual stimulation during my graduate years at Harvard, but also my interest in South Africa and my choice of Caneville for an intensive study. Edna Miller ably assisted me at various stages of the study, particularly in the collection and analysis of the data. To Hilda and Leo Kuper, J. F. Holleman, David McAllester, Ben Magubane, and Jack and Len Mann I am indebted for reading the field notes and manuscript and offering valuable criticisms and encouragement. My wife Irmgard deserves credit for her unfailing moral support, clerical assistance, and astute suggestions. The Institute for Social Research at the University of Natal extended its full co-operation to this study, particularly in preparing the manuscript for publication. Without a generous grant from the Ford Foundation, this study would not have been possible. The responsibility for the views expressed here is entirely my own, however. To all those who have helped me, I wish to express my sincere appreciation.

Durban, 1961   P. L. v. d. B.

CANEVILLE

THE AIMS, SCOPE, AND METHOD
OF THE STUDY

As ɪᴛs title indicates, this study is a sociological monograph on a small sugar town near the Indian Ocean coast of South Africa. One of the central themes of this book is that Caneville, in spite of its idiosyncracies, represents in most important respects a microcosm of the country to which it belongs. While any detailed description of South Africa clearly falls outside the scope of the present study, we shall nevertheless attempt to draw a thumb-nail sketch of the country for the benefit of the unfamiliar reader.

Modern South Africa is the highly explosive result of some three centuries of conflict. Since the first Dutch settlement at the Cape in 1652, South Africa has been the scene of violent clashes for political hegemony and economic control. The three main protagonists in the struggle have been the descendants of the Dutch settlers (known as the Boers and more recently Afrikaners), the English, and the native Africans. The Afrikaner-English conflict, which dominated the nineteenth century, receded in importance relative to the White-Black struggle after the Anglo-Boer War of 1899–1902 and the founding of the Union of South Africa in 1910. The 1909 South Africa Act became the country's constitution and determined the basic structure of modern South Africa. Although Great

Britain won the war against the Boer republics, it granted South Africa the status of an independent Dominion under the control of the White settlers. In effect, the English retained their financial interests in South Africa while the Afrikaners increasingly monopolized political power. Since 1961, South Africa has been a republic outside the Commonwealth.

The Black Africans have always remained a politically oppressed and economically exploited majority, a disfranchised helotry. The growing militancy of the African liberatory movements has been met by ever more ruthless repression, culminating in today's Afrikaner Nationalist police state with its policy of racial segregation and discrimination known as apartheid. One may safely assert that South Africa today is the most virulently racialist country in the world. The White-Black struggle has clearly become the paramount source of strain in South Africa today.

Excluding South West Africa, the Republic covers some 472,000 square miles and has a total population approaching sixteen million. Africans constitute slightly over two-thirds of the people; Whites, one-fifth; Coloureds, i.e., people of mixed descent, one-tenth; and East Indians, one-thirtieth. South Africa is by far the most industrialized and urbanized country in Africa. The three largest African cities south of the Sahara are located within its borders. South Africa is also the wealthiest country in Africa, but wealth, like political power, is overwhelmingly a White prerogative.[1]

Like all human communities, Caneville is both uniquely itself and "typical" of the larger society around it. Caneville shares with the rest of South Africa the basic elements of

---

[1] Among the best general works on South Africa are Ellen Hellman, ed., *Handbook of Race Relations in South Africa;* I. D. Mac Crone, *Race Attitudes in South Africa;* Leo Marquard, *The Peoples and Policies of South Africa;* and Sheila Patterson, *Colour and Culture in South Africa.*

its political and social structure, namely those of a racialist White-dominated society with a rigid colour bar enforced by law and observed by custom. Caneville is "typical" of the Province of Natal in the cultural, religious, and "racial" composition of its population except for the high proportion of Indians. In its economic dependence on sugar-cane planting and milling, the town is like several other "sugar belt" communities along the Natal coast. But at the same time, Caneville weaves all these common elements into an idiosyncratic pattern. Caneville is indeed unique in its elaboration of the basic South African pattern of social life, in its variations on the dominant theme. Some of these variations such as its graceful neo-eighteenth-century architecture strike the eye of the most casual visitor. Other such variations, e.g., its welfare services, profoundly affect the life of Caneville citizens. Many of Caneville's unique features make it a better place to live in than most other towns in South Africa. Important though Caneville's idiosyncrasies are in the town's day-to-day existence, and unique though the community appears to its inhabitants, the basic structure is externally determined.

As a sociologist, my primary interest in Caneville is what it can teach us in general. This work is thus primarily a monograph on the structure of a relatively small, self-contained, industrialized, heterogeneous, and stratified community. The ubiquitous factor of "race" in South Africa is no less real for its irrationality. "Race" pervades every aspect of Caneville as it does elsewhere in South Africa. For that reason, "race relations" loom large in the present work. Although there has been a vast number of community studies, such studies on racially stratified societies have been few and largely confined to the Americas.[2] The present study purports to con-

---

[2] For such studies in the Americas see: Davis and Gardner, *Deep South;* Dollard, *Caste and Class in a Southern Town;* Tumin,

tribute to the detailed comparison of multi-racial societies. Beyond that, I hope to fill in certain gaps in our knowledge of South African society. Certain aspects of South African race relations such as the economic, political, and legal ones have been abundantly documented; others such as racial attitudes and etiquette are still largely uncharted.[3]

Another problem of general theoretical interest is the relationship between an industrialized economy, a paternalist policy, and a rigidly ascribed stratification. Caneville is a perfect example of the "company town" with its virtually complete overlap between economic and political power and the monolithic nature of both forms of power. This study, then, is also an examination of benevolent paternalism in a semi-industrial context.

From a dynamic point of view, Caneville, like South Africa as a whole, has gone through an era of rapid industrial expansion, with the stabilization of a rising urban population, and the acculturation of non-Western peoples to the Western way of life. In particular, the difference in adjustment to Western life between Indians and Africans is of great interest. Present conditions, one may safely predict, are but the prelude to even more rapid and drastic changes in the political system, which will have wide repercussions throughout South

---

Caste in a Peasant Society; Colby and van den Berghe, "Ethnic Relations in Southeastern Mexico"; Wagley, *Amazon Town* and *Race and Class in Rural Brazil.* Two recent studies of multi-racial societies comprising large numbers of Indians and based on sugarcane planting offer interesting comparative material in relation to the present work. On Fiji, see A. C. Mayer, *Peasants in the Pacific;* and on Mauritius, see Burton Benedict, *Indians in a Plural Society.*

[3] The principal studies dealing with South African racial attitudes are: Mac Crone, *Race Attitudes in South Africa;* Pettigrew, "Social Distance Attitudes of South African Students"; Kuper, *The Uniform of Colour;* van den Berghe, "Race Attitudes in Durban, South Africa."

African society. From that standpoint, this study of Caneville has been made at a strategic moment in time.

This study is sociological rather than *historical* in its emphasis on the significance of the particular for the general, and in its lack of time perspective. The emphasis is not on how things came to be what they are. That would require a much more ambitious study than the present one. The primary aim is to describe and analyse present conditions. This work is sociological rather than *ethnographic* insofar as it deals more with social structure than with culture. It is sociological rather than *psychological* in that it is concerned with individual personality and motivation only where relevant to the structure of the group. This study stresses neither the legal aspect nor the economic aspect of the local situation except where directly relevant to the total structure. I do not imply that these aspects are unimportant, but as they have been abundantly and excellently documented in many studies, particularly those published by the South African Institute of Race Relations, I wanted to avoid duplication of effort and elaboration of what is already known about South Africa as a whole. The complexity of the subject matter forced me to limit the scope of my work even further. Because of cultural heterogeneity in Caneville, a study of the micro-structure of the family in the various segments of the community would have been an almost endless task. Family structure, therefore, will only be mentioned in relation to the larger structure of the town.

Social and political conditions in South Africa raise in particularly acute form the problems of scientific objectivity, and of the relationship of the investigator to the community under study. The Olympian self-image of the social scientist as the completely objective, detached, emotionless observer is, I think, impossible to achieve and unrealistic to expect. This is particularly true in the South African context, where it is impossible to live and work without taking a position on the colour issue. I must therefore make my own ideological position explicit and allow the reader to introduce any corrective that he may think necessary.

With most of my Western colleagues, I share a general "liberal" or "progressive" ethos. That is, I value such things as individualism, freedom, democracy, political and legal equality, self-determination, achievement on the basis of merit, universalism, and broad-mindedness. Conversely, I abhor any form of political despotism, economic exploitation, and colour discrimination, and I find any racial barrier to rights and opportunities repugnant. My own particular brand of "liberalism" leans towards a non-materialistic, Gandhian type of humanitarian socialism. To a doctrinaire Marxist, I am a "bourgeois reformist," whereas to a White supremacist I am at best an "impractical liberalist," and at worst a *kaffir-boetie* (literally, "brother of kaffirs"; the South African equivalent of "nigger-lover").

The reader will have to decide the extent to which my personal values have affected my findings. While I believe that any sociologist would have presented a similar picture of Caneville, there is, of course, considerable room for differences in emphasis, interpretation, and phrasing. I have, however, consciously endeavoured to avoid gratuitous inferences from the data or to impute motives without evidence. What may appear to be unwarranted imputation of motive in the text is in fact based on evidence from interviews and written documents.

The investigator's relationship to the community is of course partly determined by his values, and can also affect the findings. Most of the following remarks apply equally to my assistant, Edna Miller, and to myself. We both belong to a very rare species in South Africa, namely that of White liberals. Through our behaviour, our position became quickly clear to most of the people in town. We rejected the South African etiquette of race relations, and acted in a "colour-blind" fashion. This behaviour was not the result of a deliberate choice on our part, but was simply the extension of our normal behaviour. As it happened, any other attitude on our part would have doomed our study.

To be sure, our position on the colour issue elicited amusement, scorn, or even severe irritation on the part of a number of local Whites. Among White civil servants (railway, post office, police), co-operation with our study was reluctant at best. As most Whites were employees of the Company, however, and as the Company gave its official approval to our study, our *entrée* into the European group was relatively easy and White co-operation was generally excellent. On the whole, we were most readily and cordially received in the Indian, and, more particularly, the Hindu community. Within a short time we became fully accepted and felt most "at home" among Hindus. As English is the *lingua franca* among both Whites and Indians, language was rarely if ever a barrier among these two groups.

Among Africans, on the other hand, especially among uneducated migrants, we felt both a linguistic and a racial barrier. Due to the explosive situation in South Africa, migrant Africans generally regarded us with the same suspicion and hostility as they did other Whites. There is no question that the presence of a Zulu- or Xhosa-speaking African on the research team would have enriched the material on African migrants and, to a lesser extent, on the sedentary African population of Caneville. On the whole, however, our relationship to the community was good, and we encountered fewer difficulties and obstacles in our research than we anticipated.

I must conclude this chapter by describing briefly the methods used in this study. The period of intensive field work was preceded by several exploratory visits to Caneville. These visits confirmed my first impression that the town offered an ideal setting for a community study. Caneville was small enough to be manageable, and isolated enough to constitute a clearly defined community. The town was partly industrial, partly commercial, partly agricultural. The heterogeneity of its population added to its interest. But most of all, the paternalism of the Caneville Sugar Company offered me a good opportunity to study in detail a type of race relations which has been of theoretical interest to me for a long time. These exploratory visits were followed by a period of intensive field work extending from October, 1960, to April, 1961. Edna Miller joined me from November, 1960 to February, 1961. While I have stayed overnight in Caneville on several occasions, housing limitations prevented my living in town. Instead, I commuted by car from near-by Durban.

At the end of each day in the field, both Miss Miller and I wrote extensive field notes from sketchier notes taken during the day. We investigated existing written documents such as municipal records, Company statistics, medical files, school records, applications for state support, sales figures of merchants, property valuation rolls, and the like. Access to police records was denied us by the station commander, however. Questionnaires and small censuses yielded further data. So did an essay contest conducted at the local high school. In interviews, we utilized either short prepared schedules from which questions were read, or a more anthropological method of informal conversations with key informants. The extreme heterogeneity of the population made it necessary to use sixteen key informants with whom we established excellent rapport and whom we approached repeatedly throughout the study. Besides these key informants, and over three hundred questionnaire respondents, a further fifty to sixty persons gave more specific information on certain topics.

Of the sixteen key informants, all but one were men;

"racially" eight were Indian, four White, and four African; occupationally they were mostly teachers (five), or municipal and company employees (five), but they also included a clergyman, a merchant, a bookkeeper, a housewife, and two health assistants. The fifty to sixty secondary informants who were interviewed one to three times included disproportionately large numbers of men as opposed to women; Indians and Whites as opposed to Africans; and teachers, merchants, clerks, priests, and officials as opposed to manual workers and farmers. All major occupational groups were represented, however. In most cases, before conducting an informal interview, we made a rough list of things to ask and a "plan of action" on such matters as the order in which to ask the questions. Sometimes we took notes during the interviews, sometimes not, depending on the informant, the sensitivity of the questions, etc. Immediately after the interviews, we took cursory notes to insure remembrance of the major points and the significant quotes when writing the day's field notes in full later.

Admittedly, there was a class bias in the selection of our informants, who were mostly white-collar and professional workers rather than manual workers. This was due to the difficulty of finding articulate working-class informants in a culturally heterogeneous and partly illiterate society. In the case of the Africans, our inability to speak Zulu made our reliance on middle-class, Western-educated informants even greater than among the Indians, most of whom speak fluent English. We did, however, interview some working-class persons through an interpreter, always, we felt, with a considerable loss of the more elusive emotional material. The material on the largely rural, illiterate, and migrant field workers is particularly inadequate because of reasons already mentioned. As the migrant African workers live on the margin of the settled community of Caneville, and as the settled community constitutes the focus of the study, this inadequacy is not as serious as might be thought at first. Migrant workers will be mentioned insofar as they affect the urban community, but, unless otherwise indicated, comments on the Africans in Caneville will refer principally to those in the settled population.

The class bias of our choice of informants was in good part offset by our observational data. Sometimes we acted as participants, sometimes not, depending on conditions. Many people graciously invited us into their homes, where unobstrusive observation was quite easy. On all possible occasions, we closely observed casual behaviour of children at play, of discussion groups on the sidewalk, of customers in the market and in shops. We attended a great number of functions, both public and private, from weddings, charity bazaars, baby shows, and protest meetings to religious services, board meetings, drinking parties, and dances. On several occasions I was invited to address teachers' groups and school assemblies, to open bazaars, and the like. All of these occasions afforded excellent opportunities to observe behaviour in all social classes.

In short, most of the data for this study come from the use of standard anthropological techniques of participant observation and open interviews with informants. Because the community is so segmented and stratified, however, we had to rely on many more informants than in ordinary anthropological research. Questionnaires, short interview schedules, essays, written records, statistics, and small censuses were the main secondary sources of information.

While this book is not intended to be polemical, it does purport to offer something more than do most technical monographs. Apart from the scientific aims of this study, I hope to make a plea for reason and non-racialism by showing in detail how prejudice and discrimination affect the lives of the vast majority of South Africans who are, by genetic accident, born with a brown skin. Because of this "hybrid" nature of the study, I have tried, as far as possible, to stay clear of pedantry and jargon. For a sociologist this is not an effortless task, and in parts, I had to be theoretical and abstract rather than descriptive and concrete. I have endeavoured nevertheless to confront the educated layman with reasonably digestible prose.

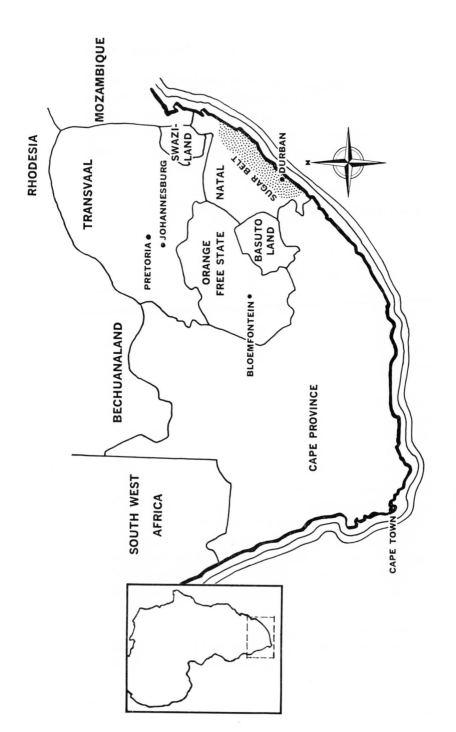

SOUTH AFRICA showing location of the Sugar Belt

Chapter II

CANEVILLE IN PLACE AND TIME

MOST South Africans have never heard of Caneville. It is but a small town in Natal the smallest province of the Union (now Republic) of South Africa. A good road map will show Caneville as a town under ten-thousand inhabitants on the main road from Durban to Zululand, a few miles inland from the Indian Ocean. The town is too far from the large harbour of Durban to be called a suburb, yet close enough to be within one hour's leisurely drive on a tarred road. The agonizingly slow and antiquated Zululand Railway also bisects the town and provides a passenger service of sorts for anyone compelled to use it. Caneville's *raison d'être*, for the outside world at least, is sugar. Natal (including Zululand) produces virtually all the sugar consumed in South Africa and exports a surplus. The Sugar Belt stretches for some two hundred miles, about two-thirds of which are north and one-third south of Durban. Caneville is near the geographical center of that belt. For climatic reasons, mostly elevation, temperature, and precipitation, the cultivation of the sugar cane is largely confined to the coastal low-lands of Natal within twenty to thirty miles of the Indian Ocean.

By South African standards, the Natal sugar industry is of considerable importance. It produces over one million tons of sugar a year from roughly ten million tons of sugar cane.

One-fourth to one-fifth of the production is exported, principally to the United Kingdom and Rhodesia. The South African sugar output accounts for only 2 per cent of the world production, but for over one-third of the African output. Table I shows that the growth of the industry has been rapid though not evenly distributed over the years. The years 1940 to 1950 showed a period of relative stagnation followed by a spectacular doubling of production during the 1950's. This increase of output brought with it the danger of overproduction and the need for output restriction under a quota system, which was introduced in 1960.[1]

TABLE I

Sugar Production in South Africa, 1859–1960

Year	Number of Tons
1859	1,300
1880	17,000
1900	18,000
1910	87,000
1920	189,000
1930	299,000
1940	596,000
1950	561,000
1960	1,043,000

Source: *South African Sugar Year Book*, 1959–1960, p. 187.

The area under cane cultivation in Natal and Zululand amounts to about 600,000 acres of which 40 to 45 per cent is harvested each year. The land is largely owned by the eighteen sugar mills which, in 1957–1958, produced 25.2 per cent of the crop, and by the same fourteen hundred European farmers who accounted for 66.7 per cent of the 1957–1958 cane crop. About two thousand Indian growers delivered 6.4 per cent, while three thousand African farmers, accounting

---

[1] *South African Sugar Year Book*, 1959–1960, p. 61.

for 1.7 per cent of the crop, barely subsist on minute holdings. The economic structure of the industry is thus clearly pyramidal. At the top, a few large mills control the processing of the cane and own large land estates averaging 7,400 acres and ranging up to 40,000 acres. The fourteen hundred European farmers with average holdings of 270 acres control most of the cane land not owned by the mills; the two thousand medium- to small-scale Indian farmers with average holdings of about thirty-nine acres make a modest living on the margin of the industry. Finally, the three thousand small African farmers earn a small amount of cash on holdings which average about five acres but in many cases are below one acre. The inequality in the distribution of land is further aggravated by the fact that European planters, through irrigation and other capital expenditures, get a yield of thirty-five tons of cane per acre compared to about twenty tons for Indian and African planters. In 1959, European planters irrigated 11.2 per cent of their cane lands, compared to only 1.2 per cent for Indian planters.

The degree of concentration on the milling side of the industry has increased over the years, as the smaller mills have become incorporated into the large ones. In 1905, there were 30 mills; in 1945, 22; in 1960, 18.[2] Of these 18 mills, one group owns 3, and another 2, so that the total number of milling companies is only 15. Of these companies, one produces one-fourth, five produce about two-thirds, and six produce some three-fourths of the total output. From the milling side, the industry can thus be described as an oligopoly.

Capital investment in the industry has increased from about £1 million in 1905 to £27.5 million in 1945.[3] In 1905 the industry employed 8,000 workers. By 1929 the number had risen to about 40,000, by 1945 to about 68,000, and by

2 Hurwitz, *Agriculture in Natal,* p. 44.

3 *Ibid.,* p. 44.

1960 to 106,000.[4] Approximately one-seventh of that labour force is employed in the mills. Of the mill workers, about 10 per cent are Europeans, 30 per cent Indians, and 60 per cent Africans. Most of these mill workers are permanently settled. The field side of sugar growing is quite labour-consuming in South Africa, where the low cost of migratory African labour, as well as the hilly nature of the terrain, has hindered mechanization. About six-sevenths of the sugar workers are employed in the fields. Originally, most workers were indentured Indians brought over to Natal for that purpose. The aboriginal African population in the nineteenth century belonged to pastoralist groups, was unused to steady agricultural work, and was found unsuitable at first. Gradually, however, Indian workers were displaced by African migratory workers, mostly Pondo and Zulu, under a staff of European supervisors and Indian semi-skilled personnel. Migratory Africans now prove more willing to work as cane cutters than the Indians, and their housing in military-type barracks is cheaper than the family housing, however poor, which the settled Indian families required.[5] Wages paid to non-European in the industry are, together with mining wages, among the lowest in South Africa, while salaries of Europeans are quite high. Field workers are entirely unorganized and unprotected by any minimum-wage agreements. Non-European factory workers fall under a minimum-wage agreement, but are not effectively organized, and African workers are denied the right to strike. The sugar companies furthermore adhere to an unspoken "gentlemen's agreement" not to raise non-European wages substantially above legal minimums. Housing and living conditions for Europeans are quite spacious and satisfactory, while, for Indian and African workers, they fall far short of the barest standards of decency and hygiene on most estates.

---

[4] *Ibid.*, p. 44.

[5] Woods, *The Indian Community*, p. 26.

In this respect, the sugar industry follows a long-established South African tradition of racial discrimination.

Centralized control of the sugar industry is guaranteed by the South African Sugar Association (SASA), a statutory body on which both European millers and planters are represented, and from which non-Europeans, whether workers or planters, are excluded. The Sugar Industry Central Board (SICB) acts as the executive committee of SASA in implementing agreements such as the distribution of quota. European planters and millers have each formed a central body, the South African Cane Growers' Association (SACGA) and the Natal Sugar Millers' Association (NSMA). Non-European planters have been forced to establish segregated associations, the Natal Indian Cane Growers' Association (NICGA) and the Natal and Zululand Bantu Cane Growers' Association (NZBCGA). These associations can make representations to the Non-European Sugar Advisory Board, which has a European chairman and a majority of White members, and which does not have any powers.

The general picture of the sugar industry is that of an oligopoly under the control of a few large firms. Europeans whether workers, planters or millers, enjoy a highly privileged and protected position. Non-Europeans are excluded from any measure of control and paid low wages. Labour is largely migratory, unskilled, unorganized, and unrepresented for collective bargaining purposes.

The Caneville Sugar Company (CSC) plays an important role in the industry. While it is not the largest sugar company, it has the largest single mill, and is generally considered the "premier" company in the industry. Its shares are among the few sugar stocks regularly quoted in the South African daily press, and its production accounts for about 12 per cent of the total output. Employees trained by the CSC are at a premium in the other companies, and the son of the CSC

President is also Chairman of the South African Sugar Association. The CSC takes pride in being the most progressive company in the industry, both technologically and sociologically.

The ancestor of the CSC, a sugar estate of some six thousand acres, was established in 1848, when the Colony of Natal was in its infancy.[6] In 1854, William Sherwood, the founder of the Caneville dynasty of sugar barons, came over from Britain to manage the estate. A small nucleus of European colonists and African workers soon gathered at what later became Caneville. Sherwood was one of the prominent Natal settlers to campaign for the immigration of Indian indentured labourers. In 1860 Caneville received its first batch of fifty-two Indian workers, and in time the town became predominantly Indian, as it is today. In the same year, the older ox-driven cane crusher was replaced with a steam-engine mill.

In 1896 the Caneville Sugar Company was formed under its present name. At that time, the Company exploited some seven thousand acres of cane-land, of which it owned some six thousand. The mill was again enlarged to a six-roller plant with a capacity of four thousand tons a year. The following year, the Natal-Zululand Railway connected Caneville with the harbour of Durban, thereby greatly facilitating transport and access of sugar to the market. In 1899, Ronald Sherwood, William's son, floated the CSC as a limited company. By 1911 the plant was again enlarged to a sixteen-roller tandem producing some eleven thousand tons of sugar a year.

While the Company expanded, slum conditions continued to prevail in Caneville, wages remained extremely low, hy-

---

[6] Unfortunately, I am not able to refer to the informative and well-written history of Caneville by one of its prominent citizens, as doing so would reveal the identity of the town. My debt to the author, who, in spite of friendly disagreements, always showed himself very kind, co-operative and generous of his time with me, is very great indeed.

giene was virtually non-existent, and the treatment of field workers housed in crowded rows of one-room windowless shacks was tantamount to slavery. Corporal punishment in the form of severe flogging remained a feature of the sugar estates until the 1920's. The indentured Indian worker was bound for five years at wages of ten shillings a month with an increase of one shilling each year. While the mass of the field workers were Indians, the sugar boilers and engineers were mostly French creoles from Mauritius.

These appalling living conditions led to the decision of the Indian government to halt the immigration of Indian indentured workers to South Africa. Meanwhile White anti-Indian agitation was mounting in Natal, leading to the iniquitous three-pound tax designed to force the repatriation of the free Indians. This tax led to the Gandhi strike of 1913, when, under the guidance of the Mahatma, the technique of passive resistance was first developed. The Indian workers of Caneville participated in the strike that lasted some three weeks, and that is remembered as the only serious labour unrest in the history of the sugar industry. Starting around that time, African migratory workers began to displace Indians as field workers.

From 1918 to 1930, the CSC underwent a period of rapid expansion. New cane lands were acquired and, in 1922, a sister factory was opened in Sugartown on the other side of the Caneville River. In 1927 all the crushing of cane was transferred to the large Sugartown mill, which, by 1930, produced about 30,000 tons of sugar a year. The Company then employed three thousand workers. Of these, two thousand were divided between nine field sections. The field workers were about three-quarter African and one-quarter Indian. The remaining one thousand workers were employed at the mill and in the transport operation. In the 1940's the CSC incorporated two smaller sugar estates and reached approximately its present size. Improved methods of cultivation, transport, and milling gradually increased production to its present level of approximately 125,000 tons of sugar per year.

In 1930, an epidemic of malaria raged along the Natal coast and Caneville was not spared. Slum conditions and lack of sanitation were among the major contributory factors in the epidemic. Starting then, the Company embarked on its "Caneville Experiment" (about which more will be said in Chapter IV). Gradually, corrugated iron shacks were eliminated, and sanitation and "model housing" were introduced. As late as 1944, a housing survey of the Indian part of town revealed that 186 buildings out of 258 were shacks. While a number of hovels still exist, the assessed value of Indian-owned properties in the township is now about £750,000.

The year 1949 stands out in the history of Natal as the date of African-Indian riots, when gangs of Zulu attacked Indians in Durban and in many other Natal towns, resulting in a toll of 142 killed and over 1,000 injured, some of it due to police gunfire. Caneville was, however, spared serious trouble. A gang of Indian youths attacking an African constituted the only incident of violence.

The post-war years brought a new phase of prosperity and expansion for the South African sugar industry and for the CSC. The 1960–1961 period during which the present study was made was, however, one of anxiety and uncertainty for Caneville as for the rest of South Africa. The great wave of African protest demonstrations against apartheid swept over the country, and the police shootings of Sharpeville and Langa have already become historical. These events were followed by a tempest of world indignation against the South African government, by a sharp decline in stock market quotations, including the sugar shares, and finally by the withdrawal of South Africa from the Commonwealth. CSC shares which stood at twenty shillings before Sharpeville in February, 1960, declined to twelve shillings in May, 1961, after Dr. Verwoerd announced his country's withdrawal from the Commonwealth. Commonwealth membership is particularly important to the sugar industry, as South African sugar has hitherto been exported to Britain at a subsidized price. This special arrangement is a result of the Commonwealth Sugar Agreement that makes it possible for South Africa to dispose of its surplus production at a more advantageous price than on either the home or the world market.

Combined with political uncertainty, the sugar industry faced the problem of overproduction after a decade of rapid expansion. A crop reduction of 25 per cent was finally agreed upon, bringing production down from its 1959 peak. The year 1960 was also one of relative drought, which affected the growth of the cane, increased the hazard of cane fires, and caused a shortage of water for both industrial and home consumption. All these circumstances had an unfavorable effect on Caneville. In addition to these general adverse conditions, several special factors combined to make 1960–1961 a difficult period in Caneville history. The CSC reduced its factory labour force by some 20 per cent because of falling profits, thereby creating unemployment in town. A serious cane fire broke out in September, 1960. Road construction, besides inconveniencing the inhabitants, diverted traffic from the commercial centre and caused serious financial losses to local merchants. All these factors combined to make the period of the study a rather lean one for Caneville. The years 1960–1961 were definitely not "normal," but then, of course, no year ever is. It must, however, be remembered that the time of the study was one of crisis, anxiety, recession, and unrest.

Having placed Caneville in the larger context of the Natal sugar industry and having sketched the history of the town, I must conclude this chapter with a climatic, demographic, and geographical description of the town.

The climate of Caneville can best be described as subtropical. The summer months of January to March are hot and humid, while the winter months of June to August are mild and dry. The mean annual rainfall between 1887 and 1959 was 38.8 inches a year, over two-thirds of which fell between October and March. The rainiest month, March, had a mean of 5.08 inches and the driest, July, 1.04 inches.[7] The annual temperature for the years 1928 to 1959 was 68.8 degrees Fahrenheit, with a mean daily range of 16.5 degrees. In the hottest month, February, the mean was 74.7 degrees, and in the coldest month, July, it was 62.2 degrees.[8] Oppressively hot weather is largely confined to a few days in January and February, and the cold is never uncomfortable except on early winter mornings when a wool sweater is welcome. Climate is of great importance to Caneville since it determines the yearly cycle of work. The sugar mill closes each year for a period of approximately four to five months between the end of December and the middle to the end of May. This period coincides with the hot and humid months for two main reasons: firstly, this is the period of most rapid growth of the cane when the sucrose content of the plant is at its lowest; and, secondly, the backbreaking labour of cutting the cane can best be done in mild dry weather.

In keeping with a common South African practice of extending the municipal limits well beyond the area of dense settlement, Caneville stretches along about 4.5 miles of the tarred national road that bisects the town following a north-south axis (or more precisely a NNE-SSW axis). The Zululand Railway, which meanders along the main road, crosses the latter three times, though only once at a level crossing. The town limits form an irregular elongated polygon that vaguely calls to mind the famous "gerrymander" of United States

---

[7] *South African Sugar Year Book*, 1959–1960, p. 43.
[8] *Ibid.*, p. 95.

politics. The longest axis of the polygon is constituted by the
road and railway, while its width from east to west varies
from one-third to one and a half miles. Township boundaries
encompass 2,079 acres of land, of which about 55 per cent
is residential, 13 per cent industrial and commercial, 29 per
cent open spaces, roads, and railways, and 3 per cent educational, religious, and governmental. The central residential and
commercial area of Caneville only extends along one mile
of the main road.

Besides the main north-south road, a narrow road connects
Caneville with the seashore five miles away from the centre
of town. A new national road under construction is going
to follow the coast and by-pass the town altogether. In addition to these public roads, the CSC has built an extensive network of gravel roads giving access to the surrounding canefields. Company canefields, interspersed with smaller privately
owned farms, extend five to six miles in all directions over
pleasantly rolling hills that slowly slope down 200 or 300
feet towards the seashore. In that area of 25 to 30 square
miles that constitutes Caneville's rural hinterland, there are
no other centres of settlement that could be called "towns."
The Company canefields are divided into thirteen sections
averaging 2,000 acres each. On each section there is a compound housing 250 to 300 workers. Along the beach, there
are a Catholic convent, school, and church, and a number of
holiday cottages. Dispersed in the canefields are private cane
farms, some quite small, some nearly as large as one of the
Company's sections. Each of these farms has its own nucleus
of workers. In addition some large Indian families constitute
isolated little hamlets of their own. However, Caneville itself
is the only town of any size within the district.

Travelling from the south, one comes first to the "Indian"
part of Caneville, which is also the commercial centre and the
largest part of the town (see map of Caneville). When local

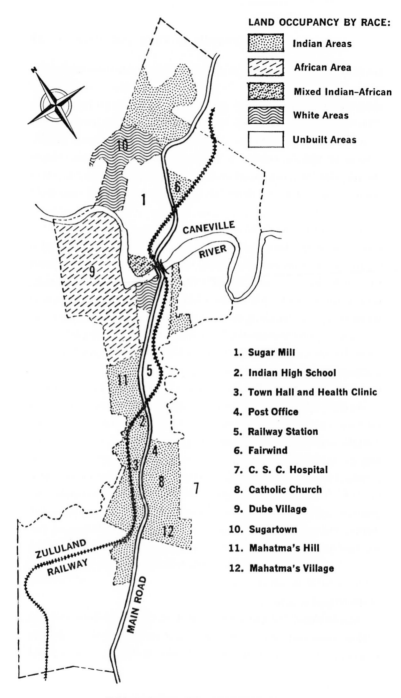

LAND OCCUPANCY BY RACE:

Indian Areas

African Area

Mixed Indian–African

White Areas

Unbuilt Areas

CANEVILLE RIVER

ZULULAND RAILWAY

MAIN ROAD

1. Sugar Mill
2. Indian High School
3. Town Hall and Health Clinic
4. Post Office
5. Railway Station
6. Fairwind
7. C. S. C. Hospital
8. Catholic Church
9. Dube Village
10. Sugartown
11. Mahatma's Hill
12. Mahatma's Village

TOWNSHIP OF CANEVILLE

people talk of Caneville, they usually mean this part of town, although the municipality of Caneville includes the "White" area of Sugartown and the "African" area of Dube Village. The "Indian" part of Caneville, or, more succinctly, Caneville Centre, consists of Main Street (in effect, the main road), where all the larger shops are found, and five other tarred streets, two of them parallel and three perpendicular to Main Street. In addition, there are several secondary untarred streets. Caneville Centre, besides its row of shops along Main Street, includes government buildings (the Town Hall which also houses the Health Clinic, the Post Office, and the Police Station), an Indian high school, and three large Indian primary schools, two small hotels, a mosque, three Hindu temples, a Catholic church with its African primary school, the covered market hall, a community centre, an Indian sports stadium, and several residential sections. Of the latter, Mahatma Village (not to be confused with Mahatma's Hill) constitutes an exclusive Indian middle-class area, occupied chiefly by teachers and other professionals.

Mahatma's Hill, to the north of the level railway crossing and to the west of Main Street is an extension of Caneville Centre and consists of a row of Indian stores (including the town's only department store), an Indian residential area, and a mosque. Bordering on the northern edge of Mahatma's Hill is Dube Village, known among Africans as "the location" by analogy with the segregated African areas in the rest of South Africa. Dube Village, besides its rows of red-brick cottages and its few white-washed houses, includes a community centre where a few small shops are leased to Africans, a club-house, athletic fields in construction, a non-denominational Protestant church, and a primary school.

Sandwiched between Dube Village and the main road is a European residential area occupied by government railway workers. The Sugartown railway station to the east of the road faces that housing area. The road then crosses the Caneville River, a shallow stream from one hundred to three hundred feet across, and one finds to the west of the road the area known as Sugartown that includes the large CSC sugar mill, barracks for the Company's non-European mill workers, and a well laid-out village with a large golf course, a church, a primary school, a club-house, a swimming pool, a bowling green, tennis courts, tarred streets lighted at night and spacious houses with garages and gardens. This Sugartown area houses most of the Company's White employees. Opposite Sugartown, on the east side of the road, there is a small Indian section known as Fairwind that includes a primary school. In addition to all the areas described above, the Company has two non-European compounds and one European village located just outside town limits, one to the north-west and two to the east. One of the non-European compounds known as Loco Village comprises a Hindu temple and a lower primary school. The CSC hospital is also to the east of the town, just outside the boundary. (A more detailed description of the social ecology of Caneville will be given in later chapters when we shall discuss racial segregation and the stratification system.)

The approximate population of the Caneville police district is 21,000. About 1,000 are classified as "Europeans" or "Whites," 10,000 as "Indians" or "Asiatics," and 10,000 as "Bantu" or "Natives"—i.e., Africans. (The terms "Asiatic," "Native," and "Bantu," though in common use among Whites, are highly distasteful to non-Europeans, and hence are avoided in this study. More will be said of the use of terms later.) The 1960 population census for the town itself gives a total of 9,919 persons, of whom 543 are Whites, 7,048 Indians, 2,325 Africans and 3 Coloureds (Table II). The population shows a rapid growth. In thirty-nine years the town has increased nearly seven-fold. The rate of growth has, however, slowed down in recent years. Whereas the increase was nearly four-fold in the first half of that period, it was less than two-fold after 1946. The Africans show the greatest rate of growth due to the influx of workers in the sugar industry. The Indians show the second highest rate of increase, largely as the result of natural growth. The over-all sex ratio for 1960 is 106.8 males per 100 females, while the ratio for Africans is 128.2, for Europeans 118.0, and for Indians 98.9. In short, the town of Caneville has about 10,000 inhabitants, 70 per cent of whom are Indians, 25 per cent Africans and 5 per cent Whites. The sex ratio shows that the urban population consists largely of stabilized families, not of migrant male workers. Of the additional 11,000 people living in the rural hinterland of Caneville about 75 per cent are migratory African male workers, 20 per cent are stabilized Indian families, and 5 per cent are stable European families.

TABLE II
Caneville Population Census

Number of:	1921	1936	1946	1951	1960
Indians	1129	1887	3700	4626	7048
Africans	196	871	1474	1482	2325
Europeans	148	96	344	360	543
Coloureds	14	17	19	26	3
Total	1487	2871	5537	6494	9919

The "racial" composition of the Caneville population is atypical both of that of South Africa (where the breakdown for 1960 is 19.4 per cent European, 9.4 per cent Coloured, 68.2 per cent African, and 3.0 per cent Indian), and to a lesser extent of that of Natal (11.6 per cent European, 1.5 per cent Coloured, 73.5 per cent African, and 13.4 per cent Indian). Caneville is, indeed, unique in South Africa in that over two-thirds of its population are of Indian origin. After Durban and Pietermaritzburg, Caneville has the largest Indian population in Natal.

These broad "racial" groups are further subdivided by

religion (Christian, Muslim, and Hindu) and by language. Six Indian tongues or dialects (Memon, Gujarati, Urdu, Tamil, Telugu, and Hindi); four main African languages (Zulu, Xhosa, Shangaan, and Nyanja); and three European languages (English, Afrikaans, and French) are spoken in that small community. In practice, however, English is the common tongue among Whites and Indians, and Zulu among Africans. Most Caneville Whites are English-speaking, and most permanently settled Africans are Zulu-speaking as is the case in Natal as a whole. The migrant African labour comes mostly from outside Natal, more particularly from Pondoland (a section of the Transkei), and to a lesser extent from Mozambique. As in the rest of Natal and South Africa, Caneville Whites are overwhelmingly Christian (at least nominally so), and predominantly Protestant. The settled urban African population is, like the White group, mostly Christian and Protestant, while migrant, rural Africans are still principally "pagan"; i.e., they follow the traditional cults of ancestor worship. The Indian population is fairly representative of that of Natal as a whole. Tamil, Hindi, Telugu, Urdu, Gujarati, and Memon are spoken in descending order of frequency. With regard to religion, Hindus are by far the largest group (86 per cent of a sample of 243 high school children), followed by Muslims (10 per cent of the sample) and Christians (2 per cent).

Caneville, insofar as it depends for its existence on the monoculture of the sugar cane, and insofar as its population is predominantly Indian, is not a "typical" South African town. Neither, as pointed out above, is the time of the study "normal." Nevertheless, I hope to show in the succeeding chapters that Caneville has enough in common with the rest of South Africa to make many of the findings more generally applicable. I also hope to show that Caneville, in its uniqueness and complexity, can make a contribution to the cross-cultural study of multi-racial societies.

Chapter III

THE CULTURAL SYSTEM

IF Caneville were located in the United States, its enterprising Chamber of Commerce would undoubtedly have placed a gaily painted publicity board at the entrance of the town stating: "Welcome to Caneville, the world's most cosmopolitan small town." Instead, a large but prosaic black board simply states "Entrance to Caneville" in white letters.

The town needs, however, no publicity, for its cultural heterogeneity is obvious even to the most casual visitors. The elegant beauty of its neo-eighteenth-century architecture with its white-washed buildings contrasts with the unrelieved drabness and lack of imagination displayed by most Natal small towns. Its fountains, lily ponds, and gardens show a concern for beauty absent elsewhere. But, most of all, the inhabitants, ranging in skin colour from dark brown to "white," witness to the meeting of three broad cultural streams in Caneville: the African, the Indian, and the European. Hindu women in exquisite saris; Muslim women in dresses and pantaloons; Pondo women adorned with beads, copper anklets, and finely braided hair; European women in shorts, slacks, or dresses, all walk past one another in the market, shops, and streets. Well-to-do Indian merchants or professionals in white shirts and ties or White Company employees in neat khaki shorts and open shirts drive past ragged African workers. Within three hundred yards of one another, the Catholic priest chants prayers in Latin, the Brahmin priest in Sanskrit, and the Imam in Arabic, all three languages that nobody speaks in Caneville and that few read with any degree of comprehension. Some thirteen different tongues belonging to four unrelated families are heard, though only two with any frequency in public places, namely English and Zulu.

All these "racial," religious, and linguistic groups (some of which overlap one another) interact in a highly complex fashion which will be analysed in greater detail in chapters VI and VII, but which may be simply described for the time being as "separately together." In the present chapter, I am not directly concerned with the day-to-day interaction of these groups or with their social structure. Rather, I intend to jump from concrete behaviour to the highly abstract level that American anthropologists have called *culture*.

It is obviously beyond the scope of the present work to describe all of the dozen cultures or sub-cultures represented in Caneville. This gigantic task would involve the learning of as many languages and a lifetime of field work. Furthermore, much of that effort would be duplicatory as the cultures of most of the groups represented in Caneville have already been studied and described. The aim of this chapter, while not simple, is much more modest. I want to describe the complex influence of these cultures upon one another and the resulting changes therein.

Three broad cultural streams have met in Caneville, as in the rest of Natal. The aboriginal African culture was conquered by force of superior European weapons. Though European penetration of Natal goes as far back as the 1820's, it was not until 1879 that the subjection of the Zulu was completed with the defeat of Cetewayo. In 1860, only some twenty years after the Europeans established a sizeable permanent colony in Natal, Indian indentured workers were imported into the Colony. Of the three cultural strains, the European (which in Natal is predominantly of English origin) remains politically and economically dominant. Belonging to the dominant culture, Europeans have imposed their religion and language on many members of the other cultures. Acculturation has thus, been most evident in the adoption by Indians and Africans of characteristics of the dominant European culture.

This schematic description of cultural contact obscures the complexity of the process. For one thing, acculturation has not been entirely one-way. For another, Indians and Africans have differently reacted to, and adopted from, Western culture. Within the Indian group, Muslims and Hindus have been differently affected by Western society, and have also influenced one another. Finally, Africans and Indians have influenced each other as well, though only to a slight extent. We must therefore examine these smaller currents to reconstruct the total picture.

Europeans in Caneville represent three local variants of Western national cultures. The English-speaking are the most numerous and include about two-thirds of the White population. The Afrikaners and the French Mauritians constitute groups of slightly less than one hundred persons each. The Afrikaners and the English are mostly Protestants and the Mauritians are Catholics. The Mauritians are in a racially marginal situation in that some of them are rejected by Whites and treated as Coloureds, but all of them are completely European by culture. The English are not only the largest White sub-group; they also largely own the CSC, and occupy all but two or three of the top twenty positions in the Company and the township. As the dominant White sub-group, the English have imposed their language, not only on the Afrikaners and the Mauritians, but on the vast majority of Indians and educated Africans as well.

Afrikaners maintain their own sub-culture through political allegiance, language, and membership in the Dutch Reformed Church. They are but a small group in Caneville, but they belong to the majority White group that rules the country as a whole. Included in this Afrikaner group are several families of old French Huguenot and German descent which were completely assimilated by the Dutch Afrikaners in the seventeenth and nineteenth centuries respectively. The majority of Afrikaners in town are transient civil servants associated with the police, the post office, and the railways, and are transferred every few years. They consequently live on the margin of the community and retain extensive ties with the outside world. Most of them belong to the ruling Nationalist Party, and their political differences with the English (who are divided between the United and the Progressive parties) reinforce the cultural cohesion of the Afrikaners as a small marginal group.[1]

The Mauritians are in a different position from that of the Afrikaners. They started to come to Natal in the second half of the nineteenth century as technicians in the sugar industry. Their group is not represented elsewhere in South Africa, and their colour status is ambiguous in a racialistic White society which is reluctant to admit some of them as Whites. These factors combine to make them seek assimilation in the dominant English group. No serious effort is made by parents to maintain knowledge of French on the part of their South African-born children, with the result that African-born Mauri-

---

[1] The United Party differs from the Nationalist Party in wishing to retain ties with Great Britain. On the colour issue both parties are in basic agreement in wanting to maintain White domination and segregation, but they differ on the methods of achieving these aims. The Progressive Party is a recent splinter party from the United Party and advocates a policy of concessions to non-Whites and a qualified non-racial franchise loaded in such a way as to keep government in what it terms "responsible" hands.

tians speak English more fluently than French. There is no French club as this would increase the danger of their being set apart as Coloureds by the English Whites. In fact, the Mauritians are internally divided between the "White" families that are accepted by the English and the "creole" families that are not. The only major cohesive factor that keeps the Mauritians together is religion. They are all Roman Catholics, and two-thirds of the White families in the parish are Mauritians. They play a prominent part in parish affairs. The Catholic priest himself is French-speaking, though he is not from Mauritius. Many Mauritian-born persons still maintain a sentimental tie to the island and to French culture, subscribe to Mauritian and French newspapers, and view the English as foreigners. But African-born persons have been almost completely anglicized.

The contrast between the Afrikaner and the Mauritian reaction to English culture is interesting. Both Afrikaners and Mauritians are small and relatively low-status groups within the local European culture. Both groups speak the language of the dominant English, as well as their own tongue. But the Mauritians seek assimilation to the English, largely because of the threat to their "White" status, whereas the Afrikaners, who belong to the group that rules the country, want to maintain their cultural distinctiveness. The presence or absence of a national reference group outside the local community seems to play an important role in attitudes towards acculturation and in its extent.

The Indian community of Caneville shows greater cultural heterogeneity than either the European or the African one. In fact, the concept of an "Indian" group is almost entirely the product of discriminatory treatment and legislation that lumps all descendants of immigrants from India into one "racial" category. The deepest cultural gulf among the Indians is between Hindus and Muslims.[2] The deep differences between the value systems of the two religions constitute a strong barrier to social intercourse, particularly to intermarriage, and to mutual understanding.

Of the two religious groups, the Muslim, numbering some fifteen hundred people, shows by far the most social cohesion, although it is itself internally split and stratified along linguistic lines. All local Muslims belong to the Sunni branch of Islam. The two mosques, each with their full-time Imam (priest) and Madrasa (Qur'anic school held in Urdu and Arabic) are well attended and constitute important social centres. The solidarity of all, regardless of wealth, in the brotherhood of Islam is emphasized in spite of internal class and language stratification. Friday noon prayers at the two mosques draw a combined weekly attendance of about 100 to 150 men. The *absolute* weekly attendance at the four main Hindu temples is roughly the same, but there are four times as many Hindus as Muslims, and Hindu temples are open to both sexes. The *proportional* Muslim attendance at places of worship is thus about eight times higher than for Hindus. It may be argued that temple attendance for Hindus does not reflect accurately the extent of religious practice, as much Hindu worship and ritual is performed at home and is connected with family events. The same applies to Islam, however, where the five daily prayers are recited at home, and where women, though not *forbidden* access to the mosques, in practice never come. The fast of the Ramadan is strictly observed by the vast majority of Muslims, and so are the dietary rules on the slaughtering of animals and the prohibition of pork. Many younger Muslims are more negligent about the five daily prayers and the prohibition of alcohol, however, although alcoholism is virtually non-existent among Muslims.

---

[2] Cf. Pierre L. van den Berghe and Edna Miller, "Some Factors Affecting Social Relations in a Natal North Coast Community."

The Ramadan, which is all the more difficult to observe in the hot summer weather, brings the solidarity of the group to a yearly climax.

The combined attendance at the two Qur'anic schools is about 180 pupils, compared to about 90 in the two Hindu schools. Of a sample of 23 Muslim children in high school, all but two had attended the Madrasa. As for attendance at weekly religious services, these figures show that the rate of enrollment is about eight times higher for Muslims than for Hindus. Not only are Muslim enrollment figures much higher, but the Madrasa stresses religion much more than the Hindu mother-tongue school. Unlike Hindu children, the Muslim child receives a solid education in the daily practice and the basic dogma of Islam. He also learns a smattering of Arabic that allows him to read and recite the Qur'an, though in most cases without full comprehension.

Muslim traditionalism also expresses itself in the use of Indian languages, which is considerably more widespread than among Hindus. In a sample of 243 high school pupils, two-thirds of the Muslims speak an Indian tongue at home, compared to only one-third of the Hindu children. Muslim women, while unveiled and allowed to appear in public, are generally seen outdoors only in groups and during the day-time. There is still a strong taboo against participation by women in public functions, except traditional ones which are segregated by sex such as weddings. In practically all Muslim homes, women never join the guests, and they remain in the kitchen. As a general rule, they do not even serve the men at table as Hindu women do. Hindu women, on the other hand, while much less "emancipated" than European women, enjoy a greater freedom of movement than Muslim women.

The common faith in Islam does not prevent the internal division of local Muslims into three hierarchically ranked language groups: the Memon, the Gujarati, and the Urdu.

These groups are almost entirely endogamous, overlap largely with differences in wealth, and form separate social cliques. Nevertheless, the brotherhood of Islam overrides these internal distinctions and acts as a powerful cement of in-group solidarity and out-group rejection. Conservative Muslims are inclined to regard non-Muslims, and more particularly Hindus, as idolatrous, polytheistic pagans from whom one must dissociate oneself.

Hindu culture contrasts markedly with Islam on a number of basic values. The extreme religious tolerance of Hinduism that accepts all faiths as different paths to the same goal makes Hinduism a vague cultural tradition to which one claims an ill-defined adherence. Islam, on the other hand, with its simplicity of dogma and its precise moral and religious precepts, makes for a rigidly defined community. Hinduism, in its philosophical sophistication and its extremely complex but often conflicting and outwardly irrational ritual and rules of conduct, fails to act as a strong integrative force. This is clearly illustrated in Caneville. Here the vast majority of Hindus are ignorant of the most basic concepts of their religion, which becomes little more than a vague cultural allegiance and a domestic cult performed mostly by women.

Though conservative families regularly practice Hinduism at home and abstain from meat on certain days of the week, the younger and the better educated Hindus come into contact with religion only at Diwali and at weddings and funerals. Even Diwali, the Hindu festival of lights, has been greatly secularized. Many "Hindus," while still claiming the cultural allegiance, openly ridicule Hindu ritual, caste practices, etc., without any comprehension of Brahminic philosophy. At a teachers' party at the end of the school year, for example, a teacher presented a parody of Hindu ritual, which aroused hilarity among all but one or two of his colleagues. The performance took place early in the party when everyone was sober. Religious instruction is largely limited to a smattering of the Gita in an English translation. Attendance at both temples and mother-tongue schools is dropping steadily. Furthermore, in the absence of any clear-cut dogma, many sects, currents, and movements of Hinduism are represented in Caneville. While the more orthodox Sanathanists are in the majority, Arya Samajists and Saivists are also represented. The Divine Life Society, an extremely tolerant and eclectic reform movement opposed to caste distinctions, is strong in Caneville and includes several prominent members of the community.

The complexity and tolerance of Hinduism, in contrast to Islam, lead to three major differences between the two religious communities. The first difference is in the extent of internal cleavages, which are deeper in the Hindu group. There is a wide cultural difference between the South Indian language groups (Tamil and Telugu) and the North Indian groups (Hindi and Gujarati). Although these language groups are *less* strongly hierarchized than the Muslim language groups, they are separated by strong barriers not only to intermarriage, but also, in a lesser degree, to social intercourse.[3] Beyond these linguistic groups, *varna* and caste membership still play some divisive role among Hindus.[4] (These internal cleavages have been the object of two separate studies already referred to, and will be treated in greater detail in a later chapter.)

The differences between Islam and Hinduism also influence the extent to which the two groups affect one another. On the whole, there has been little acculturation either way. Muslim bridegrooms wear garlands of yellow flowers at weddings, which is a Hindu custom. Muslims have adopted in a modified form some of the caste prejudice of Hindus in that the Urdu-speaking Muslims, many of whom are low-caste converts from

---

[3] van den Berghe and Miller, *op. cit.*

[4] Rambiritch and van den Berghe, "Caste in a Natal Hindu Community."

Hinduism, are looked down upon by many Muslims of older stock. Conversely, Hindus have virtually discarded the caste system (except for endogamy) under the combined impact of Islam, Christianity, and South African material conditions. Gujarati is spoken by both Muslims and Hindus. Nevertheless, Muslims and Hindus have remained two clearly distinct groups.

A number of individuals, however, have crossed the line, and that almost exclusively in one direction. As may be expected, Islam, with its vigorous proselytism, its insistence on conversion in the case of mixed marriages, its appealing simplicity of dogma, and its opportunity for escaping low-caste status, has exerted a stronger attraction on Hindus than the other way around. While many Muslim families, a few of them prominent ones, are known to have converted to Islam within the past four generations, the opposite move is exceptional. A number of these conversions were motivated, at least in part, by the desire of low-caste Hindus to escape inferior status. In one case brought to my attention, that of a marriage between a Hindu man and a Muslim girl, the bridegroom converted to Islam and the children were brought up as Muslims. In three cases of concubinage between Muslims and Hindus, the Hindu partners and the children became Muslims. In two additional cases of concubinage, the Muslim women converted to Hinduism. In spite of the fact that Muslims are a relatively small minority in relation to Hindus, they have managed not only to retain their own identity, but also to attract a number of Hindus.

Finally, the contrast in outlook between Hinduism and Islam expresses itself in differing reactions to Western culture. Both the Muslim and the Hindu groups have been influenced by the dominant European culture surrounding them, but the degree of acculturation is greater for the Hindus. Both groups are exposed to a Western educational system in which English is used as the medium of instruction. Knowledge of English, the language of the dominant group in Natal, is indispensable in the economic sphere. In spite of its racial segregation, the Western school system has probably been the major acculturating factor for both Muslims and Hindus. The economic advantage of English education has long been recognized by all Indian leaders, and no other community in South Africa has made such efforts and sacrifices to render that education available to its children in the face of the government's discriminatory treatment of non-White children. Three of Caneville's six Indian primary schools were built by the initiative of the local Indian people. Had the Indian community relied only on the government schools, many Indian children would not get any education at all for lack of space. Although education is not compulsory for non-Europeans in South Africa, virtually all Indian parents, no matter how poor, make sacrifices to give their children at least four to six years of Western education. But Hindus have, on the whole, attached a greater importance than Muslims to post-primary English education, with the result that Hindus are over-represented in teaching and in the other professions.

Both Hindus and Muslims have favoured boys in education, but Muslims have given their girls even less education than the Hindus. I know of only one Muslim woman in town with a complete secondary education compared to at least thirty Hindu women. Several of the daughters and wives of well-to-do Muslim merchants have, until recently, been illiterate either in all languages or in English. In these cases, conservatism rather than economics was obviously the barrier. In regard to Western education it may be said broadly that Muslims discriminate against girls for reasons of conservatism, and that Hindus favour boys for economic reasons. While the Hindus have stressed Western education more than the Muslims, the Muslims have emphasized religious education in their mother tongue more heavily than the Hindus. This differential stress in the type of education between the two religious groups accounts in large part for the lesser Westernization of the Muslims.

The choice of language is perhaps the most important criterion of acculturation. While the vast majority of Hindus below the age of thirty speak English more fluently and more readily than their mother tongue, this is not true of Muslims. A substantial percentage of Muslim women, even young ones from well-to-do families, speak little or no English. Among Hindus only old women from the poorer classes speak no English. In the vast majority of middle-class Hindu homes, English is spoken in the family circle, except perhaps in the presence of the grandparents, whereas middle-class Muslim families generally speak an Indian language at home.

As far as dress is concerned, both Hindu and Muslim women wear their respective traditional garb, but Muslims start to do so at school age while Hindu girls do so only after adolescence. Furthermore, many middle-class, educated Hindu girls and young married women no longer wear saris except on such occasions as formal evening affairs or weddings. Their Muslim contemporaries all wear pantaloons, at least in public. Among Hindu men, only an occasional elder is still seen in turban and loincloth, though officiating priests still wear the loincloth as a rule. On the other hand, most of the Muslim men over fifty wear the fez in public, and quite a few wear special prayer robes at the mosque.

In cooking, Hindus and Muslims have been equally conservative. Western-type cooking is rare even among Christian Indians.

The family and kinship structure remains largely traditional in both groups, but, at least in the middle class, Hindus are more Westernized than Muslims. Women still play a distinctly subordinate role in both religious groups, but Hindu women have a much greater freedom of movement in such matters as attendance at public functions. In a number of Hindu families in the professional occupations, the host's wife stays in the parlour with the guests though she rarely takes an active part in the conversation. I have only observed this in one Muslim family, and the family was exceptional in that both spouses were highly educated.

Adoption of Christianity is another index of Westernization. Few Indians have adopted Christianity (in part because conversion does not confer any privilege in the White South African society), but those who have are virtually all Hindus. As in the case of conversion to Islam, low-caste Hindus have thereby escaped low-caste status and they have often adopted Christian surnames. Islam and Hinduism are not comparable in this respect since the egalitarian creed of Islam eliminates the one practical incentive for conversion that a Hindu finds in Christianity. But Hinduism itself has been deeply influenced by Western culture in a way that Islam has not been. More will be said of the virtual disappearance of caste in Caneville in Chapter VI. Undoubtedly the material impossibility of preserving the caste system in a Western economy is the main factor responsible for the disintegration of caste restrictions. But the egalitarian values of the broader Western culture (as opposed to the narrow racialist South African variant thereof) have also contributed to the condemnation of caste among Hindus. A special study of caste points out the tragic paradox of the Hindu rejecting caste on the basis of Western egalitarian values, but finding himself in a White-dominated, quasi-caste society that rejects him on colour grounds.[5]

Besides the elimination of caste, Hinduism has been influenced by European culture in several other aspects. Reform movements such as the Divine Life Society and the Rama-

---

[5] Cf. Rambiritch and van den Berghe, *op. cit.*

krishna attempt to create a syncretism of Christianity and Hinduism. The personality of Krishna is widely identified with that of Christ. The flexibility and complexity of Hinduism make that syncretism relatively easy, whereas the rigidity and simplicity of Islam doom any such attempts to condemnation as heresies.

I am not suggesting that the differential acculturation of Muslims and Hindus is due only to religion. In both groups, acculturation naturally increases with formal Western education, but, holding education constant, Hindus still tend to be more Westernized. Acculturation to the European way of life also increases with class status. Here the two groups cannot be closely compared because the Muslim middle class of Caneville is largely mercantile, while the Hindu middle class consists mostly of members of the professions. To be sure, the Gujarati Hindu merchants are as traditional in their behaviour as Muslim merchants, and are much more conservative than the other Hindu groups, which would indicate that religion is not the only factor affecting acculturation. Accepting these qualifications, Caneville does show how the broad ethos of a religion determines to a considerable extent the acceptance or rejection of an alien culture.

Of course, as mentioned earlier, acculturation has not been entirely one way. For example the local European culture has adopted a few Indian words in its vocabulary, such as *sirdar* (overseer); and curried foods occasionally appear on the table of White families. By far the major trend has been towards the Westernization of Indians, however. In the case of the educated Hindu middle class the process is virtually complete except for a vague cultural and religious affiliation.

While the general trend is clear, one must not assume that all the forces are on the side of Westernization of the Indian population. There are at least two counter-acculturative forces retarding the process. The first force is White rejection of all non-Europeans on the basis of skin colour and irrespective of the degree of Westernization. Not only is the Indian, even the Christian Indian, socially rejected by most Whites, but he is segregated in ghettos by law and custom, he is forced to attend segregated schools, etc. This European rejection has created a "racial" group of the Indians, and has evoked a degree of cohesion between heterogeneous Indian groups that would not otherwise have existed. The fact that the two main Indian political organizations are non-sectarian illustrates this point.

The other factor retarding Westernization might be termed "cultural pride," that is, the consciousness of belonging to a rich and ancient tradition. Muslims look to Mecca and the Islamic world as their cultural centre, and Hindus look to India; but both share a strong feeling, if not of cultural superiority, then at least of cultural equality with the West. This feeling of pride found its political and nationalist realization when India and Pakistan became independent.

The Indian does not, as a rule, seek assimilation with the European group as does the majority of South African Coloureds, for example. For one thing, he knows that assimilation is impossible under present conditions. But even if it were possible, complete assimilation would not be viewed as desirable. The average Indian accepts the necessity of speaking English and of adjusting himself to many aspects of the dominant Western culture, and he rejects certain aspects of his own culture, such as the caste system. But he nevertheless retains, often self-consciously, certain outward marks of Eastern culture. The most emacipated Hindu women continue to wear saris, at least on formal occasions. Families otherwise completely Westernized continue to cook Indian food and often eat with their fingers, though they are well versed in Western table etiquette. One often finds this interesting paradox among educated Hindus: in depth they are almost completely Westernized and their ignorance of Indian culture is almost as abysmal as that of most Europeans; yet, through pride of Indian cultural heritage, they retain some outward and superficial marks of Eastern culture.

This feeling of cultural pride is not a "sour grapes" reaction to European rejection. The latter certainly slowed down acculturation by limiting inter-racial contact and denying educational and economic opportunities to Indians. But this pride reaction, reinforced when India and Pakistan became independent, would be found, I am sure, even if social assimilation into White society were possible.

We must now turn to the third broad current in the Caneville cultural kaleidoscope, namely the African. Unlike the Indians who came from an urban, sedentary, and literate society and were introduced into Natal as agricultural workers, the Africans belonged to semi-nomadic, pastoral, militaristic, and non-literate cultures. They were conquered by force of arms in the nineteenth century, and have since been kept at the bottom of the South African racial hierarchy by the ruling White minority. As a powerless, defeated group, the Africans have not exerted much influence on the other two main cultural streams. A few words from Bantu languages have been adopted into English and most Natal place names are Zulu. Furthermore, a corrupted and impoverished form of Zulu known as *Fanagalo* or "kitchen Kaffir" is used as a *lingua franca* between Africans of various language groups and between Africans and non-Africans. A small minority of Europeans and even fewer Indians speak proper Zulu or Xhosa, the two main African tongues spoken in Caneville. Certain African staple foods such as "mealie meal" are also eaten by Europeans. For all practical purposes, however, acculturation has taken the direction of Westernization of the Africans.

At first glance, one is surprised that Islam has made no inroads into the African culture. In view of Christianity's failure to practice the equality it preaches, one might have expected that Islam would have made some appeal to the masses of Africans as it has in other parts of Africa. This has not been the case, partly because of lack of contact between Indians and Africans, and also because the Indians, who are themselves a subjugated group, have little to offer the Africans. The Caneville "location" does have a small group of eight Black Muslims, but they are not local Africans. They are the descendants of East African slaves captured from a slaving vessel by a British man-of-war, liberated by the British government, and disembarked in Durban, where they have since been known as Zanzibaree. The South African Government, in its classificatory zeal, has alternatively decreed them to be Indians and Coloureds, but physically they are indistinguishable from local Africans.

In Caneville, the Zanzibaree live in Dube Township and have been largely assimilated into Zulu culture. All the Zanzibaree are adult men. They are married to Zulu women. In only one case was the marriage according to Islamic rites. The wife converted to Islam and the children are brought up as Muslims. In the other cases, the Zulu women and the children are Christians and speak Zulu. The Zanzibaree men have remained Muslims, however, and attend the mosque, where they are treated as equals. They are also invited to Indian Muslim weddings, but otherwise live among Africans. They all speak Zulu with varying degrees of fluency. The children attend the African primary school in the location.

A few Africans have lived in such close contact with Indians that they have become Indianized. I met one old African man of sixty-four who was brought up by Indians, spoke Hindustani, and now manages a farm for Hindu owners. In three cases of extra-marital unions between African men and Hindu women, the children have taken their mother's surname and are being brought up as Hindus in the Indian part of town. They attend the Indian schools and are accepted in the Hindu community. A few Africans have gained a measure of acceptance among Indians, but, as a general rule, no Africans can be accepted into White society, except as servants or as menial workers in White enterprises. This itself has limited the scope of acculturation, and has often determined the kind of Western values most readily adopted by the African majority.

All African men are incorporated into the wage economy, pay taxes in cash, and have become accustomed to thinking in terms of money. They wear European clothing, often in various stages of disrepair, as the most visible sign of Western contact. Their material needs are virtually all satisfied by the products of European-owned factories. The food they eat is largely grown on European farms but with the help of African labour. Even European liquor, a black-market commodity for Africans, is often preferred to such indigenous beverages as "kaffir beer" to which they have ready access. When speaking the vernacular, Africans have absorbed some Afrikaans and a great many English words, such as numerals and the official terminology pertaining to the unpopular system which regiments their existence in the urban areas. All are aware of the vast machinery of White supremacy, and give at least tacit allegiance to protest movements such as the African National Congress which base their liberatory platforms on a Western ideology of democracy and equality. All these elements constitute the common denominator of Westernization among Africans.

Over and above this level of acculturation, African absorption of Western culture varies greatly. Of a sample of 35 migrant field workers, 29 speak little or no English and are illiterate. The permanently settled residents of Dube Village are much more Westernized. A few women are still seen wearing beads and traditional hair styles, but 95 per cent of the location dwellers dress in Western clothes, often ragged ones because of extreme poverty. Of the 214 heads of house-holds in Dube Township, 33 per cent have been living there for over ten years and a further 37 per cent between five and ten years, showing a relatively high stability and, hence, high exposure to an urban and non-tribal environment. About 26 per cent could be described as having a fair knowledge of English and a further 22 per cent as speaking at least some English. Of a sample of 108 applicants (mostly adult men) for housing in the township, 72 per cent were literate, at least to the extent of being able to sign their names. While the vast majority still follows the traditional custom of marriage by bride-wealth (*lobola*), 70 per cent are married by Christian rites as well. Excluding the few Zanzibar Muslims, 88 per cent claim allegiance to Christianity, and, of these, more than three-quarters belong to orthodox Christian denominations. Less than one-quarter belong to various "Zionist" denominations which incorporate a mixture of tribal and Christian beliefs and rites.[6] The majority of children receives a minimum of two or three years of lower primary education which insures at least semi-literacy. However, only about one child out of seven who enters school completes Standard VI. No African in Caneville can be described as either completely Westernized or completely tribal. A small group of twenty to twenty-five teachers, nurses, health assistants, and ministers speak fluent and correct English; have, for the most part, some secondary education; and have largely acquired middle-class European tastes in clothing and diet. Because of discrimination in salaries, however, they are forced to live on a much more modest scale than equally qualified Whites. But even this small emergent middle class is not completely Westernized in that these professional workers still speak their mother tongues, no matter how fluent their English, and remain

---

[6] For a treatment of African Separatist Churches see B. G. M. Sundkler, *Bantu Prophets in South Africa*.

African in some of their basic values, their mode of expression, their sense of humour, etc.

Following that small élite, one finds an intermediate group, perhaps three or four times as large, of people who have clearly broken their bonds with tribal culture, but who through lack of education speak only a little English. They are Christians, wear only Western clothing, and have acquired many Western tastes. The mass of the Caneville Africans, including the lower strata of the permanent Dube inhabitants as well as the migrant field workers, while far from purely tribal, retain ties in the rural "Native Reserves," are illiterate, and speak only African tongues (generally three or four of them).

It is interesting at this point to compare African and Indian reactions to Western culture. The difference is both qualitative and quantitative. Whereas a substantial segment of the Hindu population is completely Western in all aspects but religion and a few outward symbols of Eastern culture, there is no comparable African group in Caneville. Except in the field of religion, the process of acculturation to the West is more advanced in the Indian than in the African population. As Hilda Kuper points out, the Indian immigrant had the initial advantage over the African of coming from an urban, literate, and highly diversified society based on a money economy and exposed to the West for a long time. The traditional Indian social structure is more akin to and adjustable to the Western structure than are the pastoral, nomadic, non-literate African societies.[7]

A further factor mentioned by Kuper is the special legal and administrative treatment to which Africans have been subjected. On the one hand, African traditional institutions are utilized (but inevitably corrupted) by a system of rural administration, which offers little scope for development in the Western sense, and for this reason has become deeply suspect

[7] Kuper, *Indian People in Natal*, pp. 262–271.

as a scheme to keep the African masses backward and to turn their chiefs into puppets. On the other hand, Africans have been subjected to countless legislative measures that curb their freedom of movement, their earning capacity, and the scope of their education. Indians, to be sure, have also been the target of much discrimination, but not to the extent that Africans have. Neither has the Government utilized traditional Indian culture to rule Indians as it has done with Africans. Indian education in particular, while inferior to that of Whites, is far superior to that of Africans, particularly since the passing of the Bantu Education Act of 1953.[8] Another factor favouring the Indians over the Africans has been that the former have not been subjected to the disruption of family life and social ties that the migratory-labour policy has imposed on Africans.

In one important respect, the Africans have become acculturated faster than the Indians, however. Over 90 per cent of South African Indians retain their allegiance to Islam and Hinduism which provide cohesive systems of religious belief that can successfully compete with Christianity. Indigenous African religions, on the other hand, have failed to provide an effective alternative to the religion of the White conquerors. Africans have also been the object of greater missionary efforts than Indians. Less than 40 per cent of the Africans in the entire country are still classified as "heathens," and virtually all the others claim allegiance to Christian denominations.[9] The majority of Africans have accepted the Christian values of brotherhood, charity, and love of one's neighbour, and these values are now used to challenge the White man's claim to supremacy. Nearly one-third of the African Christians belong

---

[8] For a treatment of Bantu Education see Muriel Horrell, *A Survey of Race Relations in South Africa*, 1958–59, pp. 254–281; 1959–60, pp. 209–240.

[9] See Muriel Horrell, *A Survey of Race Relations in South Africa*, 1959–1960.

to a multiplicity of "separatist" churches, many of which have strong nativistic and revivalistic elements. It would be a grave mistake, however, to interpret the existence of these churches entirely as a return to tradition. More importantly, they represent a reaction to disillusionment with the failure of the established White-controlled denominations and White society generally to "practice what they teach."[10]

All these factors help to account for the faster rate of acculturation of Indians as compared to Africans except in the area of religion, but they fail to account for the qualitative differences in the way the two groups have reacted to, and selected from, Western culture. An important factor here is the evaluation of one's own culture. I have already mentioned how *cultural pride* among Indians leads to the paradoxical position where the middle-class educated person, who is completely Western in outlook and values, self-consciously retains certain superficial and outward symbols of Eastern culture. Among Africans the reverse position exists. Having suffered the crushing blow of military defeat followed by endless vexations and humiliation, and, having been treated as helots, many Africans came to harbour an inferiority feeling. Most urban Africans no longer feel inferior nor respect a White person simply because of their differing skin colours. The majority of Africans today challenge the White man's "divine" right to *baasskap,* but the claim of Western *culture* to superiority over African culture remains largely unchallenged. Unlike West Africa, where nationalist movements have been coupled with cultural revivalism, virtually all South African Black leaders have thought in terms of a Western type of society, the superiority of which they have implicitly assumed.

The reverse of this attitude is a sense of *cultural shame* in

---

[10] See B. G. M. Sundkler, *op. cit.*

respect to African culture. This factor of cultural shame is found mostly among Westernized Africans. There are remaining pockets of tribal Africans chiefly in the Transkei and in Zululand, who exhibit considerable cultural resilience and conservatism, and who reject not only the White machinery of oppression, but also Western culture and Christianity. In the Eastern Cape, this leads to a sharp cleavage between the Westernized peasants known as the "school" people and the tribal conservatives, known as the "red" people.[11]

Westernization is viewed by urbanized Africans as a process of cultural improvement from a stage of backwardness to one of civilisation. To be sure, there has been a certain amount of African revivalism for example, in the Zionist churches, but only as a minor counter-current to the dominant Western aspirations of the vast mass of Africans. The major stimulation of cultural revivalism and idealization of tribal society has come from the Nationalist Government in its deliberate attempt to perpetuate cultural differences and in its stubborn refusal to recognize non-tribal African nationalism that is essentially Western. The failure of the Government to elicit a favourable response to its "Bantustan" schemes clearly illustrates my argument. In his striving toward Western culture, the African, contrary to the Indian, adopts all visible and outward symbols of the West such as clothing, furniture, table manners, food, etc., even though he is, on the whole, less Westernized in depth (except for religion) than the Indian who self-consciously retains symbols of the Eastern culture.

It would be erroneous to interpret this strong African desire for Westernization as a desire to "be *White*." A few African women in large cities use hair-straighteners and bleaching face creams, but, in general, there is no feeling of *racial* inferiority such as is found among many Coloureds or American Negroes.

---

[11] Cf. Philip Mayer, *Townsmen or Tribesmen*.

African aspirations are cultural; they want to be Western, not White. Educated Africans in Caneville, for example, generally speak English together even if they both share the same mother tongue. They also strongly resent being talked to in Zulu by Whites, even by those few Whites who speak it fluently. The great emphasis on clothing gives another illustration of the urge to achieve Western middle-class standards. Much as the middle-class American Negro often "out-Babbitts" his White compatriots, the educated Caneville African often dresses more formally than the European in a similar or higher position. At meetings of the Bantu Consultative Council (BCC), for example, the Africans are generally dressed in coats and ties, even in the sweltering summer heat, while the Whites are in shirtsleeves. Similarly, while the White chairman invites informality in the proceedings, the African members comply only reluctantly, and would obviously prefer stiff formal proceedings. These illustrations tend to modify the common European stereotype that the African merely "apes" the Whites. Rather, the middle-class African conforms to his image of the Western middle class. He often does so with a certain time lag and "overshoots the mark," but there is a sound basis for that. The White is secure enough in his dominant status to be able to dress in khakis without loss of prestige, whereas the African is not. To phrase this point as a general proposition, reliance on external symbols of status appears to be inversely related to security of status.

So far, I may have given the erroneous impression that Caneville Africans are culturally homogeneous. They are probably more homogeneous than the Indians in that they are not as religiously or linguistically divided. Most Caneville Africans claim allegiance to Christianity and speak related Bantu tongues. They are, however, at least as heterogeneous as the European population. Of the 2,470 African field workers employed in the adjacent districts by the CSC, 86 per cent are

Pondo, 8 per cent Zulu, 4 per cent Shangaan, and 2 per cent Nyasa. Of 206 heads of household in Dube Village, 47 per cent are Zulu, 23 per cent Tonga, 7 per cent Nyasa, 6 per cent Shangaan, 6 per cent Pondo and 4 per cent Xhosa other than Pondo; 7 per cent belong to other groups such as Sotho, Swazi, and Ndebele. In the district as a whole, the Pondo are the largest single group, but as they are transient, they do not exert much influence on the other groups. Their "tribal homeland" (to use a government phrase) is in the Transkei, 150 miles south of Durban. They speak Xhosa and belong, together with the Zulu, to the large Nguni group of southern Bantu. Xhosa and Zulu are closely related tongues that are mutually understandable.

On the other hand, among the settled population of Dube Village, the Zulu constitute the largest group. Culturally they are clearly dominant. In relation to the African community, they are what the English are in the local European group. Nearly everybody in the township speaks Zulu, though the "foreign Natives" (to use a government semantic monstrosity) from Mozambique such as the Shangaan and Tonga, and the Nyasa from the Central African Federation often speak Zulu with an accent and with varying degrees of fluency. Zulu is the main medium of instruction at the government primary school, and most children either already speak the language when they come to school or quickly learn it. Not only is Zulu used in the location as a common language to the virtual exclusion of other African languages, but non-Zulu of the same ethnic group often speak Zulu together. Zulu has a distinct prestige value, and the use of another language sets one apart as an outsider. In the field districts, however, Pondo workers speak Xhosa among themselves.

The strength of Zulu culture in Caneville is such that it attracts not only Africans from other linguistic groups, but also some persons who could otherwise escape the status of Africans altogether and be classified as Coloureds. I have already mentioned the few Zanzibaree Muslims who are married to Zulu women, and whose children are with one exception brought up as Christian Zulus. These men would have experienced great difficulty in finding spouses among the Muslim Indians, but they could have sought accommodation outside the African location and had themselves classified as Coloureds. The same applies to a few Christian Coloured families who also live in the location and send their children to the African school. One of these children would be considered quite fair-skinned by Coloured standards. She is in fact just a shade too dark to pass as White. She speaks English at home, but she is as fluent in Zulu. When somebody suggested to her dark-skinned Coloured father that he should try to have himself classified as a Coloured, he emphatically rejected the idea, calling himself an African.

It is true that, except among the Mauritians who all try to pass as Whites and would reject any other Coloureds, there is no Coloured community in Caneville in which these people could find a place. Nevertheless, the incentive to escape the complex of restrictive laws (notably the pass and liquor laws) to which Africans are subjected is such that one would expect these Coloured families to move out of Caneville altogether.

Let us now summarize the entangled process of acculturation found in Caneville, and see what contribution Caneville can make to the theory of culture contact. Three broad cultural traditions, further subdivided into religious and linguistic groups, are found side by side, and hierarchically ranked. While, in theory, each of the three main cultural strains could have markedly affected the other two, only the dominant European culture has done so to any significant degree. This is, of course, in conformity with what happens all over the world: the main stream of acculturation flows from the technologically backward to the technologically advanced culture.

The interesting complication of Caneville in this respect is that the three main streams are on a scale of technological complexity in which Indian culture occupies an intermediate position. African culture bears little mark of Indian influence, however. One may argue that the Gandhian concepts of passive resistance and non-violence have permeated African political movements, notably the African National Congress. But since these political movements are otherwise largely Western in ideology and organization, and since the Mahatma himself was to some extent a product of the West, this is not a clear-cut example of the influence of Hindu culture on African culture. Numerical proportions, while of some importance, are not a major factor in the speed or extent of acculturation. While in the country as a whole Indians are a small minority, locally they form the majority. If numbers were the determining factor, then one would have expected Indian culture to have exerted more influence on the Africans than European culture whose members are in minority both locally and in the country as a whole. The hypothesis that technological development determines the main direction of acculturation is well established. But it remains to be tested in other cultural situations whether this "short-circuiting" of the process from the culture at the simplest technological level to that at the most complex level is a general finding. If this short-circuiting is a general phenomenon, the reasons for it must be explored further. Clearly, political dominance is not the whole answer, for there are many examples in history of conquerors adopting the culture of the conquered.

Caneville also throws some light on the factors making for the selectivity and the rate of acculturation. The existence or absence of an outside reference group in the larger society and the political or social position of that reference group seems to be an important determinant of acculturation. This factor is illustrated, within the European group, by the different reactions of the Mauritian and Afrikaans sub-groups. Both sub-groups share the fact that, in the local European society, they are relatively small, powerless, and of low status. But the Afrikaners, who belong to the group in power at the national level, resist anglicization; whereas the Mauritians, without such a powerful outside reference group, seek assimilation with the locally dominant English.

Within the Indian group, the difference in the rate of acculturation between Muslims and Hindus shows clearly the importance of in-group solidarity in retarding the process. Again, the lack of importance of group size is illustrated. If size were important, one would have expected the much smaller Muslim group to become assimilated fastest. In fact, the reverse has happened.

If in-group cohesion or solidarity seems to be a retarding influence, what I have called "cultural pride" does not appear to have that effect. In spite of cultural pride, the Indians, more especially Hindus, have become Westernized faster than the Africans, who exhibit cultural shame. This shame-pride aspect seems to affect the *selection* rather than the *rate* of acculturation. The shame reaction leads to the most commonly observed acculturation sequence: at first, the superficial, outward, material symbols of the dominant culture are eagerly adopted; to be followed by the "deeper" and less manifest aspects of that culture. That sequence is locally observed among the Africans. The pride reaction, on the other hand, reverses the sequence; outward symbols of the traditional culture are self-consciously preserved even though depth acculturation has already taken place. This phenomenon is found among the educated middle-class Hindu in Caneville. I believe that this shame-pride aspect is not only important, but must be clearly distinguished from the aspect of solidarity. Both Muslims and Hindus exhibit cultural pride, but only the former show a high degree of in-group solidarity or corporateness. The Africans show considerable group solidarity, a solidarity that now tends to transcend ethnic divisions. It is brought about by common subjugation and resentment of the White regime, and finds political expression in African nationalism. Yet, since most Africans also exhibit cultural shame, the two factors must be regarded as independently variable.

Another problem that I should like to raise in this chapter is the effect of status ascription on acculturation. Does the almost complete impermeability of the South African racial barriers impede Westernization, and, if so, how much? Caneville shows that even the most rigid colour bar has not prevented Westernization. Neither has it caused the rise of revivalistic or messianistic movements on a large scale. Admittedly, a number of tiny marginal Zionist African groups display revivalistic elements, and there is some evidence of a highly sophisticated revivalism among a small segment of the Hindu intellectuals. But in Caneville, as in the rest of South Africa, the possibility of large-scale revivalism or messianism seems remote. Not only have traditional institutions been undermined by industrialization to an extent unparalleled elsewhere in Black Africa, but the association of tribal revivalism with the policies of the government leads Africans to regard this kind of movement as reactionary.

If colour barriers have not brought about large counter-acculturation movements, have they retarded the adoption of Western ways? Certainly, racial discrimination, by limiting opportunities for non-Europeans, has slowed down the acquisition of Western material culture, education, and language. At a deeper level, the colour bar probably contributes to an increasing rejection of the institutionalized, White-controlled, Christian denominations among both Indians and Africans. With the partial exception of Catholicism, churches in South Africa have failed to reconcile their discriminatory practices with their egalitarian teachings. Among Africans, the reaction to institutionalized "White" Christianity first led to the formation of the separatist churches, but now begins to assume the form of secularization of the intelligentsia.

While many Africans have increasingly rejected White leadership in institutionalized religion, they have not, as a whole, rejected the basic tenets of Christian belief. Similarly, the White South African variant of Western culture, while provoking widespread and mounting opposition to White political domination, did not shake non-European belief in the broad principles of Western democracy, equality, justice, and opportunity. Indeed, it is the absorption of these Christian-Western values that gives impetus to the opposition to White domination in South Africa. In other words, the internalization by non-Western peoples of the basic values of the French Revolution and the basic ethics of Christianity leads to an interesting South African paradox. As a reaction to racial discrimination, the non-White peoples, particularly the Africans, have selected from Western civilisation those elements with which they could challenge the legitimacy of White supremacy. Conversely, the dominant White group, while claiming to be the custodian and repository of Christian-Western culture, has deviated from the most fundamental values thereof. This paradoxical process has now reached the point where teachers might well learn from their pupils.

Racial discrimination, then, has reduced the practical opportunities for Westernization, but not the incentive for it. Indeed, at the level of many fundamental values, discrimination has, in some respects, *accelerated* the process of acculturation. Such appearance of rejection of Western culture as exists, is only a rejection of the White South African variant of the European way of life. Unlike many of the South African Coloureds, neither Africans nor Indians want to be White. They all want to see the end of White domination. Nevertheless, Africans and Indians are becoming increasingly Western and for the most part strive in that direction. White domination is doomed in South Africa, but Western civilisation will unquestionably survive in the foreseeable future. This is not to say that some elements of Western culture will not be reinterpreted and modified, so that the end result will be a new variant of Western culture. Indeed, this will probably happen, in a similar way to the evolution of Afrikaner culture as a variant of Dutch culture.

Yet another facet of this complex problem of the relationship between status ascription and acculturation concerns White attitudes towards the Westernization of non-Whites. These attitudes have ranged from the active evangelization of the English missionaries of the nineteenth century to the traditional *trekboer* opposition to the sharing of Western culture with non-Whites. The main weight of attitudes seems to have been anti-acculturative, however, certainly since the Nationalist Party came into power. In 1959, the Minister of Bantu Education defended his Government's official policy in these terms: "It is the basic principle of Bantu education in general . . . to keep the Bantu child a Bantu child. . . . The Bantu must be so educated that they do not want to become imitators [of the Whites, but] that they will want to remain essentially Bantu . . . ."[12] This attitude is one of the many sources of contradiction and tension in South African society. On the one hand, Africans are denied political and economic rights on the ground that they are "uncivilized," while, on the other hand, the Government attempts by all means to reverse the Westernization process and "to keep the Bantu essentially Bantu." The Nationalists alternatively belittle and glorify traditional African culture, depending on circumstances. They profess to fear cultural "swamping" while keeping the number of Westernized Africans as small as possible.

---

[12] Horrell, *A Survey of Race Relations in South Africa, 1958–59*, pp. 254–255.

Through its recognition of "Native Law," the South African state has in certain respects retarded Westernization among Africans. Such basic traditional institutions as the *lobola* (bride-wealth in cattle), communal land tenure, and the chieftainship system have thus been retained in modified form to facilitate government of the rural masses. Although these institutions have, in many cases, changed their function so markedly as to make them parodies of the traditional system, the recent government-sponsored revivalism of "Bantu culture," and the long-standing cultural conservatism of previous South African governments have probably slowed down the pace of acculturation of Africans to the West. Paradoxically, it is also true that the government, by misunderstanding tribal institutions or reshaping them to suit the needs of "Native Administration," has contributed to the breakdown of the traditional structure without substituting a Western system in its place. In many cases the result is a pseudo-Bantu culture manufactured by White officials in Pretoria. A Zulu teacher told me, for example, that the Department of Bantu Education constantly coins "Zulu" words that are entirely unknown to Zulu linguists.

White South African attitudes are in marked contrast to the theory of assimilation held by the French, Portuguese, and Spanish. This theory was a logical deduction from the colonizer's feelings of cultural superiority and of contempt for the aboriginal cultures, coupled with a non-racial outlook. The colonial populations were viewed as primitive savages, but endowed with the capacity to absorb the blessings of the "superior" European culture. In South Africa, racialism led to the identification of colour and culture. The cultural "inferiority" of the "Natives" came to be accepted as a proof of their inherent genetic inferiority, and, hence, of their inability to become anything but "imitation Europeans." When acculturation of Africans to Western culture disproved the myth of black inferiority and, hence, threatened the legitimacy of White domination, the Nationalist government systematically attempted to "keep the Bantu essentially Bantu." The aim of that policy was not to maintain cultural pluralism for its own sake as the apologists of apartheid claim, but to maintain the myth of White superiority and the reality of White domination.

A final remark imposes itself here. In this chapter I have implicitly relied, for the sake of simplicity of presentation, on a rather mechanistic model of culture contact. I have dealt with contact between Caneville's various groups largely in terms of acculturation, i.e., of selective borrowing (usually in modified form) of elements from one culture by members of another. However, culture contact is not simply a process of "shopping" for items from another culture; and acculturation, in this restricted sense, does not exhaust the changes brought about by contact. Not only do cultures "borrow" from one another, but they also adjust and react to each other in terms of their own internal dynamics. As different cultures become integrated into a larger society characterized by what Durkheim called "organic solidarity" (i.e., interdependence of functionally heterogeneous and specialized parts), these cultures undergo profound transformations generated from inside.

In a colonial situation, hierarchization is one of the dominant aspects of the way Western and non-Western cultures have been welded together in a pluralistic society. By virtue of its dominance, European culture in Caneville and South Africa has been deeply modified. The Caneville English have developed a quaintly anachronistic colonial way of life. Their style of life, their political outlook, and their racial attitudes are much more reminiscent of bourgeois Victorian Britain than of contemporary England. We shall return to those aspects of local English culture when we deal with social stratification and race relations. Conversely the subordinate status of Africans has not only stimulated borrowing from the dominant culture, but also entailed cultural changes from within, for example, in the structure of authority, in the position of women, in family relationships, etc.

"Detribalization" is, thus, not simply the product of selective borrowing, with or without reinterpretation, from Western culture. It is also a process of cultural dislocation and disorganization initiated by the impact of external forces (such as industrialization and political subjection), and a process of readaption of traditional institutions to new conditions. Much of what is sometimes interpreted as cultural borrowing is in fact the result of internal readaptation to change. For example, the increasing predominance of nuclear as opposed to extended families among urban Africans is not so much an "imitation" of the European type of family as an adaptation imposed by urban conditions, restrictions on internal migration, etc.

The present chapter falls very short of an adequate account of culture dynamics in Caneville. Such is not the major focus of our study. We have simply tried to show that a bewildering variety of cultures are represented in Caneville, that these cultures are integrated into a pluralistic society, and hence, that the various cultural traditions are profoundly affected by mutual contact.

Chapter IV

THE POWER SYSTEM

WRITING about "power" is always a difficult task, for the concept has malevolent undertones. Yet, de-emphasizing the importance of power, as so many American sociologists have done, necessarily distorts social reality. Here I shall follow Max Weber's notion of power as the ability to enforce one's will despite resistance.[1] Still following the Weberian analysis, I shall isolate the political component of social life from both the economic and the status components. As will become clear in the next two chapters, these three components are very closely allied in Caneville. In particular, the virtually complete convertibility of power and wealth or, if one prefers, the near identity of economic and political power, immediately strikes the student of Caneville. As a monolithic "company town," Caneville exemplifies in miniature Marx's capitalist society. This close identity of power and wealth in Caneville is thus the result not of a Marxist bias on my part, but of the reality at hand. In fact, I reject the Marxist notion that power and wealth *necessarily* coincide. The most that can be said is that there is a long-range tendency for the two to go together. South Africa as a whole shows a sharp distinction between capital held largely by the English and political

---

[1] Max Weber, *The Theory of Social and Economic Organization.*

power in the hands of the Afrikaners. Power and wealth just happen to coincide in Caneville.

Another ideological misunderstanding that needs clarification from the outset concerns the Machiavellian, conspiratorial view of power. This aspect of power does of course exist; as a theory of power, however, it is a seductive oversimplification. While I disagree with the theory and practice of power in Caneville, I am not writing in order to "expose" anything. I shall merely try to analyse a particular type of political system as I found it.

The Caneville political system can best be described as paternalistic, or, in the words of the town's "Leader of the Opposition," a benevolent dictatorship. Donald Sherwood, the "ruling monarch" and an admirer of Nietzsche, describes himself as "a Fascist, a paternalist or whatever you want to call me." The exercise of power in Caneville follows a deliberate plan, referred to as the "Caneville Experiment." It is based on a definite theory of politics and human behaviour. In analysing the practice of power, it would be a mistake to disregard the theory on which that power is legitimized. Before we turn to Caneville proper, however, we must put the local situation within the framework of the Province of Natal and the Union (now Republic) of South Africa.

The powers of the central and the provincial governments circumscribe the sphere of local autonomy within well-defined limits. Central government maintains a monopoly of coercive force (locally represented by the South African Police), and controls most means of communication (post, telephone, telegraph) and rail transport. The laws of South Africa restrict the freedom of its citizens to live where they please, to move about, to marry or to have sexual relations with whom they choose, to own property, to vote, to compete in the labour market, to go on strike, to express opposition to the Government, to use certain public facilities, and (until 1962) to drink certain beverages. The central government imposes its taxes, determines the administrative structure of the sugar industry, and mediates in labour disputes. Through the departments of Bantu Education and of Bantu Administration and Development, which together constitute a partly autonomous and arbitrary colonial state within the state, the central government regiments almost every aspect of the lives of the voteless mass of its Black subjects. The state controls the African schools, the freedom of movement of Africans through the notorious "pass system," and the whole machinery of Bantu authorities, chiefs, and advisory bodies. Finally, the central government, through its secret police (known as the Special Branch), its dawn raids and house searches, its powers of arbitrary arrest, banishment, and detention without due process of law, its confiscation of property, and its tapping of telephones, casts its shadow on the public and private lives of all its citizens.

The powers of the Natal Provincial Administration are much more limited. The Province levies certain taxes, builds certain roads, controls primary and secondary schools (other than the African schools), and determines to a large extent the structure of local government other than African.

The main legal powers of the local Town Council are to levy rates on real estate, to grant trading licences, to spend the town's revenues, to control sanitation, to impose certain standards on the erection of buildings, and to zone certain areas for specified purposes. The township also operates the municipal beer hall for Africans, supervises street construction and maintenance, water supply, drainage, and hygiene inspections, carries out raids against illicit brewing among Africans, allocates housing in the African location, and runs a municipal housing project for Indians. The Town Council is also empowered to act as a judicial body in appeals against trade-licencing decisions or real estate assessments. This list of statutory powers of the local government does not, however, exhaust its *de facto* power, for the local authority is closely linked with the CSC, as will become clear later.

The sphere of local autonomy is thus clearly limited by the powers of the central and the provincial governments, mostly of the former. What relationship exists, then, between these three levels of government? The relationship between the local authorities and the Natal Provincial Administration is a close and amicable one. Although the local authorities pride themselves on being more progressive than the rest of the country, both the Province and Caneville are dominated by conservative English interests that find their political expression in the United Party, and to a lesser extent, in the Progressive Party. The president of the CSC, Donald Sherwood, through his position in the sugar industry, is an influential person in Natal politics, and he maintains close relations with the Administrator of Natal and other prominent local politicians. He has served on government commissions appointed by the United Party government of Smuts. His daughter-in-law, the wife of the "Crown Prince," Reginald Sherwood, is a close relative of a Member of Parliament for Durban.[2] The link is, in fact, so close that, in 1944, the Provincial Administration amended the Local Government Ordinance to meet what Donald Sherwood considered to be the requirements of Caneville. We shall describe that arrangement in greater detail later.

In contrast to this amicable relationship with the provincial government, the ties between the local and the central authori-

---

[2] My use of royal terminology in reference to the Sherwood family is not gratuitous. Several informants in Caneville used the simile of the British Royal Family when talking about the Sherwoods. The Zulu nickname or title of "Red King," now applied to Donald Sherwood, has become hereditary in the family. Donald's grandfather was the first to be given the title by the local Zulu.

ties are tenuous if not tense. They have been so since the Nationalist Government came into office in 1948. The reasons for tension do not arise from a basic policy disagreement, at least not in colour policy. Indeed, the "Caneville Experiment" presented the Nationalists with a blueprint of apartheid several years before they came into office and before the very word "apartheid" was coined. The difficulty is basically three-fold:

1. The local authority resents the increasing interference of central government in township affairs.

2. The Nationalists have little sympathy for the United Party English, and distrust the English capitalists, whom they view as a challenge to Afrikaner Nationalist power. Conversely, the locally dominant English view the Nationalists as semi-barbarous political *parvenus* who cannot speak the King's English and who are on a lower plane of civilisation.

3. The local English élite, while in agreement with Nationalist policies of racial segregation and discrimination, considers that the Nationalists are too frank and tactless about the implementation of these policies. It fears that the utter inflexibility of the "Nats" might precipitate a revolution, and, hence, endanger White supremacy. It believes that a few minor concessions or palliatives would prolong White domination for the foreseeable future.

While the central government is used as a convenient scapegoat and is constantly criticized in private by Company and Town officials, the necessity of reaching a *modus vivendi* with it is inescapable. The "foreign policy" of the Company and of the Town Council, as formulated by the Sherwoods and implemented by Roger Hancock and Thomas Whitehead, is, in broad outline, to minimize outside interference and blundering in the Caneville Experiment, and to safeguard the interests of the Company. To achieve these aims one must remain on polite terms with the central authorities, and compromise informally with them, so as to forestall any coercive moves that might threaten the interests of the Company. This policy of cautious containment often involves anticipating the wishes of the Nationalist Government so as to bring about change with a minimum amount of disruption and cost to the Company.

Let us take two examples of this containment policy. A South African Police force of some fifteen men under an Afrikaner sergeant is stationed in the centre of Caneville. The force is about equally divided between African, Indian, and European constables. The latter (who alone are allowed to carry firearms) are young, lowly-educated Afrikaners whose traditional colour outlook is to "keep the kaffir down" by means of deliberate discourtesy, punitive raiding and searching of houses, mass arrests on purely technical grounds, and sometimes physical brutality. The Town Council endeavours, with some measure of success, to minimize the number of South African Police raids in Dube Village, by raiding the location itself. Jan Swanepoel, the Town Secretary and Bantu Supervisor of Dube Village, organizes these raids with the help of the municipal policemen. The Africans do not consider that they benefit from this arrangement. To them, it matters little who conducts the raids. Even a highly conservative African clergyman characterized the liquor raids as "a blot on the good name of Caneville." The Company does benefit, however, by retaining a greater amount of direct control over the population and by curbing illicit brewing.

Another illustration of the Company's containment policy concerns residential segregation of racial groups under the provisions of the Group Areas Act. As I have already mentioned, there is no conflict in basic policy between the Company and the Nationalist Government on the issue of segregation. Here again, the Company anticipated Government policy.

However, the Caneville Experiment did not provide for quite as rigid a segregation as the Government would like to see. For one thing, the Company is limited by financial considerations in segregating people, an aspect which the Government is apt to discount in pursuing its policy.

More specifically, the Caneville Experiment failed to satisfy the Group Areas Board on two main counts. In some of the Company's non-European barracks, Africans and Indians live together or close to one another. That problem was easily settled by reshuffling the workers to the satisfaction of the Board. The second problem was more difficult to solve. A few Europeans not employed by the CSC were found to be living among Indians. A special area had to be found for them. The Company recommended to the Group Areas Board that the small area of Fairwind, now occupied by Indians, be declared a European area for the purpose of settling those few Europeans. The Indian residents of the area, one of whom is a prominent foe of the Company, are all opposed to being uprooted. The Company has tried to persuade them to accept equivalent properties on the "Indian" side of the Caneville River—so far, however, without success.

By recommending the displacement of these Indian residents, the Company openly violated one of the avowed principles of the Caneville Experiment, namely that segregation should be voluntary and not forced. The Company knows that, once the Government declares an area for occupation by a certain racial group, all other persons have to sell and vacate their properties, often at a large financial loss. Yet it has recommended such a move in order to avoid a conflict which might be detrimental to it. It must be added that, even accepting the principle of racial segregation, there is no need to expropriate any Indian residents. The Company might have recommended the expropriation of a few of its 37,000 acres of land for that purpose. As one Indian businessman bitterly pointed out to me, there is a large European golf course opposite the Fairwind area, which is nearer to the present European residential area of Sugartown, and which is more than large enough for the purpose. The Company eventually withdrew its recommendation to make Fairwind a European area because of the difficulties involved in displacing the large Indian primary school located there.

A letter written in 1955 by a high Company official to the Group Areas Board summarizes the relationship between local and central government rather clearly. In that letter, the official expresses "appreciation of your Board's readiness to co-operate and to meet our point of view whenever it was possible to do so and of the agreeable manner in which the discussions were conducted." The same official, whose dislike for the Nationalist Government is intense, told me verbally, "You have got to work with those people whether you like it or not."

So far, I have tried to put the local political system into the broader context of the provincial and central governments. Now I must turn, first to the theory, and then to the practice, of political power in Caneville. The Caneville Experiment was initiated in the 1930's and has largely been the work of three men: Peter du Plessis, then the Company physician; Donald Sherwood, the prime theorist of the Experiment; and Thomas Whitehead, who as vice-president (now retired) of the CSC and mayor of the town, acted, as it were, as "His Majesty's" trusted First Minister. In presenting the theory of the Experiment, I shall rely heavily on quotations from Sherwood's and Whitehead's writings.[3] The aim of the Caneville Experiment is to create "a perfect sugar undertaking in an ideal multi-

---

[3] As mentioned earlier, I cannot give the references for the quotations without revealing the identity of the town and of the authors. Changes of names have been introduced in the quotations for the same reason.

racial community," and its proponents hope "that the story of Caneville may be of use in promoting similar co-operation between the races, not only in Africa but throughout the world."

The explicit premise of the Experiment is that democracy can only work in the Anglo-Saxon "race" and cannot be exported to other "races," and, indeed, that democracy is not such a desirable aim. Donald Sherwood states:

> We all know that it is the genius of, shall we say, the Anglo-Saxon race to absorb democracy. Many of us know that no Englishman fully appreciates why other people cannot equally easily be democratic. I think you will agree that it is somewhat problematical as to whether democracy has been of use to either of these two great European nations, the French nation or the Italian nation. Therefore how much more dangerous it is to assume that the Indian population of this country, that has been subject for generations to oppression, will be able to understand and fully absorb the benefits that the Anglo-Saxon people derive from democratic government. . . . Our own district of Caneville . . . has some 10,000 Indian inhabitants. I think you will agree that the vast majority of these people know nothing whatsoever about democracy. Perhaps not the vast majority but certainly the majority are unable to read or write. Would not the inevitable result of applying the democratic principle be that the Indians of this district would be represented by a demagogue who stood on a box and talked communism?

Implicit in the above quotation is a hierarchy of "races," with the Anglo-Saxon on top. Because democracy does not work for other European "races" which stand just below the Anglo-Saxon race in this hierarchy, therefore, it is unthinkable that it can work for the Indians who are still one rung lower in the hierarchy. It is even more absurd to expect that democracy can work for the "Natives" who are at the bottom of the racial pyramid.

Sherwood goes on to say:

> The democratic principle is equally foreign to the mind of the Bantu male, for in patrilineal tribal rule the chief or headman is right, whether he is altruistic or tyrannical. When the Native tries to conceive the idea of an election his tribal mind thinks of some form of mortal combat between the candidates . . . he sees in democracy a way for the demagogue to rob him of his birthright. . . . [Under universal franchise] it is the majority and not the whole that governs; both universal suffrage and common roll franchise—since the demagogue inevitably panders to the lowest in the electorate—put power into the hands of the inferior and the incompetent.

Elsewhere, Sherwood approvingly quotes a biographer of Augustus:

> He [Augustus] was free of egalitarian whimsies, a malady from which the ancient world did not suffer. He did not believe in that deterioration of democratic theory which imagines that there is a peculiar inspiration in the opinion of the ignorant and a singular nobility in the character of the penniless.

Having made these statements, Sherwood oddly contradicts himself:

> Like Augustus, I see no merit in egalitarianism; but I believe in government by discussion and for that purpose I am prepared to accept any person, irrespective of race, colour, creed or sex, on the grounds of excellence alone.

It will become abundantly clear, however, that the principle of "excellence" only applies within the White group, and that colour rather than merit determines a person's opportunities in Caneville. Moreover, those qualifying as "excellent" on grounds of education are most likely to reject Sherwood's aristocratic principles.

On the functions of local government, Sherwood says:

> Local authorities are established to protect the interests

of property-owners—that is, ratepayers—and to improve the lot of the less fortunate members of the community.

Thomas Whitehead, who by all but White South African standards is a conservative, but who is nevertheless considerably more liberal than Donald Sherwood, describes at length the Caneville Experiment:

> Remember first that Caneville is constituted as one community, a unity of people, a holistic synthesis of vastly varying human beings. The object is to maintain that unity.

The way to maintain that unity, according to Whitehead, is to "aggregate" people in racial groups:

> Agrarian partition, or zoning, for the purpose of locating race groups has proved, in Caneville, to be a sound, orderly, efficient, economic, and equitable way of providing housing and amenities for mixed populations, and as a system it has the co-operation of all groups . . . . This was not segregation—not Apartheid. Segregation implies breaking down, severing, or isolating parts from a whole; it is amputation . . . . But there is nothing repugnant about the idea of the sorting of individuals into groups or classes or clubs by aggregation. Members of such groups are bonded by similarities in race, religion, traditions, interest, custom, trade, and occupation.

Another high Company official expressed the theme of "aggregation" in the following terms:

> Before this government came into power, there was friendly separation on a give-and-take basis here in Caneville. That's the way people like it. Each wants to associate with his own people who have the same outlook. Muslims want to keep together as opposed to Hindus, Natives as against Indians, Europeans as against Natives. But before [the Nationalist Government] it was not rigid. I believe that the Progressive Party has the right approach. The Liberal Party would throw the country into chaos.

The majority of educated non-White Canevilleans, however, fail to see anything in "aggregation" except a play on words to avoid the now unpalatable word "segregation." For non-Europeans "aggregation" in Caneville is no more voluntary than in the rest of South Africa, nor is it based on anything besides skin colour and hair straightness. No non-European employee of the Company could elect to live in the White area of Sugartown if he wanted to. Under law no African except a domestic servant can live on Indian or European premises without a permit which he is only granted because of housing shortage in Dube Village. Christians of different skin colour may not live together, but Christians and Hindus of the same "race" must live together. Doctors and ministers may not live together if they belong to different "races," but an African minister must live next door to an illiterate African worker because they are both Black. (This subject will be treated in detail in Chapters VI and VII.) Let us now examine the other elements of the Caneville Experiment.

Government by consultation with appointed representation by racial group is the political side of the theory. More will be said about the composition of the Town Council shortly. Recently Sherwood presented a cautious plan for a highly qualified franchise (limited to people of high income and with ten years of education) with separate voters' rolls for each racial group. On the whole, however, progress is viewed mostly in economic terms. Whitehead writes:

> The vital role of economics in the sociological development of this community of Caneville has been strongly emphasized, because it means the build-up of personal prestige as well as family welfare, and because the somewhat widespread idea that the non-European's chief target is political emancipation is not true. The immediate problem is economic.

Donald Sherwood summarizes his programme for Caneville as follows:

First of all we must raise the standard of living and make continuous efforts in this regard. Secondly, we must improve housing, building homes that as far as possible will be modern in 40 years time, the period of amortization of a Government housing scheme loan; for without good housing it is difficult for family life to thrive. Thirdly, we must reduce the fear of economic hardship or catastrophe, which can so easily occur in the working man's home through the death or incapacitation of the wage-earner. Even the serious illness of one of his family can cause an insupportable burden of debt. There must therefore be free medical attention; provision for old age, and security of employment. The fundamental necessities, then, are food, family life, and freedom from fear. But this is not enough if "the ultimate aim of life is right action." We must add a fourth necessity—Beauty.

So much for the theory of the Caneville Experiment. Let us now turn to the exercise of power. Like the old Habsburg empire, the Caneville domain is bicephalous; it consists of the Company and the Town, under a joint monarch. Through its economic power, the Company controls the Town. Donald Sherwood, known as "The President," lives in regal isolation in a large mansion on top of a hill surrounded by a large park. He lives there alone surrounded by his retinue of non-European servants who attend to his needs and luxuries. While he takes an active part in the management of the CSC, he delegates his power to Thomas Whitehead in the township. He is rarely seen at public functions which he studiously avoids and where his son Reginald, or Whitehead, represents him. As a town resident put it to me: "It's like the British Royal Family. You never see Princess Margaret and Queen Elizabeth together in public." Donald plays the role of the distant but benevolent monarch and thereby diverts direct hostility from himself. Reginald, affectionately known as "Mr. Reg," is the easily approachable, sympathetic person who listens to people's troubles. Whitehead is the man of action who implements the policy in the township, and who in the process bears the brunt of people's criticisms. One of the most common criticisms directed at Whitehead is that he lives in a neighbouring town, not in Caneville, that he owns no property in Caneville, and hence is an outsider.

The power structure of the CSC resembles that of all limited companies. A Board of Directors of ten persons sits monthly with Donald Sherwood as chairman, and Reginald as vice-chairman. In addition, four high Company executives or retired executives also sit on the board, either as full members or as alternates for the two absent British directors. The remaining four members are outsiders to Caneville. With one exception, all the directors are of English or Scottish descent. On the executive side, Donald Sherwood is president and Reginald Sherwood is vice-president (the position occupied by Whitehead before his retirement when Reginald was still a student). Below that top, quasi-hereditary level, the Company is sub-divided into three sections: Factory, Office, and Field, each under a manager. Of the three managers, Roger Hancock, although much the junior of the Field manager, is given senior status, and is being groomed to step into Reginald's shoes when Donald retires.

Hancock's right-hand man, the assistant office manager, will most likely succeed him. Each of the managers in turn has several deputy managers. All these officials, together with the medical officer, constitute the top executives who sit monthly as a management committee of thirteen members, and whose function it is to implement the policy decisions arrived at by the directors. The top executive includes only one Afrikaner and no Mauritians. Below the top executives are found a few junior executives, the field supervisors, the office clerks and typists (mostly women), and the skilled artisans and technicians. Together they constitute the highly paid European staff of about 215 employees. A group of perhaps 80 minor clerks, technicians, and heavy-vehicle drivers, almost all Indians, constitute the élite of the large non-European staff. A larger group of some 300 to 400 non-European (mostly Indian) semi-skilled workers and foremen rank a notch above the mass of some 3,000 cane cutters and other unskilled labourers. The unskilled working force is predominantly African. The Company employs some 3,500 full-time non-European workers, of whom 1,000 are Indian and 2,500 African, in addition to about 600 casual workers (mostly women and children).

The Company's power structure is typical of a modern business bureaucracy, with the added element of the rigid South African colour bar in employment. All positions requiring initiative (and quite a few others besides, such as clerical jobs) are reserved for Europeans. The high executives and the directors are mostly English.

As the only sizeable industry in Caneville, and the only large employer, the CSC completely dominates the town. This is the result of a deliberate design. When Caneville had grown large enough in the 1940's to become incorporated as a township, Donald Sherwood persuaded the Natal Provincial Administration to change the Local Government Ordinance to suit his wishes. The amendment allowed the creation of a Town Council that would be entirely appointed, technically by the Administrator of Natal, in fact by Donald Sherwood upon Whitehead's recommendation. This arrangement suited perfectly Sherwood's autocratic notion of government by "consultation."

Caneville's Town Council, while entirely non-elective, is one of the few in South Africa to have non-European members.[4] A five-member all-European Council was first formed

---

[4] Cape Town and Stanger also have non-White city councillors, and they are elected, not appointed. In the overwhelming majority of cases, South African towns are administered by all-White

in 1945. In 1946 this body was enlarged to seven members, including two Indians. Subsequently two Africans were co-opted to the Council without the right to vote. The Council now consists of nine members, of whom five are Europeans, who are all connected with the CSC. In keeping with the racial thinking of the Experiment, the Indian and African members are supposed to represent "their races." Sectional representation is carried one step further in that one of the Indians is a Hindu and the other a Muslim; of the Africans one is a Zulu and the other a Xhosa. This arrangement is informal, not statutory. As only two of the four non-Europeans on the Council have a right to vote, there is no possible danger of the Whites being outvoted and of CSC policy being rejected. One of the arguments used by the Company to defend its complete control of the Town Council is that the CSC is the biggest taxpayer in Caneville. In fact, the Company pays 40 per cent of the town's taxes but controls *all* the votes on the Council. At the same time, by comparison with other South African towns, the arrangement gives the appearance of liberalism.

A quotation from Whitehead proves that the system is intended to maintain White supremacy. Explaining why the two Indians were not asked to join the Council in 1945, when the body consisted of five members, Whitehead writes:

> The effect of the amendment was that Caneville could have implemented its declared policy of providing the Indian inhabitants with direct representation in July 1945. For two reasons it did not immediately do so; first, to have asked two of the Europeans who had held office on the Health Committee to stand down in order to make way for two Indian members would have caused resentment

councils elected by White voters. The presence of an *elected* Indian councillor in neighbouring Stanger is often referred to by educated Indians in Caneville when they attack the appointive system of Caneville.

and dissatisfaction; second, it was essential that European control of the affairs of the township should be maintained; a board composed of three Europeans and two Indians was not considered sufficiently weighted in favour of European domination.

Whitehead, as mayor and trusted lieutenant of Donald Sherwood, sits in the chair of the Council, and to a considerable extent exercises his own judgment in running the town. His influence largely determines who sits on the Council and he has, during the period of the study, replaced two members, one to fill a vacancy through retirement and the other because he thought that the incumbent was not suitable. Hancock, as the up-and-coming bright young man in the CSC, is also active on the Council. He is a conservative United Party person, considerably less "liberal" than Whitehead. At present he is chairman of the finance committee. Whitehead and Hancock, together with Reginald Sherwood, who also sits on the Council, constitute the inner circle of the body, the triumvirate that effectively runs the township. The other two European members are Dr. L. Woods, the Company physician who heads the hygiene committee; and Richard Miller, a minor Company official who sits on the Council in his capacity as chairman of the Bantu Consultative Council.

The Hindu member of the Council is B. L. Goshalia, the town's wealthiest merchant. When he accepted the post he was expelled from the Natal Indian Congress, a political organisation which aims at achieving a non-racial democracy in South Africa. Since then he has taken the cautious, conservative position of co-operating with the authorities in the hope of bringing about gradual concessions. The former Muslim representative, Mohammed Kassim, was a conservative, non-political merchant who, while a cultivated Arabic scholar, had little English education. Since his retirement, he has been replaced by Dr. O. B. Khan, a young, dynamic, overseas-trained physician. One of the African representatives is a highly conservative Anglican clergyman, Reverend Ambrose Mvusi, who can best be characterized as a local Booker T. Washington. He is the only African in Caneville who still regularly uses the words "Bantu" and "Native" in reference to Africans. Speaking about the relationship between the Company and the local Africans, he said, "The Bantu are like children under a trusted father. The mission of the father is to uplift gradually his children." The other African on the Council, Julius Ngubane, has previously been active in the African National Congress (the main African liberatory movement), but has now withdrawn from politics and prefers to play a cautious game of co-operation with the local authorities. Though Dr. Khan shows signs that he does not intend to be completely acquiescent to Company policy, none of the non-White members of the Council has yet challenged Company rule.

Under the tactful and firm chairmanship of Mr. Whitehead the Town Council, meeting monthly, serves as an efficient instrument of White policy. Most important decisions are made prior to the meetings by informal consultation between the members of the triumvirate, who nearly monopolize the discussion during meetings. I am not suggesting that other members are not given the *opportunity* to speak. They have this opportunity but are not active participants. Only minor points are thrown open for wider discussion. On the rare occasions when there is any threat of open disagreement between members of the Council, Whitehead skillfully avoids verbal clashes through conciliation or evasion. No formal votes are taken, and resolutions are passed "unanimously" by the chairman asking a perfunctory "Agreed?" During the meetings I attended, I never heard a dissenting voice. On most matters of general interest, Whitehead simply asks for the advice of Hancock and "Mr. Reg." According to the theory of racial representation, Indian and African members are only asked for their opinions on matters that affect "their own people." This applies most particularly to the Africans, who almost never participate in discussions on matters of general interest. In other respects also, there are perceptible differences in the treatment of White and non-White members. For example, when tea is served by an African cleaner during the meeting, the cups are distributed following the racial hierarchy: all the Whites are served first including Swanepoel and the typist who do not belong to the Council, then the two Indians, and finally the Africans. The chairman largely regulates the speed at which business is transacted. Proceedings are technically open to the public, for whom benches are provided, but the fact is not publicized and I have never seen any spectators during Council meetings.

Under the machinery created by the central government, Africans are governed as an entity separate from the rest of the population. "Bantu affairs" always form a special part of the Town Council's agenda and a special advisory body, the Bantu Consultative Council (BCC), purports to represent African interests. The BCC is a completely powerless body consisting of six African members under a European chairman. Of the six African members, two are appointed by the local authorities, and four are elected by the heads of households in the African location. The vote is not secret, as each voter must state his choice orally in front of the White location supervisor. The BCC exercises no control over location finances or any other matter affecting "its people." Its sole functions are to act as a sounding board for members' opinions and to advise local authorities.

In Caneville, the two African members of the Town Council also sit on the BCC. With Mr. Miller, the chairman of the BCC, these men act as the liaison between Dube Village and the rest of Caneville. In addition to the BCC members and their European chairman, Swanepoel and Whitehead generally attend meetings as well. When the chairman is away, Swanepoel takes the chair, although he is not a member of the BCC. Swanepoel, in his dual role of location supervisor and town secretary, takes care of the day-to-day administration of Dube Village as well as the town as a whole. He has only such authority as Whitehead delegates to him, and makes no major decisions himself, but in the granting of trading licences, housing, and various permits he wields considerable power over the average Caneville resident. Swanepoel also conducts the liquor raids in the African location. In Dube Village, Swanepoel is assisted by an African clerk who is also secretary of the BCC. In the Town Hall, he has a staff of two European women typists and three Indian clerks.

Meetings of the BCC deal only with minor matters, such as the brewing of municipal beer, leaks in the church roof, the uniforms of the Bantu Band, complaints over trespassing, and the granting of trading licences. No vote—not even a perfunctory passing of resolutions—is ever taken as the BCC has only advisory functions. Whitehead does much of the talking when he is present, though he is not a member. Mvusi and Ngubane are the only Africans to speak with any frequency, but since they dislike one another, they rarely attend meetings together. The general tone of the discussion is one of subservient gratitude for all the Company does for the Africans. In Whitehead's absence, the African members become more talkative, the tone of the debate is less restrained, and the discussion franker, though still inhibited by the presence of Swanepoel.

Another body in the African village is the School Committee, the composition of which is almost identical to that of the BCC, but with an African chairman, under the terms of the Bantu Education Act. The Dube Village Committee is a subsidiary body of a larger Bantu School Board. The

Town Council has no direct jurisdiction over the African School Committee, which falls under the Bantu Education Department.

It must not be inferred from the above description that Caneville's system of local government is entirely or even largely detrimental to the inhabitants' welfare. Such a picture would be a gross distortion of facts. The exercise of power in Caneville is wholly autocratic, but benevolently so. Both Whitehead and Reginald Sherwood are always willing to listen to people's grievances, and whenever suggestions do not conflict with Company policy or threaten in any way its authority, action is promptly taken to meet "reasonable" requests. In many respects, Caneville is, indeed, a model community, certainly by South African standards. Both through the private philanthropy of the Sherwood family and the public philanthropy of the CSC, Caneville exhibits a number of remarkable achievements, most notably in the fields of sanitation and hygiene, recreational facilities and housing.

A health clinic, operated by Dr. du Plessis and a staff of several nurses and health assistants, caters to the needs of the non-Europeans. The building was donated by the Sherwood family, as two large oil portraits of Donald and his father in the entrance hall remind the visitor. In recent years the clinic, which is financed by the central government, has been forced by budgetary restrictions to retrench its activities. The CSC operates a very good hospital where its employees are given complete medical attention free of charge. The Town sponsors an extensive health programme, including antimalaria spraying. In the recreational area, ample athletic fields exist. Housing of non-Europeans in Caneville compares very favourably with that of most other South African towns; and for architectural attractiveness, Caneville has few rivals. For all these achievements the CSC expects the non-Europeans to be grateful. These achievements are real enough, but they leave the power monopoly of the CSC unaffected. The political system remains one of benevolent despotism, and any potential threat to it is dealt with swiftly through a series of mechanisms which we shall examine shortly.

Nor does the benevolence of the system alter the tight control that the CSC exercises through the Town Council. A single illustration will suffice. One of the White municipal officials is highly unpopular among the inhabitants for his callous and discourteous treatment of non-Europeans, whom he openly calls "coolies," "kaffirs," and "monkeys." While Whitehead has reprimanded him, he is retained in office because he administers policy with a strong hand. On the other hand, Mr. Miller's predecessor as chairman of the BCC, a courteous, considerate person, well liked among Africans, was removed from his post because, in the words of a high Company official, "He let things run their own course. You have to force people to do things for their own good. They don't do it by themselves." The official reason given for his removal was that he was transferred to a more distant field section of the CSC.

Another factor which detracts from the philanthropy and benevolence of the system is that the underlying philosophy is one of racial discrimination in which a radically different standard is applied to Europeans and non-Europeans. The former enjoy considerably higher salaries and better facilities, housing, and employment opportunities than the non-Europeans. This dual standard is based on racial classification, irrespective of merit. Such a state of affairs is taken completely for granted by all but a tiny minority of Europeans. Two little quotations will illustrate this dichotomous thinking. A minor Company official was praising the non-European cottages built by the CSC. "These are very nice houses," he said. "I wouldn't mind having one of those as a cottage on the beach." Another Company official, a highly educated senior executive, explained how hard-pressed the widow of a European employee would be with a pension of only £25 a month. Half an hour later, when talking about non-European old-age pensions of £2 to £3 a month, he called these "not bad when you consider how many of them there are and what a liability it is for the Company." Yet it would be wrong to believe that these men are consciously callous. They are simply the products of a socially conditioned way of thinking that makes one see non-Whites as altogether different human beings. Non-Whites are held to have far fewer needs than Whites, and to be able to live adequately on a fraction of what a White person requires. Caneville shares the colour fixation of the larger White South African society.

Let us now turn to a closer examination of the methods used by the CSC to maintain a monopoly of power. Here, too, Caneville is not unique but follows a pattern familiar to the student of politics. Nor do these methods belong to a carefully calculated Machiavellian scheme of oppression. In some cases their use is deliberate, in others unconscious. Even when these techniques are applied deliberately, it does not follow that their users are cynical power-mongers. The methods employed are often considered normal and legitimate means of ameliorating the physical lot of those whom Donald Sherwood calls "the inferior and the incompetent."

I shall label these mechanisms of political power and then illustrate them one by one:

1. The "Bread and Circuses" device.
2. The "Family Affair" device.
3. The Co-optation device.
4. The "Control of Potential Opposition" device.

1. The first device is too well known to require much explanation. Basically, it is founded on the premise that diver-

sionary entertainment and economic well-being are substitutes for political rights. In Whitehead's words, "The somewhat widespread idea that the non-European's chief target is political emancipation is not true. The immediate problem is economic." As Reginald Sherwood once remarked to me, "In order to maintain the capitalist system you have got to keep the masses amused."

To what extent the "Bread and Circuses" technique is successful, I shall examine later. The fact is that, of all the devices used by the Company, this is probably the most widespread and conscious one. Indeed, it underlies the whole philosophy of paternalism or benevolent despotism, wherever it is found. We must, therefore, examine its application in detail. The phrases: "Our workers are happy here," "We must keep our workers happy," "You have never seen a happier bunch of Natives," "The Pondos are a contented lot" recur as a leitmotiv in the conversation of White Company employees. Symptomatically, I have never heard it expressed by an Indian or African. White officials are convinced of the truth of their assertions, and their belief is reinforced by the apparent gratefulness and bland smiles of non-Europeans in their dealings with Whites.

The aim to "keep the workers happy" in Caneville is pursued mainly in four different ways. The first two are the provision of good medical care and of well-balanced, nutritious rations. These measures also pay an immediate dividend in labour productivity. One White official rhetorically asked me, "How can you expect a Native to do a day's work on an empty stomach?" Nevertheless, when Reginald Sherwood recently suggested at a meeting of the Board of Directors that field workers be given breakfast, his proposal, though finally accepted, met with considerable opposition. Some of the directors argued that the "Natives" were not used to eating breakfast and, hence, did not want any. This rationalization was exploded when breakfast was introduced and the workers availed themselves of it.

The third application of the formula is the provision for family housing. This represents a heavy capital outlay to the employer, since employees are all given free housing. A "model" non-European four-room family cottage costs about £400, compared to the average capital outlay of about £25 per migrant worker in military-type barracks. The settling of the labour force has so far been confined to the mill workers, and the Company still resorts to migratory labour for the mass of its field workers. Costly though the initial outlay for family housing is, a stabilized labour force pays considerable dividends in the long run. The CSC has recognized its benefits with regard to semi-skilled and supervisory personnel. The Company still believes, however, that, for its unskilled field force, the gain in productivity of labour would not outweigh the capital expenditure for permanent housing. The field force therefore remains migratory, thus perpetuating the disruptive influence of this labour system upon African family life.

Turning to the "circuses" part of the age-old formula, the Company organizes and controls a well-run recreation programme. For the field workers it takes the form of weekly soccer matches and monthly *Ngoma* dancing feasts. Both kinds of events are organized on a section basis. Each of the thirteen field sections has a team that competes against the others. For the dancing events, the Company slaughters oxen and supplies ample quantities of "kaffir beer." Those events, held on Sundays, draw large crowds of spectators, mostly Pondo field workers. The White field personnel also attend them, in a patronizing manner, as the management of the Company expects them to show an interest in the welfare of their workers. Similarly, the performance of the various teams is taken as an index of sectional loyalty and of the efficiency of management by the White section heads. The whole recreation programme is rationalized on the military principle that men, particularly single men, must be kept busy if they are to stay out of mischief, and that healthy sporting competition maintains *esprit de corps*. One section head put it this way:

> The poor devils, they have no other entertainment. We [Whites] can go and play golf or cricket or go to the bioscope [cinema], but they don't have anything else except soccer and dancing. They love their dancing and singing, these Natives do. That's why we encourage it.

Another field official, who is an ex-sergeant, drew from his Army experience and put the principle in a nutshell:

> It's just like in the Army. You've got to occupy their minds so that they don't think evil. One strong head can ruin a whole compound. You've got to keep them busy to keep them happy. . . . The Native loves discipline and routine.

In addition to soccer and dancing, the workers are also shown open-air cinema films, mostly old "Westerns" ("They love them, they are just like children") and films on tribal custom, safety, or first aid. No effort is made to impart to field workers the rudiments of education through literacy classes. It must be added, however, that the CSC did contribute to some extent to non-European education in the public schools and has regularly pleaded with the Government for the extension of the highly inadequate non-European school facilities. At the same time it fails to provide employment outlets for educated Africans and Indians. As one African teacher put it to me, "What is the good of education if you have got to carry sugar bags in the factory?" Many of the White field personnel (who, on the whole, are poorly educated and largely unskilled persons whose principal qualifications for the job are physical ruggedness, a knowledge of Zulu, and a white skin) express a distinct preference for the "raw kaffir" with tribal roots and no "strange ideas." The ex-sergeant expressed that preference in these words:

> Detribalization is the worst thing that can happen to a Native. He becomes a wandering Jew without prestige back home. The tribal Native with his cattle and his wives has prestige. He also has roots and he is a solid character. My father who farms up-country would never take a boy [i.e., an adult African worker] who didn't have cattle.

In addition to the sports activities for the African field workers, the Company has provided sports facilities on the basis of a three-way segregation for Whites, Indians, and Africans. Not only are these facilities segregated, but they are unequal. The Whites enjoy by far the best facilities, although they represent but 5 per cent of the population. This state of affairs is considered normal and desirable by virtually all local Europeans. Sports are organized through two main Sports Associations, one for Europeans, one for non-Europeans. In both Associations, the Company, through a yearly grant of £100, exerts a great deal of control. The European association has a colour bar in its constitution, and is ruled by a committee of thirteen members, of which the Company appoints three, including the treasurer. The Association's secretary is paid directly by the CSC. Club affairs at the monthly meetings are run in the perfunctory manner that characterizes the Caneville brand of paternalism.

In the non-European Sports Association, where the danger of disagreement with the Company is greater than in the European group, the CSC control is even closer. The Company nominates six of the fifteen committee members, including the chairman, both vice-chairmen, and the treasurer. The secretary is the only elected officer of the association. The chairman is Jan Swanepoel who, until very recently, is reported to have run the club along completely autocratic lines.

An all-Indian club is being formed at present, the Whitehead Stadium Committee, to regulate the use of the Indian athletic grounds. In that committee the Town Council is going to appoint eight of the fifteen members.

2. The "Family Affair" argument runs roughly as follows: "We are all one big happy family. If you have any grievances, you are completely free to come and see me [Whitehead or Reginald Sherwood]. You know that we have your interests at heart. So don't get together to foment opposition. Above all, don't call in outsiders, don't take legal action against us, etc. Just come and see us, and we will settle our differences peacefully." The reasons for that attitude, though perhaps not explicitly formulated, are very clear: first, legal or collective protest action is viewed (quite rightly) as an open challenge or defiance of the system; and second, collective protest action defeats the aim of any autocratic government, which is to deal with unorganized individuals, or, in other words, to divide and rule.

Let me give two illustrations of the "Family Affair" technique. When real estate valuation was recently increased, a number of Indian taxpayers appealed against the new tax increases. The appeals had to be lodged with the Town Council acting as an appeal board. Those appellants who argued on the basis of personal duress and who adopted a humble attitude were treated much more sympathetically than those who argued on the basis of general principles of equity which conflicted with the local system of government. The latter appellants quickly became the target of sarcasm and abrupt interruptions on the part of the Council. I am not for a moment accusing the Council of partiality in reaching decisions. Indeed, the evidence is that the Council examined each case on its objective merits. I am simply referring to the way in which the appellants were treated.

The other illustration concerns a threat of legal action undertaken by four businessmen against the Town Council.

The claimants argued that, through negligence of the Council, road construction in the township was delayed, and that in consequence they suffered avoidable losses in their business. The merit of their case is beside the point here. The fact is that, instead of going to see Whitehead about it, they sent, through their lawyer, an aggressive letter to the Town Council. As Whitehead himself stated at the subsequent meeting of the Council: "I took a bad view of the letter, particularly because I am always available for discussions with the taxpayers. I took strong exception to the letter which constitutes a threat." According to his own report, Whitehead summoned the four complainants to his office, found out who the "prime mover" of the action was, and through diplomacy convinced the other three to desist from taking legal action; thereby isolating the instigator of the move, who demurred and did not pursue the matter further.

Other aspects of the "Family Affair" device are impatience with criticism and lack of adequate consultation with, and informing of, the local public. The Company is very conscious of *outside* public relations, and propagandizes the Caneville Experiment through a superbly printed magazine. But, apart from the routine posting of notices on bulletin boards, no attempt is made to keep the town's inhabitants informed about local government. Nor is the public consulted about decisions, except nominally through appointed representatives. Not only is the mass of the people deemed incapable of contributing usefully to the local government, but, in the absence of a franchise, the tenure and exercise of power is unaffected by local opinion, which can thus be safely ignored. The assumption is not that local government exists to serve the people, and that it is open to criticism and scrutiny, but, rather, that the Town Council protects the interests of "property owners" and condescendingly dispenses material benefits to the "less fortunate members of the community" as a mark of regal largesse. The people must accept decisions uncritically and benefits gratefully.

Many informants complain, justifiably so, that their correspondence with the Town Council is left unanswered. They charge that the water supply is cut off without warning. Even such small matters as the naming of streets is done without any consultation with the residents. There are signs of impending changes and growing challenges, however. The new Muslim member of the Town Council, Dr. Khan, is apparently taking his role as representative seriously, and has made cautious suggestions during meetings that the people should be better informed. Shortly before the time of this writing, the Taxpayers Association sent a delegation to a meeting of the Town Council. The Council, unaccustomed to spectators at its meetings, seemed to be taken by surprise and went into closed committee when discussing certain matters.

Through the "Family Affair" technique, the Company attempts to isolate the community from outside influences and to prevent the organization of collective opposition by dealing with single individuals. Channels for personal requests or grievances are open, but there is no mechanism which insures that the authorities will be responsive. Furthermore, fear of disfavour prevents many people from using the available channels and expressing their views frankly. The Town Council tries to avoid court litigation and, by so doing, to remain both judge and party to disputes. Without the check of elections, the authorities can afford to disregard local opinion and to neglect informing the people. Existing channels of consultation are ineffective because power is not shared. Paternalism makes, in fact, perpetual wards of citizens.

3. Co-optation is another stand-by of autocracy, and a favourite topic of political scientists since Machiavelli. It consists of taking the opposition or potential opposition in on

one's side, either by giving it some special rewards or by giving it the appearance of a share in power. In Caneville the system of placing non-European representatives on the Town Council described above is a clear-cut example of co-optation. By granting non-Europeans seats on the Council, the fiction of government by consultation and direct representation can be maintained, while in no way endangering the power monopoly of the CSC.

At another level, the choice of who is appointed to the Council gives an insight into the process of co-optation. When Mohammed Kassim, a completely "safe" collaborator, retired, he was replaced by Dr. O. B. Khan, a highly articulate, intelligent and cultured young man who was unlikely to be a yes-man. He belongs to an influential Muslim family and his elder brother has been an outspoken critic of the CSC regime for many years. His brother's opposition was one of the main reasons for Khan's being offered a post on the Council. Whitehead remarked to me one day that the elder Khan, who had previously been "truculent," had become more "restrained" since his brother had been on the Council. Whitehead and Hancock obviously hoped to neutralize the man who is probably the second most vocal and influential opponent of the CSC by co-opting his politically non-committal brother. The latter could, at the same time, be used to answer the criticism that the non-European Town Councillors are all yes-men, without threatening the existing power system.

A final example of co-optation at yet another level is the Council-sponsored Whitehead Stadium Club. The avowed intent is to create an élite bourgeois Indian club. The CSC thereby hopes, by granting special prestige to the Indian middle class, that the middle class (consisting mostly of teachers and merchants) will remain a conservative, stabilizing force in the community and will identify its interests with those of the CSC. To eliminate any chance of the scheme backfiring on the CSC, the latter ensured itself the right to nominate a majority of the committee members.

4. The control of potential opposition is the mainstay of all autocratic regimes. Co-optation, as we have seen above, is one of the more subtle methods to control opposition. A brief review of potential sources of resistance in Caneville and the methods used to control them will complete the analysis of the power system from the CSC point of view. The first threat to the management of a large industrial undertaking is the organization of labour. In this respect, South African legislation and custom give the industrialists an enormous advantage. The non-White proletariat, while allowed the right to organize, is denied the right of effective collective bargaining. Collective bargaining procedures, providing for compulsory government intervention and mediation, greatly favour the employer. Furthermore, striking is a criminal offense for Africans. The European artisans may both organize and strike, but their highly protected and privileged position has (to use a descriptive but cacophonous word) "deproletarianized" them. Racial segregation in the labour unions, job reservation along racial lines, legislative restrictions on non-European workers, and the privileged position of the White élite proletariat have emasculated the South African labour movement, and protected the employers to a degree unmatched in any other advanced industrial country.

The CSC shares with the rest of South African industry this highly advantageous situation from the employer's viewpoint. Reginald Sherwood candidly admitted with characteristic understatement that "the employee has been taken for somewhat of a ride." With the exception of the great Gandhi Strike mentioned earlier, there has never been a work stoppage in Caneville. Though there have been, and there still are, many differences between management and both the White and the non-White unions, labour relations are described by management as good. The European Artisans' Union has long unsuccessfully demanded a closed shop. The non-European union is negotiating for a wage increase, the first in many years, and probably will receive it. Both the White and the Indian shop stewards adopt an accommodating attitude to the Company. Through a number of devices, the CSC extends an even greater control over the unions than South African laws provide. For example, the Company provides office accommodation to the unions, and deducts union fees from the workers' pay. Again, these practices are not unique to the CSC, nor are they malevolent in their intention. Like many other control devices, they constitute an empirically evolved *modus vivendi*, the benefits of which are by no means one-sided. In this particular case, the labour union itself asked the Company to deduct dues from pay. The union benefits from the arrangement through ease of collection and greater membership.

Restricted as union activities and powers are for factory workers, the field workers are *entirely* unorganized and unprotected by minimum wage agreements of any kind.

Cane planters' associations are segregated along racial lines. They are in a weak position in relation to the mills in that, through quota agreements, they have to deliver their cane at a specified mill. However, while White cane planters have a strong direct representation in the administrative machinery of the sugar industry, the non-White association has none. In Caneville, the relations between the planters and the CSC are again described as good, though Indian planters have been the object of various forms of discrimination in the past. The Company exercises some control over both associations by providing them with office premises.

The Company's control of sports associations has already been described, as well as the plan to control the social club of Whitehead Stadium. It is important in this connection to emphasize that, while Europeans are systematically given preferential treatment, all employees regardless of race are handled in the same benevolently despotic fashion.

Yet another illustration of the CSC's attempt to control such local politics as are allowed to exist is provided by the attempted secession of the Dube Village School Committee. The latter is the only official African body in Caneville which falls altogether outside the jurisdiction of the municipality (it is responsible to the Department of Bantu Education). Without Whitehead's knowledge, the deep antagonism between Mvusi and Ngubane had come into the open over the issue of whether the local School Committee should secede from the larger regional Bantu School Board. This move was within the limited statutory powers of the Committee, a majority of which favoured secession. When Whitehead learned of the dispute, he expressed annoyance at not having been informed of it, and quickly maneuvered to prevent secession. The reasons for Whitehead's action were several. He feared that secession would antagonize the central Government, with which he was negotiating for an expansion of the African school, and he was concerned about disharmony between the Company-chosen African "representatives." With the overlapping memberships of the School Committee, the BCC, and the Town Council, the entire façade of harmonious co-operation within the African community, and between its appointed "representatives" and the Town Council, was threatened. Moreover, Whitehead felt that his authority as mayor had been challenged and circumvented.

Generally speaking the social clubs, the welfare groups, the church bodies, and the women's organizations have escaped direct CSC control. There has been, however, an attempt to influence the main Indian welfare organization, and the African religious denominations are dependent on the Town Council for official recognition and permission to use the premises of the non-denominational chapel. The Catholic Church is independent, but, as its membership does not include any of the local "top people," its influence is limited. Its declared policy of non-racialism is in conflict with CSC policy, but the contentious area is confined to the premises of the little Catholic church building.

By far the main source of opposition which the Company has not succeeded in controlling is the Indian Taxpayers' Association. The Association has no colour bar in its constitution but is, in fact, entirely Indian in membership. The main body is, in turn, subdivided into several neighbourhood groups. The Association owes its outspoken stand against the Company largely to a prominent and effective politician, Mr. L. S. Sham. Sham is a leading member of the Natal Indian Congress and a political "prison graduate." He was one of 156 persons accused of treason and Communism in a trial that lasted from 1956 to 1961 (the evidence was so inconclusive that all the accused were acquitted by a bench consisting of Nationalist appointees). As chairman of the Indian Taxpayers' Association, he was the unofficial local Leader of the Opposition, whom a high Company official described as "a thorn in my flesh." Recently he was replaced in office by the Association's former secretary. The Taxpayers' Association is the only local organization to present anything resembling an opposition platform to the Caneville Experiment. The Association follows the general policy of the Indian Congress, which favours a non-racial, democratic government based on universal adult franchise, and further holds that:

1. Appointed representation on the Town Council is a sham and must be replaced by elective representation.

2. Taxation without representation is tyranny.

3. Segregation in any form is wrong in principle.

The extent to which that opposition has been effective will

be examined presently as we turn to the receiving end of the Caneville Experiment, namely the citizens of the town.

Assessing the effect of, or the reaction to, Company policy in Caneville is a difficult task, for the population is as heterogeneous politically as it is culturally. Opinions range from arch-conservative to radical, from politically apathetic to hyper-sensitive. One salient conclusion emerges from our study, however: Caneville is a politically *atomized* community. Before substantiating this statement, I must clarify it, and try to account for the phenomenon. In its efforts to deal with isolated individuals rather than with organized groups, the CSC has, perhaps unwittingly but certainly effectively, used the old device of *divide et impera*. Helped by circumstances, the Company has been largely successful. For one thing, initial cultural differences contributed to the division of the community, irrespective of Company policy. The latter simply perpetuated cultural differences by entrenching a rigid system of racial segregation (or "aggregation" to use the Company's term), and of racial and ethnic representation. The tactless enforcement of many measures, such as the exclusion of Indians from the African village, has the clear (though probably unwanted) effect of creating friction between the two groups. The theory or rationalization on which segregation is based in Caneville as well as in the rest of South Africa is that inter-racial contact brings friction and not harmony. This fallacious notion runs counter to a great deal of experimental evidence collected in the United States.[5]

Caneville is not only *segmented*, however; it is also politically *atomized*. The considerable success of the Company in controlling possible opposition groups means that citizens face "the Establishment" as powerless individuals. A direct consequence of this atomization is the absence of organized public opinion as found in a democratic system. By absence of public

---

[5] Cf. G. W. Allport, *The Nature of Prejudice*, pp. 261–282.

opinion, I do not mean that people express no opinions, or that a majority opinion could not be obtained by polling. I mean, rather, that people's views being irrelevant to the political process since there is no franchise, nobody finds it profitable to organize the amorphous body of opinions or to arouse awareness of the issues at hand. In Donald Sherwood's words, an autocratic system such as Caneville's knows no "demagogues standing on boxes." To paraphrase his words: "The people know nothing about democracy" (since they live under oppression), and this lack of experience is used as a circular argument to withhold democratic rights indefinitely.

In a stable democratic system, though opinions are almost as numerous as citizens, most issues tend to polarize the variety of views into two opposing camps. When there are more than two political parties in existence, coalitions tend to bring the situation back to a fundamental dichotomy. Public opinion can be quickly mobilized, influenced, and mastered to support one of the contending parties. Alignments and lines of cleavage may change continuously, but the basic dichotomous pattern remains. Under an autocratic regime, on the other hand, since there is no direct machinery whereby mass opinion can determine policy, public opinion remains unorganized. The basic cleavage is between the state and its atomized subjects.

One case study of an unsuccessful protest movement will illustrate the political atomization of Caneville. This case is the only one, during the time of the study, in which the threat of large-scale concerted opposition to the Company arose.[6] It involved the Taxpayers' Association, the only local

---

[6] The call by the Congress Alliance for a "stay-at-home" of non-Whites on May 29–31, 1961, in opposition to the Nationalist Government, was largely a failure in Caneville, as it was in most of South Africa. The CSC had decided to ignore the threatened strike altogether and to carry on as usual. In doing so, the Company again missed an opportunity to express concretely its avowed

body potentially capable of "de-atomizing" the community.

The issue arose from a substantial increase in the valuation of property for municipal tax purposes, and from a change in the rate of taxation of lands and buildings. These changes were passed by the Town Council without consultation with the public, but after a considerable study of the possible effects of these changes on the taxpayers. I am not concerned here with the merits of the various views, but rather with the course of the abortive controversy.

When the Taxpayers' Association became aware of the impending change, first through rumours, then through an official notice posted in the Town Hall, a committee meeting of the Association was convened. Most members present expressed hostility to the Town Council in general, and the Indian representatives in particular, and reiterated the position of the Taxpayers' Association. As there was no quorum, no formal decisions were taken, but it was informally decided to convene a mass meeting of taxpayers to air the views of the public, clarify the issues at hand, and take a concerted stand against the Town Council. A mimeographed sheet, on which taxpayers could lodge their objection to the new taxation system with the Town Council, was also circulated. Of a total

---

opposition to the Nationalist Government. There was no absenteeism at either the factory or the field sections, and the Company was thus completely unaffected. Some two-thirds of the Indian and African schoolchildren did not attend classes on May 29, however, and about 90 to 95 per cent of the parents declared their opposition to their children receiving the medals issued by the Government for "Republic Day." Strike pamphlets were distributed in Caneville and I heard unconfirmed reports of verbal threats by strike organizers, but there was no violence. Between 1:00 and 2:00 P.M., on the twenty-ninth, after several hours of very dull trading, most Indian shops began to close down, following the lead of Mr. Goshalia, as a "token of sympathy" for the Africans. Employees of the Town Council and of Indian merchants reported for work as usual.

of some 300 taxpayers (nearly all Indians), about 100 persons lodged objections involving 115 properties.

In the meantime, several neighbourhood groups of taxpayers met to determine how the new rating system affected each individual. A number of persons then discovered that the new rates left their taxes largely unaffected. Some would even get a slight reduction of taxes. This discovery understandably created a conflict of interest between those who would have to pay higher rates and those who would not, and eliminated the possibility of a united stand against the Town Council. The proposed general meeting was called off, and the Taxpayers' Association decided not to engage legal counsel in its appeal against the changed rates. Every individual would present his own case in his private capacity. A prominent member of the Association dissented, and was asked to resign his office in the organization, thereby causing a split in the leadership. The dissenting member subsequently replaced Sham in the chairmanship of the association.

The final stage of the controversy was reached when the Town Council sat as an appeal board to hear the appellants. The majority of objectors had either withdrawn their written objections or failed to appear before the appeal board. The result was that only about forty objectors were present. Mr. Whitehead, as chairman of the board, opened the meeting by stating that there could be no legal appeal against the new rates themselves (that is, the amount to be paid per pound of valuation), but only against the value at which properties were assessed. This announcement took most of the objectors by complete surprise. As many had prepared their cases mainly as an appeal against the new rates, they were forced to change their appeal at very short notice, and were caught off balance.

Only one group of eighteen residents, those of the middle-class district of Mahatma Township, presented a united front against the Town Council; with two exceptions, the board rejected their pleas for lower assessment. Other appellants spoke either for themselves or for their relatives, and the board handled their cases individually.

In the example just cited, the major cause of the collapse of the concerted opposition to the local authority was the conflict of interests within the opposition. Some taxpayers stood to lose by the new rates, others to gain. In a democratic system, people are not less motivated by self-interest than under an autocratic regime. But in a democratically elected system, public opinion would probably have polarized into a pro- and anti-administration camp, and the relative numerical strength of the two camps would have determined the issue. In an autocratic system such as that of Caneville, the cleavage takes the form of the administration *versus* the people. Initially, many Indian taxpayers had used the rates issue as a convenient means of venting their general latent hostility to the local government. At that stage, the individual implications of the new measure had not been considered. When these did receive attention, they caused a division within opposition ranks, and the conflict of personal interests foiled the possibility of a united stand against the administration. Those individuals who stood to benefit by the new rates did not, however, become supporters of the local government as they would in a democratic system. They remained hostile or at best indifferent to the Town Council, because an autocratic body, by its very nature, can never be "of the people" no matter how much it tries to be "for the people."

The structural consequences of such a situation are obvious. Not only does an autocracy perpetuate itself by excluding any constitutional means of political change. It also intrinsically prevents the emergence of effective constitutional opposition for two main reasons. First, as constitutional opposition has no prospect of replacing the existing regime short of revolution, the incentive to organize opposition becomes smaller. Without the prospect of achieving power by legal means, politics, in the democratic sense, becomes unrewarding, and must turn to revolutionary means. Second, an autocracy, by remaining aloof from the mass of the governed, can so manipulate conflicts of interests in the mass as to prevent concerted opposition movements even in the face of nearly unanimous hostility. Even where there is no conscious manipulation, conflicts of interest among the governed are almost sure to arise unless the autocracy becomes entirely repressive, which is certainly not the case in Caneville. All the above factors make, at the same time, for the strength and the weakness of autocracy. The complete control of constitutional opposition generates revolution.

We have just seen the effect of paternalism on the formation of opinion in the mass of disenfranchised subjects. Before concluding this chapter, however, we must study in greater detail the various types of reaction of individuals to the local power system, a task that is made all the more difficult by the amorphous state of public opinion. Let us start with the White group, whose attitudes are easiest to characterize. In the case of the Whites, Company paternalism has achieved considerable success. The motto "Our workers are happy here" certainly applies to the majority of the European employees. I have only met one White family that was openly critical of the Company, and that family occupies a marginal position in the European community. Most Whites openly praise Company policy, have adopted its underlying philosophy as their own, and quote Company slogans with great relish. The one criticism that they voice with frequency is that "the Company does too much for the Natives and the Indians and not enough for us." At the same time, some middle-class Whites take pride in the "liberalism" of the Company, and claim to share the "enlightened" attitude of the local White upper class.

In view of the fact that Europeans enjoy a highly protected

and privileged position, and a standard of wages and amenities which is approximately five to six times as high as that of the non-European employees, this White resentment of welfare benefits for the non-Whites throws a rather sinister light on the outlook of most South African Whites. Racial segregation and vastly inferior treatment of non-Europeans are taken for granted. The dual standard is deeply internalized. Any attempt to reduce, let alone remove, the disparity between White and non-White standards is viewed as a threat to White supremacy. On the whole, the lavish paternalism that the Company has dispensed to its White employees has satisfied them. Many of them probably realize that this paternalism is an effective way of checking non-European political advancement and of entrenching White privileges. For this they are willing to sacrifice their participation in local affairs in a similar way to that in which the White opposition electorate in the country as a whole has supported much of the repressive legislation of the Nationalists to "keep the kaffir down," even at the cost of loss of civil liberties to all.[7]

Of the three "racial" groups, the Africans are probably the most politically conscious and the most acutely dissatisfied, although the Indians are, on the whole, more educated and better organized in voluntary associations. The degree of African antagonism against Whites seems unrelated to either sex or education. Dissatisfaction appears to be as high among illiterate field workers as among teachers, as prevalent among men as among women. Unlike White or Indian women, African women are, as a group, politically conscious and resentful. The reasons for greater dissatisfaction among Africans than among Indians

---

[7] The United Party has, of course, opposed many pieces of Nationalist legislation, but it has also supported the Government in such dictatorial measures as the Suppression of Communism Act, the Public Safety Act, and the declaration of the State of Emergency in 1960.

are obvious. While the Indians are also oppressed, powerless, and discriminated against, they do not suffer the same measure of vexation and humiliation that the Africans do as the result of the pass and liquor laws. For an African, unpleasant contact with the police and imprisonment for technical offences are frequent and unavoidable occurrences. Not so with the Indian. Furthermore, the well-to-do and educated Indian can, to some extent, protect himself from unpleasant contact with Whites in a way in which the middle-class African cannot. He may also avail himself of certain facilities. In Durban, for example, there exist many Indian clubs that discriminate informally against Africans and that provide recreational outlets unavailable to the African middle class.

In Caneville, anti-White hostility has so far remained latent, and is concealed in everyday contact with Whites under a cover of outward subservience and "happiness." I have often encountered initial fear and suspicion among Africans merely on account of the colour of my skin. A frequent reaction of a group of Africans on seeing a white skin is to stop talking and to look blank, much as at the sight of an enemy uniform in an occupied country. Only fear prevents that hostility from being openly expressed. There is an almost complete rupture of communication between Africans and Whites.

The vast majority of Caneville Africans are supporters of the African National Congress. On the whole, and with the exception of a few elderly gentlemen like Reverend Mvusi who have accepted the system of oppression to the point of deeply internalizing their inferiority feelings, Caneville Africans see the local pattern as not different from that in the rest of South Africa. As elsewhere, they are paid low wages, the privacy of their homes is invaded in frequent liquor raids, they are arrested for not carrying their "reference book," they are discourteously treated by White officials, and they are obliged to live either in a segregated "model" township (a part of which still has no electricity) or in military-type barracks. Dube Village is referred to as "the location," the common term used elsewhere in South Africa. (The term "location" is studiously avoided by high Company officials, who like to stress their conviction that Dube Village is quite different from other segregated African urban areas.)

A few sample reactions to the question, "What do you think of Europeans?" will illustrate the feelings of some largely illiterate cane cutters. So long as I worked through an interpreter, the stereotyped evasive answer was: "I have nothing against them." As soon as the African interpreter was left alone with the workers, the answers became: "They are my worst enemies," "All the trouble in Pondoland is caused by the European," "Why not give us a chance?" "I hate them," "Do they ever think of going back to their country?" "Why don't they let us alone?" "I hate them because they pass laws without consulting us," "If it wasn't for the Europeans, I would not be here cutting cane for only ninety shillings a month," "They are only good to me because they give us money," "I will feel much better when I am dead than being ruled by the Europeans."

It is perhaps significant that, after thirty-five workers had reluctantly answered the questions, the other field workers boycotted my study, which, they thought, was connected with the government census. Earlier in 1960, the Pondo workers, in Caneville as well as in Pondoland, had boycotted the official census. This boycott was perhaps the largest overt protest action that Caneville has seen since the Gandhi Strike of 1913. As in the case of my interview study, the census boycott was obviously a well-organized movement because the non-co-operation order quickly spread between distant and relatively isolated workers' compounds. The fact, however, that the study was undertaken during a wave of violent anti-government unrest in Pondoland undoubtedly heightened both the political consciousness and organization of the migrant Pondo in Caneville.

African opposition to the local system in Dube Village is also very widespread, though kept underground by fear and lack of leadership. One of the White officials is bitterly hated for his rudeness. The Africans nickname him "Monkey" in retaliation for his use of the term in reference to them. The Bantu Consultative Council is recognized as the parody of representation that it is. Only about one-fifth of the eligible voters bother to show up for the elections. It is not even possible to find enough candidates to fill the four elective seats. In the last election there was only one candidate for four vacancies. As a result, incumbents were reappointed to the Council, and only one member was elected.

In an atmosphere of sustained tension, suspicion and rumours are rampant. The members of the BCC do not, with two exceptions, have the confidence of most inhabitants of Dube Village. They are generally regarded as representative only of themselves and as powerless tools of the White administration. BCC members are accused of not taking the interests of the people to heart, and of ignoring complaints made to them. Many popular grievances centre around the municipal beer hall and the poor quality of the beer served there. In common with all other municipalities in South Africa, Caneville has its African beer hall. Private brewing is illegal except under restricted permits, and the municipal beer is sold to Africans at a profit. These profits are then used for segregated public facilities in the African location, and the people have no deciding say as to how the money is spent. The underlying principle is that each racial group has to finance its own facilities, a principle that results in regressive taxation. Africans, who are the poorest group, pay the heaviest taxes proportionally.[8] In Caneville, beer profits until 1960 averaged about £4,000 a year, thereby making Dube Village completely self-sufficient. The White Company and Town Council officials consider the principle of each racial group paying for its own segregated facilities as self-evident. They also consider it self-evident that the White officials should decide how the money is spent. Another result of the municipal beer halls is the extensive illicit brewing, which is countered by police raids. These raids were a frequent source of riots in South Africa; however, since this study was completed, liquor restrictions against Africans have been abolished.

Widespread though African political consciousness is, it remains locally unorganized and leaderless, except among the Pondo. The government ban on African liberatory movements (notably the African National Congress and the Pan-African Congress) may have rallied mass support for these organizations, but the intimidation and arrest of "agitators" have probably scared potential local leaders into inactivity. Ngubane, who had been active in protest politics, has lost any popular support he may have had, and is viewed with great suspicion now that he has compromised himself with the local authorities. Only two of the members of the BCC, both elderly clergymen, can be said to enjoy any degree of confidence on the part of the location residents, but the influence of one of them is on the wane, and the other is too conservative to have a political following. Neither of them can be described as a leader, except within his religious denomination. Teachers, who enjoy no security of tenure, cannot afford to antagonize the Company, the government, or the BCC; so this potential source of articulate leadership is closed. Almost all other

---

[8] For a careful documentation of the burden of discriminatory taxation on Africans see *African Taxation, Its Relation to African Social Services.*

location residents are employees of the Town Council or the Company. They can be dismissed from their job, evicted from their houses, and even deported from the area altogether, if they become "troublesome" to the authorities. There are, of course, several persons who are influential in certain circles, such as sports clubs and religious sects. Others enjoy wide respect for their education or wisdom, but, for the reasons just given, there is not a single local African who could be described as a "leader of the community."

The reactions of the Indian community to Town Council policy are by no means as uniform as those of either the Europeans or the Africans. The Muslim merchants are generally accused by the Hindus of being apolitical and only interested in making money. The criticism certainly applies to several of the prominent Muslim families who believe in co-operation with the Company, but it also applies to many Hindu merchant families. It is not so much religion as occupation that is the important factor in determining political consciousness. On the whole, merchants are more conservative and more willing to co-operate with the Company than other segments of the Indian community. However, L. S. Sham combines the roles of businessman and politician, to the detriment of his business.

The professional group, consisting mostly of teachers, show the greatest political awareness. The majority are Indian Congress supporters but there is a small left wing of Unity Movement sympathizers, and a small right wing of Natal Indian Organization adherents. Among these educated people there is nearly unanimous agreement that the Indian members of the Town Council represent only their own interests, and that the local government is completely autocratic. A few of the older teachers, however, believe in co-operation with the Company, not because they agree with Company policy but on grounds of expediency. It was mainly the professional group which applied pressure on Goshalia and Khan not to accept posts on the Town Council. For an Indian, acceptance of a seat on the Council is tantamount to committing political suicide. Goshalia was expelled from the Natal Indian Congress when he accepted the position in spite of opposition. One of the high school teachers, who accepted a post at a Government-sponsored, segregated college for Indians in Durban, was also under strong pressure and criticism on the part of his colleagues. The fact, however, that this articulate and politically minded group of teachers is debarred by profession from active participation in politics has substantially contributed to the maintenance of Company autocracy.

Among the majority of Caneville Indians who are poorly educated manual workers or small farmers, the level of political consciousness is lower than among the Africans. This applies even more to women than to men. One can safely say that 90 per cent of the Indian women are apolitical. Working-class men are generally dissatisfied with their low wages. Of twenty-two workers interviewed at the factory, fifteen spontaneously complained about low wages. Quite a number of the older workers, however, are accommodated to their humble status and are grateful to the Company for adequate housing and other benefits. The younger generation, on the whole, is resentful of the limitations that skin colour imposes upon them, particularly in the occupational field. They know and bitterly resent that there is no scope for promotion to a responsible post in the CSC.

Attitudes towards residential segregation range from passive acquiescence by the older, poorly educated people who cannot conceive of anything else, to extreme opposition by others to a system considered to be discriminatory and humiliating. Virtually all the educated men fall in the latter category. They view the Company motto of "aggregation" as a typical piece of English United Party hypocrisy. They accuse the Company and the United Party of having shown the Nationalists the practice of apartheid. The Company, they say, made a blueprint for apartheid before the Nationalists came into office. The Company dogma that "everybody wants to be aggregated" is emphatically rejected by most articulate Indians, who also repudiate the belief that segregation in Caneville is more voluntary than elsewhere in South Africa.

The Town Council is widely accused of hypocrisy and duplicity in dealing with the Group Areas Board on the Fairwind issue mentioned earlier. Finally, most Indian property holders are fully aware of the economic cost they have to pay for segregation. Indians are prevented by law from buying "European" land. This creates an artificial scarcity of "Indian" land, the value of which is grossly inflated as a result. Indians generally have to pay much more than Europeans do for a good building plot. Recently an "Indian" business plot of about one acre changed hands for £8,000, though Caneville is a small, partially undeveloped town. These inflated property values constitute the basis of evaluation for local taxation, which is thus clearly loaded against Indian property holders. Indian taxpayers are, of course, aware that this tax discrimination is the result of segregation, and inflated value was one of the recurrent themes in rate appeals against the Town Council.

Essays on the topic "Caneville, 1975" were written by forty-two adolescents in the upper two standards of the Indian high school. Of the seventeen students who mentioned housing segregation, fifteen were unqualifiedly opposed to it, and two thought that Caneville was better than other South African towns. Of sixteen students who expressed views on the Town Council, only three were favourable and thirteen unfavourable. The main negative criticisms concerned the inefficiency of the Town Council (mentioned by four people), the poor roads (six times), and the undemocratic nature of the Council (five times). Attitudes towards the Company were more favourable, however; sixteen students expressed positive comments, five gave negative views, and six were mixed in their responses. General improvement was attributed to the Company thirteen times, and good housing five times. Favourable reactions were also elicited about sports facilities, the attempt to beautify the town, and sanitation. Poor housing and low wages led among the negative criticisms of the Company.[9]

Direct quotations ordered from favourable to unfavourable will capture the flavour of the essays better than a set of statistics:

> Today Caneville has grown with the assistance of the C.S.C. A striking method adopted by this concern is that they intend to make Caneville a place of beauty.
>
> Today Caneville is a model town in that it is not affected by the Group Areas Act.
>
> The C.S.C. has aided in improving Caneville.
>
> A good example of what the Sugar Company has done for non-Whites is the stadium.
>
> The main people responsible for developments are the big men of the C.S.C.
>
> Although the Town Council at present is multi-racial, the members are nominated and as usual they are yes-men to whatever the Council proposes.

---

[9] A 1955 essay contest in the same school yielded much more favourable reactions to the Company and the Town Council. The growth of non-European political consciousness in the intervening years probably accounts for some of the difference between the two sets of essays. Another important factor is that the earlier essays were signed and the pupils had reasons to expect that the essays would be read by local White officials, as indeed they were. In the more recent essays, anonymity was complete, and I stressed the fact that the study was completely unrelated to the government or the Company. As there are no high school facilities in Caneville for White and African students, comparable essay material on these two groups is not available.

Caneville should be represented by Indians, Europeans and Natives and all laws passed should be for the welfare of all.

I wish the Town Council officer would be thrown out of office immediately. The Town Council is not doing its work efficienctly.

It would be nice if we could be *free*.

The houses along the road look quite attractive . . . but those that are not in sight of the public have a shabby appearance.

The system is something like Feudalism practised in the 15th century. . . . Segregation in Caneville is creating three camps with different ideas and ideals.

One girl of nineteen writes in a tone that is both bitter and balanced, and that sums up the general mood rather well:

If I were a governor or a premier of this town of ours, I shall bring about various improvements. Firstly, I shall do away with the hateful apartheid policy. After all, we are God's creatures and why shouldn't we live . . . with greater freedom. Although this policy is not so bitterly practised in Caneville, nevertheless this policy may turn out for the worse. . . . Most of the Europeans of this town are not so ill-disposed towards the non-Europeans as in other parts of South Africa. Some of them are always willing to help the poor instead of discriminating against them. Yet, we have another class of Europeans who look down upon the non-Europeans with great contempt. It is time that such aggressive policies were forgotten and all the people, whether black or white should unite and fight for freedom together.

Other symptoms of dissatisfaction among Indians are recurrent complaints against the Town Council. Mahatma Village residents are bitter about the unpaved and pot-holed streets in the area, and argue with considerable cogency that if the area were White the streets would have been tarred long ago. Water shortages are another source of complaints. The water is supplied to the Caneville Township by the Company.

During the dry months, when shortages are common, the water supply is often cut off without warning. Discourtesy on the part of some White officials is another common complaint. The telephone exchange (run by central government postal employees) provides Indian residents with another common source of irritation. With justification, people accuse the Post Office employees of deliberately letting non-Europeans wait before putting their calls through.

While a number of people praise the Company for its efforts to make the town look attractive, others criticize the Company style as unprogressive and wasteful. The new high school built in the Company style on a site donated by the Company is a target of intense criticism on the part of virtually all of the teachers and students. The school is popularly nick-named "The Central Gaol," and is held to be most un-functional, damp, and unhygienic. Its site is said to be the worst conceivable, between a busy road and a noisy railway. The Company chose the site, people say, because the school is right next to the main highway for all visitors to see.

A few of the merchants co-operated with the Company by building in the local style, but some of the Indians reacted by building in a militantly modernistic style.

To sum up the attitude of the Indians to Company and Town Council policies, one could say that the working class is outwardly acquiescent though dissatisfied about wages, that much of the merchant class is opportunistically co-operative, and that the intelligentsia is strongly opposed to a system which it considers oppressive. An Indian teacher summed up his feelings in the following terms: "When we talk of White-head and Hancock, I think of the master group. If one could attune to living as a servant group, on could be happy." In contrast to the African group, political consciousness among Indians is largely confined to the men.

Unlike the Africans, several prominent Indians emerge as

political leaders in Caneville. Foremost among them is L. S. Sham, who is widely recognized as a clever and outspoken politician. His imprisonment after the nation-wide wave of protest demonstrations in March, 1960, has probably enhanced his prestige. Although many people disagree with him for a variety of political and personal reasons, he is generally viewed as the leading opponent of the Company in town. He is called upon to address official functions, he is influential in school committees and he has been the chairman of the Taxpayers' Association. Together with two or three other local members of the Natal Indian Congress, he has taken a firm stand against the Company in such matters as representation on the Town Council. Sham's main personal antagonist is B. L. Goshalia, a former member of the Natal Indian Congress who was expelled from that organization when he accepted a post on the Town Council. Goshalia is influential through his wealth, but generally unpopular.

Dr. O. B. Khan's elder brother, A. B. Khan, is, next to L. S. Sham, the town's leading opponent to the CSC. He is also active in school matters, and has generally taken a common stand with Sham on most political issues. He has led the fight against expropriation at Fairwind where he is one of the landowners, and he was opposed to his younger brother's joining the Town Council. Both A. B. Khan and Sham strongly condemned one of the high school teachers who accepted a post at the new apartheid university for Indians in Durban. In recent years Khan has become more conservative and has withdrawn from active political life, and his influence is probably on the wane. His brother's position on the Town Council is also a political liability to him. Mohammed Kassim, Dr. Khan's predecessor as the Muslim representative on the Council, has always been conservative and apolitical. He is a respected member of the Muslim group because of his piety, but he has never been a community leader.

As among the Africans, none of the Indian "leaders" recognized by the Company exerts any popular influence. The mere fact that they collaborate with the Company jeopardizes any claim to leadership they may otherwise have had. Whereas no political leaders have yet emerged from the African group, several Indian leaders have gained popular support by opposing Company policy, even though their opposition has not yet been successful. Below this top level of community-wide political leadership, a number of persons exert influence and enjoy respect in more restricted groups. The elderly retired Imam at one of the mosques is treated with great reverence among Muslims; the various Hindu priests have their little circles of devotees; several of the older teachers and principals play an important role in school matters; some persons occupy key positions in voluntary associations; some of the larger planters have a hand in a number of community activities; but the influence of these people does not extend beyond their own small groups. The principal of the high school, a gentle, devout, cultured Hindu sage, has withdrawn from most social activities, and, while generally esteemed, is accused of being too "soft" on the students and of failing to maintain discipline. Despite the importance of his position, his influence is largely confined to the ranks of the Divine Life Society, a Hindu reform movement. Through his undisputable selflessness and honesty, he is in the anomalous and unique position of being friendly with Whitehead without arousing the suspicion of his fellow townsmen.

In the autocratic political structure of Caneville there is a clear divorce between leadership and power. Those in power, i.e., the incumbents of official positions in the governmental structure, are not leaders. The power figures attempt to legitimize their rule through a theory of their own making, but this theory is rejected by the governed. Conversely, the leaders who emerge from the community and who represent popular sentiments are debarred from access to the official machinery of power. When these leaders accept co-optation into the power group (without effectively sharing power with the ruling group), they almost automatically cease to be leaders. The rupture between leadership and power thus seems to be built into the political structure of an upper-caste, ascribed autocracy such as that of Caneville. (The analysis does not apply to a *popular* autocracy wherein leaders have risen from the ranks and entrenched themselves into power.) In such a system, co-optation is an effective device to neutralize the influence of a popular leader, but it cannot effect a liaison between the rulers and the ruled, because of a built-in incompatibility of roles. This divorce between leadership and power in a Caneville type of autocracy makes "government by consultation" impossible, unless the co-opted leaders are given an *effective*, not a fictitious, share of power.

The above considerations are also related to the problem of what Weber calls legitimization of power. In a relatively static society, a traditional paternalistic aristocracy can maintain its rule without resorting predominantly to force, so long as the governed do not question the aristocracy's right to rule, or, in Weberian terms, so long as they consider the basis of power legitimate, or, in Marxist terms, so long as the oppressed do not develop class consciousness. In the rapidly changing South African society, the vast majority of the subjugated non-White groups reject White supremacy as illegitimate. Bantu authorities, advisory councils, and the like are recognized as parodies of representative government. The same applies to the local fiction of "government by consultation." No amount of benevolence alters the basic nature of autocracy, which must resort to punitive sanctions or the threat thereof, to the extent that it does not rest on consent. The benevolent aspects of paternalism tend to become rewards for subservience; but, at this time in history, people increasingly prefer (to quote the old *cliché*) self-government to good government. They are rarely satisfied with, much less grateful for, material rewards without dignity and self-determination. That is the reason why, under paternalism, benevolence can never be a substitute for consent of the masses who must, in the last resort, be ruled by force.

We have seen that the Caneville power system is one of autocratic paternalism complicated by a three-way segregation and discrimination on grounds of colour. All racial groups, including the super-ordinate White group, are subjected to this policy of centralized paternalism. In that sense the system is monarchic, not aristocratic. But the Whites enjoy material benefits the value of which is five to six times greater than those of non-Europeans. The Company, through a variety of devices (some of them conscious, others not), has succeeded in controlling most sources of opposition and in fragmenting the community.

I must repeat once more that this chapter is not meant to be an indictment against paternalism, but an analysis of it as I saw it in Caneville. Other sociologists with different political views would undoubtedly have phrased the findings differently, but I believe that the broad picture they would present would be the same. I have quoted at length the architects and apologists of the system, and they agree with me that the local power system is intended to be "sufficiently weighted in favour of European domination," and to be denied to the "inferior and the incompetent," i.e., according to Donald Sherwood, the vast majority of Caneville's citizens.

If this chapter can be interpreted as an indictment, it is not directed at Caneville in particular, but at South African society as a whole. Caneville is but a small part of that larger system of discrimination. It is only natural that the thinking of the Whites of Caneville should be determined by the pattern of the larger environment. Even if those locally in power could emancipate themselves from these wider influences, they would not be free to alter radically the local system until the collapse of the whole machinery of White oppression.

Benevolent despotism has, of course, its positive aspects. Material conditions are undoubtedly better in Caneville than in most other South African towns, and certainly than in all other sugar towns. These benefits are widely recognized by the people of Caneville, but they do not change the basic premises of the Caneville Experiment. One person put it to me as follows: "They give us as charity what we have earned in wages." An intelligent schoolteacher summarized his feelings thus: "Although the CSC has done a lot for the people, it did nothing to uplift the people. In that respect, it has been very unprogressive. They talk about natural apartheid but it is apartheid like everywhere else, only they thought about it long before the government."

Up to the present, the CSC has been successful in its aims of making profits, maintaining a monopoly of local power, and atomizing potential opposition groups. The Company has been powerfully aided in those aims by the former United Party Government and to a lesser (but still considerable) extent by the Nationalist Government which it professes to abhor, but which it would, as a last resort, support against a democratic revolution. In a future which I consider to be near, Company paternalism must fail, irrespective of its ethical merits or demerits. It must fail because paternalism, as a stable system, can only exist in a static, isolated, agrarian society where people through generations of serfdom have internalized their inferiority feelings and accepted their subservient place without envisaging the possibility of escaping it.[10]

With urbanization and industrialization, South Africa has

---

[10] For a theoretical discussion of paternalism, see P. L. van den Berghe, "The Dynamics of Racial Prejudice" and *The Dynamics of Race Relations*.

entered a phase of race relations which I have called "competitive."[11] Any attempt to enforce an anachronistic political system in a rapidly changing society is doomed to fail. As our nineteen-year-old schoolgirl phrased it, "the system is something like Feudalism." The dominated majority of the people of Caneville and South Africa are *not* satisfied with their humble lot as "less fortunate members of the community." Material welfare is not a substitute for political rights and human dignity. The masses of the governed do not accept White domination, and do not feel grateful for what is "done for them." In the words of an educated Indian technician, "Why should we feel grateful to the Company? They are only giving us back with one hand what they have taken from us with the other." If anything, material welfare whets the appetite for these other less tangible but no less real commodities. What happened to the "model colony" of the Congo is tragically before us. The deceptive short-run success and the dismal long-range failure of what has probably been the greatest paternalistic experiment of the twentith century should be a lesson.

The basic ingredients and leitmotiv of the Congo Experiment and the Caneville Experiment are the same: "Father knows best," "They are not yet ready for it," "Look at what we have done for them," "It is bread they want, not votes," "They have no idea of democracy," "Look how happy they are, not a worry in the world. Honestly, they are just like children." The blindness of ruling classes on the eve of revolutions is a recurrent historical phenomenon. Not only are the basic ingredients of the two Experiments the same, but the phase of industrial development and political awareness is much more advanced in South Africa than in the Congo. If paternalism failed dismally in the relatively backward Congo, it must fail all the more in Caneville.

---

[11] *Ibid.*

Chapter V

THE ECONOMIC SYSTEM

T HE DISCUSSION of the political system has already shown how closely the exercise of power in Caneville is tied to the economic structure. Indeed, Caneville is a type-case of the company town with its unitary and centralized control. Still following the broad Weberian schema, I shall analyse in this chapter the economic component of the town's social structure.

With its authorized capital of £3,000,000, its 3,700 full-time employees, and its 37,000 acres of land, Caneville Sugar Company is one of the five large enterprises which together account for two-thirds of the South African sugar output. The Company assets within the Town limits alone (which include the factory and residential housing) are valued at £527,000, i.e., 39.5 per cent of the total assessed value of real estate in Caneville. (The assessed value, however, is considerably below market value in most cases.) Of the 64,500 acres of cane land in the district of Caneville, the Company directly owns and exploits some 22,000 acres and leases a further 10,000 to private planters. Excluding the African migrant workers, and assuming an average of five dependents per male employee, it can safely be estimated that at least 40 per cent of the permanent inhabitants of the district directly depend on the CSC for their subsistence. Indirectly, the livelihood of virtually every Caneville resident (with the exception of the teachers) is dependent on the Company.

The ownership of the CSC is divided between 40,000 cumulative preference shares of £1 held by 88 shareholders, and some 4,350,000 ordinary shares of 10 shillings owned by 968 persons. Eighty-eight per cent of the capital is owned in South Africa, 11 per cent in the United Kingdom, and the remaining 1 per cent elsewhere, largely in Rhodesia. Of the 839 South African shareholders, only three are non-Whites; they own a total of only 500 ordinary shares. None of the local non-Whites owns any CSC shares. To all intents and purposes, the Company is owned and controlled by South African Whites who are mostly English-speaking. As in all limited companies, the effective control of the CSC lies in the Board of Directors, and not in the mass of the shareholders. The Sherwood family retains control of the Company, not so much through the size of their shareholdings, as through control of the Board of Directors. Donald is chairman of the Board, and Reginald vice-chairman. Two additional directors are present or retired executives of the Company, and two other Company executives sit on the board as alternates for two absent English directors. In effect, six of the ten directors who meet in South Africa can be expected to support the Sherwood family. An unsuccessful attempt to displace Donald Sherwood as Chairman was made a few years ago. As Board meetings are secret, I am unfortunately not able to analyse this important aspect of Caneville's power structure in greater detail.

Like all economic enterprises, the sugar industry has its ups and downs, and Caneville is always affected by them. After a period of boom and rapid expansion in the 1950's, a number of factors combined to make 1960 a lean year for Caneville. While the drop in the value of the CSC shares did not directly affect the mass of the people, the Company's considerable retrenchment in the labour force did. This retrenchment affected mostly non-Europeans, and was the result partly of labour reorganization making for greater efficiency, partly of the output restriction imposed by the 1960 quota agreement. The non-White labour force was reduced by more than 20 per cent between 1959 and 1960. This affected both factory and field employees. While those who first lost their jobs were mostly temporary or migrant workers, unemployment among permanent inhabitants undoubtedly increased. Throughout the period of the study a group of unemployed Indian youths gathered daily in the shade of trees in front of the Town Hall and passed the day in conversation. Unemployed Africans do not remain in Caneville because "redundant Natives" (to use the official jargon) are periodically rounded up in pass raids and deported to their "tribal homelands." This mass deportation of Africans from urban areas is euphemistically known as "influx control," and is part of a vast scheme to prevent too many Africans from entering the "White areas," and to settle as many as possible in the already over-populated and desolate "Native Reserves." These Reserves are, by governmental decree, assumed to be the "homeland" of all Africans, even of the three million people who are more or less permanently urbanized.

Apart from these long irregular cycles of boom and depression, Caneville's economic life goes through a regular yearly cycle. The four to five months during which the factory is not crushing cane are lean. While European wages remain largely unaffected, the vast majority of non-White workers have greatly reduced earnings during that period. From January to May, the town settles into its yearly summer torpor. Most businesses experience a drop of about 20 per cent in cash sales during the summer months, and the same applies to the sale of "kaffir beer" in the municipal beer hall. The migrant African cane cutters are particularly affected, as they earn only their basic wage of £4.10.0 a month during the off-season. The virtual absence of secondary industry in Caneville and the almost exclusive reliance of the district on the monoculture of the sugar cane, make the local economy particularly subject to cyclical ups and downs.

Not only is the CSC a large concern, but it is the only concern of any size in and around Caneville. A handful of European planters employ up to fifty or sixty African cane cutters. A rice mill owned by Mr. Goshalia is the largest industrial concern after the CSC, but it only employs some forty workers when in operation. The whole Goshalia business, which includes a garage, a sizeable department store, a spice mill, and a rice mill, employs less than one hundred persons and is dwarfed by the sugar company. Apart from the two Goshalia mills, a large mechanized bakery, employing about fifteen workers and owned by a Greek family, exhausts the list of secondary industries in Caneville, and none of these concerns comes within even one-twentieth of the size of the CSC.

The CSC seeks to maintain its economic paramountcy as jealously as it maintains its political monopoly, for the two go together. Recent events have made Company officials crucially aware of the dangers of monoculture, and the Company itself is beginning to diversify its activities in a small way (for example, through the breeding of pigs). This internal diversification does not, of course, change the extent of Company economic control. The CSC is also aware that, since the population of Caneville continues to increase, and since the Company is reducing its labour force, an ever greater percentage of the population will have to leave Caneville, be unemployed, or find local employment in other enterprises. The Company professes to encourage the last alternative, but is adamantly opposed to any sizeable outside industry settling in town. If other large industries were allowed to develop in Caneville, they would presumably be subsidiaries of the CSC and be dependent upon some of the by-products of sugar, such as molasses.

The reasons for the Company's opposition to the settlement of large outside concerns are obvious. Not only would its power monopoly in the community be endangered, but secondary industry would present a serious threat of wage competition. The sugar industry, like all other primary industries in South Africa (notably the mines), thrives on the extremely low wages paid to unskilled migrant workers. The CSC is no exception; it pays non-European wages that are considerably lower than those paid in secondary industry in near-by Durban. The *rationalization* given for the CSC's objection to large outside interests coming to Caneville is that such interests might not maintain the high standards of housing and sanitation that the CSC has created for its non-White employees. The reasons given by two high Company officials are less idealistic: any large secondary industry in Caneville would have the effect of raising non-White wages, and threatening the monopsonistic position of the CSC in the labour market. The various sugar mills and the European cane planters also avoid competing with one another for labour by informally agreeing not to exceed the legal minimum wages or the currently prevailing wages. The employers who break this "gentlemen's agreement" become the victims of much unpopularity and even targets of hostility on the part of other employers.

The CSC offers, however, a solution which reconciles the need for a more diversified local economy on the one hand, and the desire to maintain a monopoly of power on the other hand. The Company advocates the development of small-scale Indian industries. This plan is rationalized on the White South African pattern of thinking, namely, that "charity begins at home," and that it is up to Indian businessmen to help "their own race." Again, the real reason for the proposal is different: because of the relatively weak financial position of Indian enterprise, its necessarily small-scale ventures could not upset the local labour market. Thus, the monolithic economic structure of Caneville, which first developed by accident, is now being maintained by design.

While secondary industry is therefore undeveloped in Caneville, a sizeable merchant class lives from commerce and other services. The town has some eighty retail businesses, mostly fresh produce stalls or small general dealer's shops, three hotels with bars, a couple each of tearooms and barbershops, and a few more specialized businesses, such as a bakery, two jewelry shops, four garages, two butcher shops, a photographer's studio, and the like. Except for the bakery and the hotels which are owned and operated by Europeans, the Company trading store, a butcher shop run by a Coloured Mauritian, and about a dozen minute African enterprises in Dube Village, all the retail business of Caneville is in the hands of Indians. The vast majority of Indian stores and all of the African shops are small concerns with a low volume of trade. In many cases the shops are operated as family ventures to supplement the income of wage earners. Overtrading, in spite of municipal control of the issue of trade licences, is a major problem; many shops are unprofitable and cannot support the owner's family adequately, let alone in comfort.

A handful of merchants could be described as well-to-do; they include three Memon Muslims, and four Hindus (of whom two are Gujarati and two Hindustani). With assets of between £5,000 and £50,000, the families owning these businesses can be said to live in comfort though not in luxury. These concerns are usually run by a group of brothers, or a father and sons, and consist mostly of large general dealers' shops. One of the merchants, however, is a jeweller who lends money at high interest rates. Two families also operate a garage in addition to their shop. With the exception of one self-made businessman, the owners of the other leading businesses have inherited much of their wealth.

Another twenty-odd Indian merchant families derive the basic necessities of life from their business and are reasonably sheltered from the threat of poverty. Most undertakings, however, are marginal, and many go bankrupt through the burden of debt at high interest rates. Fresh produce gardeners who sell at the market place also fall in the category of minor enterprise. The few African businessmen have a precarious existence. They buy their goods at relatively high prices and in small quantities from Indian stores, and resell them at a fractional profit. As most basic necessities are manufactured goods, small artisanal trade in Caneville, except for a few cobblers, masons, carpenters, a jeweller, garage mechanics, and a few African herbalists, is underdeveloped. South African legislation largely restricts artisanal work to Europeans, and virtually all artisans in Caneville are employed by the Company or by the South African Railways.

The Indian merchants, together with the professionals and the private farmers, are the only sizeable group of people in Caneville not *directly* dependent on the Company. But even for them, independence is largely illusory. Their fortunes fluctuate with those of the Company and the sugar crop. Through the municipality, the Company can exercise various means of pressure on the merchants. The most important of these is the power to grant or to refuse trading licences, a power that leads to frequent criticisms against some Town Council officials. The patronage of White Company employees is also a factor to be reckoned with. For these reasons, the merchants find it unwise either singly or collectively to organize into an economic pressure group against the Company, and, on the whole, advantageous to toe the Company line.

The municipal valuation roll gives an idea of the pyramidal

distribution of wealth in Caneville. From a town population of some 10,000 persons, only 294 are listed as owners of real estate. No African owns such property as he is denied the legal right to do so in Caneville as practically everywhere else in the country. Only thirteen of the taxpayers in Caneville are Europeans, because most local Whites are relatively transient Company or Government employees who are housed rent free by their employers. The vast majority of property owners are thus Indians. While the latter may only acquire and occupy land in certain restricted areas, and suffer under many other legal disabilities of an economic nature, Caneville is unique in South Africa in that most of the residential land is owned and occupied by Indians. Most landowners have small assets, however. Table III, which excludes the Town Council, the Company and the South African Railways, shows that 39.5 per cent of the taxpayers own property assessed at less than £500, and 53.8 per cent at less than £1,000. Only 6.4 per cent hold properties exceeding £5,000 in assessed valuation.

As is generally true of the South African Indian population as a whole, Muslim owners are over-represented in the high property brackets by comparison with Hindus, the majority of whom are small owners. Forty-one per cent of the Muslim owners are in the £2,000-plus category, compared to only 26 per cent of the Hindu owners. Europeans are also over-represented among the large property owners. Altogether, only five Caneville Indians have properties assessed at over £10,000, compared to two private European concerns plus the Town Council, the South African Railways, and the CSC. The assessed valuation of the Goshalia properties (the second largest group after the CSC) amounts to only nine per cent of the CSC town properties (which exclude most of the 37,000 acres of Company agricultural land). The Company alone pays about 40 per cent of the town's taxes.

The distribution of cane land in the Caneville district,

TABLE III

Number of Owners of Real Estate in Caneville by Assessment Category (1960)

(Percentages in Parentheses)

Assessed value of property (£)	Hindus	Indians Muslims	Christians	Europeans	Total
0– 499	99 (42.7)	13 (28.3)	0 (0.0)	4 (30.8)	116 (39.5)
500– 999	34 (14.7)	5 (10.9)	0 (0.0)	3 (23.1)	42 (14.3)
1000–1499	25 (10.8)	7 (15.2)	0 (0.0)	0 (0.0)	32 (10.9)
1500–1999	15 (6.5)	2 (4.3)	0 (0.0)	1 (7.7)	18 (6.1)
2000–2999	38 (16.4)	8 (17.4)	3 (100.0)	0 (0.0)	49 (16.7)
3000–4999	12 (5.2)	6 (13.0)	0 (0.0)	0 (0.0)	18 (6.1)
5000 and over	9 (3.9)	5 (10.9)	0 (0.0)	5 (38.5)	19 (6.4)
TOTAL	232 (100.2) *	46 (100.0)	3 (100.0)	13 (100.1) *	294 (100.0)

* Because of rounding, percentages do not add up to exactly one hundred.

shown in Table IV, points to the same pyramidal pattern of wealth distribution and emphasizes the racial disparity in the size of landholdings. A total of 878 planters (not including the CSC itself) delivers its cane to the Company mill. Of these planters, 75 are Europeans, 606 are Indians and 197 are Africans. The latter come from more distant tribal reserves. The figures shown in Table IV include only the 431 European and Indian planters in the Caneville district. Although the Indians constitute 86 per cent of the planters in the district, they own only 23 per cent of the land. Ninety-four per cent of the European planters own cane lands amounting to more than one hundred acres, compared to only 7.4 per cent of the Indian farmers. Nearly sixty per cent of the Indian planters live on farms of twenty-five acres or less, which, for a cane farm, is barely a profitable proposition.

Another economic aspect of racial stratification concerns

TABLE IV

Number of Cane Planters in the Caneville District by Size of Holding (1960) (Percentages in Parentheses)

Area of farm in acres	Europeans	Indians	Total
0– 10	0 (0.0)	72 (19.5)	72 (16.7)
11– 25	1 (1.7)	148 (40.1)	149 (34.6)
26– 50	1 (1.7)	81 (22.0)	82 (19.0)
51– 100	2 (3.2)	41 (11.1)	43 (10.0)
101– 250	11 (17.7)	21 (5.7)	32 (7.4)
251– 500	27 (43.5)	5 (1.4)	32 (7.4)
501–1000	12 (19.4)	1 (0.3)	13 (3.0)
Over 1000	8 (12.9)	0 (0.0)	8 (1.9)
TOTAL	62 (100.1)*	369 (100.1)*	431 (100.0)

* Because of rounding, percentages do not add up to exactly one hundred.

employer-employee relations. With a few minor exceptions, Whites are in the position of employer in relation to non-Whites, and Indians in relation to Africans. I know of no African who employs either Whites or Indians, if one excepts White civil servants from the definition of the employer-employee relationship. In South Africa, White civil "servants" are in fact in the position of masters over non-Europeans. In Caneville, only the White Post Office officials have to perform direct personal services for non-Europeans. In Caneville, unlike Durban, there are few White shop attendants. White Town Council employees are technically employed by the taxpayers the vast majority of whom are Indians, but, here again, these Whites act as masters, not as servants, in relation to non-Whites. Only two clear-out reversals of the White–non-White relationship in a normal employment situation have been brought to my attention. The Goshalia business employs on a part-time basis a White artisan at the rice mill. One informant mentioned with much gusto how another Indian merchant occasionally employs a European whom he described as "a bum" to perform such odd jobs as painting.

Survey after survey conducted in recent years in South Africa has conclusively shown what anybody who casts the most cursory glance around him already knows, namely, that the vast majority of the population lives in poverty. Caneville is no exception to the general pattern. Nor is Caneville unusual in its enormous racial disparity in the distribution of wealth. There exist no income data covering the entire population, nor did I carry out an economic survey myself. But several sources of readily available data give a reasonably clear picture of the standard of living of the mass of the population.

A sample of 108 African applicants for housing in Dube Village, who can be considered to be a fairly typical cross-section of the permanent African residents of Caneville, shows a mean family wage income of £8.11.6 per month. As the

1960 census gives an average of 5.74 persons per family in Dube Village, the mean monthly per capita income is just under £1.10.0. Most of these people receive neither rations nor free housing from the Company, and must pay a monthly rent averaging about £1.10.0 per family, leaving some £7 a month for an average family of close to six persons. Of 148 rent payers in the location, only 35 pay an "economic" rental, which is payable if the total family income exceeds £15 a month. Over three-quarters of the residents thus earn less than this amount. It must be added, however, that a number of families supplement their meagre income to some extent by illicit brewing.

A sample of 173 Indian parents applying for free school books for their children provides information on the standard of living of the Indian working class. Since parents have to prove "indigence" to be entitled to free books, this sample is biased towards the lower income groups. As application forms were filled by the parents of about 40 per cent of the school children, the sample may be taken as indicating the economic position of the lower one-third to one-half of the Indian population. It is possible that the applicants under-represented their income to obtain grants, but the risk involved in doing so probably minimizes the error.

The mean monthly per capita income comes to £1.2.4 and the mean family income to £7.12.0. Apart from old-age pensioners, 9.3 per cent of the family heads were unemployed. Seventy-five per cent of the applicants worked for the CSC and received free housing and, in some cases, rations. The latter are, however, completely inadequate to feed a family of more than two persons. If one included the value of housing and rations, the mean family income would probably rise to about £11 a month. On the whole, then, Indians are better off than Africans, but this advantage is partly counterbalanced by the fact that Indian families are larger than

African families. Both the Indian and the African traditional family group are of the "extended" variety (mostly patrilocal), but the African extended family has broken up in urban areas to a much greater extent than the Indian extended family. This, combined with a lower infant mortality rate for Indians, makes for a larger Indian than African family. Of a sample of 58 Indian families 62.1 per cent included relatives other than spouses and children, compared to only 41.7 per cent of the settled Dube Village families. The Pondo field workers, are, of course, separated from their families. For a sample of 1,034 infants born in Caneville between 1943 and 1953, the infant mortality rate for Africans was 127.5 per 1,000 live births and for Indians 47.0. These mortality figures are well below the national average, and point to the relatively high standard of public health in Caneville. The average Indian wage earner in the sample had 6.75 dependents compared to 5.74 for Africans. Furthermore, Indian families do not supplement their income through illicit brewing as many Africans do. Eighty-seven per cent of the families earn £12 or less in cash a month. The modal family earning for the Indian sample is in the £4 to £6 category (for cash wages alone).

On the whole, however, the Indians are economically better off than the Africans. This generalization is certainly true if one includes the sizeable Indian merchant, professional, and farming class. Indian school teachers average about £40 to £50 a month. A couple of Indian physicians and a few of the merchants must exceed the £100-a-month bracket. None of the Africans approach that income category. For an African teacher, nurse, or other semi-professional, £40 a month is about the maximum he can reach. Confining the comparison between Indians and Africans to the working class, Indians are again better off, though not *much* more, because Indians are given preference over Africans in semi-skilled, minor clerical and supervisory positions. The Africans are more heavily concentrated among the unskilled labourers. The gap between African and Indian income is not nearly as great, however, as the gap between White and non-White income, as we shall see presently.

One may safely conclude that 90 per cent of the Africans and 60 per cent of the Indians in Caneville live in such poverty as to make adequate diet (let alone the less basic necessities of urban life) impossible. (These figures do not include the migrant labourers who are fed well-balanced rations, but whose earnings are insufficient to support their families adequately.) Any visit to an African or Indian school will convince one much more poignantly than a set of statistics of the extent of malnutrition among children. Of all the single sources of ailment in Caneville, malnutrition comes second highest, after scabies and before bilharzia, gonorrhea, and epidemic diseases such as chicken pox, measles, and whooping cough. In 1959, 187 cases of malnutrition (mostly children) had degenerated to the point of showing advanced clinical symptoms and requiring medical treatment.

If the earnings of most non-Europeans are insufficient for adequate diet, they obviously do not allow for any form of economic security against unemployment, old age, or death. So long as a person is employed by the Company he gets adequate medical care, but pensions for non-Europeans are either entirely absent (as in the case of migrant field workers) or grossly insufficient. Those who receive pensions have an average income of about £2.10.0 a month. While the White employees receive very adequate pensions paid for entirely by the Company, the non-Whites who get any retirement pay at all receive a mere pittance which is partly deducted from insufficient wages during their working life. Security against unemployment is also virtually non-existent for non-Whites. Moreover, due to legislative and customary restrictions, a non-White worker has practically no prospect of escaping his poverty and of improving his material lot to a level that even remotely approximates that of the most unskilled White workers. The frustration and despair generated by such a situation are obvious.

The major sources of information on the standard of living in Caneville are the CSC wage rates and other benefits. These data clearly illustrate the enormous disparity between the White and the non-White standards of living. Before examining the facts, I must briefly state the reasons for that racial disparity. It is true, of course, that Europeans, through greater opportunities for both general education and technical training, have on the whole a higher level of productivity than non-Whites. But the wage disparity is much greater than the difference in productivity. The common complaint of White industrialists that non-White labour is inefficient in South Africa by comparison with labour in Western Europe is valid for many obvious reasons such as malnutrition, climate, the migratory labour system, lack of skills, and lack of mechanization. This inefficiency is used to justify low non-White wages. What is rarely mentioned is that *White* South African labour is also inefficient, although it is highly paid. The wastefulness and incompetence of the South African Railways and Post Office are notorious. Each time I went to the Sugartown railway station during working hours, for example, I saw groups of White artisans in overalls sitting idly on benches. In the sugar mill, White artisans have non-European "boys" (in effect, perpetual apprentices) to do the heavy work for them.

Evidence of the inefficiency of White artisans is also provided by a recent change of wage policy concerning overtime. The Company suspected that many White artisans were doing much unnecessary overtime work. Management then decided to add the White artisans' average overtime wages earned in the past to their basic monthly pay, but, thereafter, to stop paying for any overtime. Since that measure was taken, the amount of overtime work performed has, by Reginald Sher-wood's own admission, greatly decreased. The conclusion is inescapable that South African labour inefficiency by comparison with other industrialized countries is by no means confined to non-White labour. White workers are, on the whole, more productive than non-Whites because the opportunity to acquire skills is denied to the latter; but, holding skill level constant, South African labour, irrespective of colour, is less productive than labour in many other countries. The huge wage gap between White and non-White workers is in great part the result of discrimination, not of free competition, in the labour market. In terms of free-competition economics (and quite apart from Marxist surplus-value arguments), many White workers are overpaid and non-White workers underpaid.

The entire structure of South Africa entrenches economic as well as other privileges of the Whites in such a way as to prevent, or at least retard, the tendency for the racial gap to narrow. Not only are the segregated White schools vastly superior to the non-White schools, but the non-Whites with their low wages are not able to avail themselves of existing opportunities nearly to the same extent as Whites. Opportunities are largely determined by skin colour, not by merit. In industry, White labour is given much greater freedom to organize than African workers, who are forbidden to go on strike, for example. Skilled occupations in some industries, notably in mining, are restricted by law to Whites. While there is no legal job reservation on the basis of colour in the sugar industry, the high minimum wages for skilled labour have the same effect of maintaining the privileged White position. Where no specific industrial colour bar exists, employers can be relied upon, through their own colour prejudices, to hire only Europeans in the highly paid jobs. This is what happens in the sugar industry.

At the bottom of the economic hierarchy of the CSC are the African cane cutters who constitute nearly two-thirds of the total labour force. They are housed free of charge in single men's barracks and are fed a nutritious (if simple) diet that is undoubtedly superior to the average rural diet. Their standard basic wage, earned by 75 per cent of them, is £4.10.0 for a full thirty days of work. Only 3 per cent of the cane cutters earn more than £4.10.0 in basic wage, while 22 per cent earn less. For this basic wage they have to cut a daily "task" of three thousand pounds of cane. They receive a bonus for anything cut in excess of the task, at the rate of 1d per one hundred pounds. While the actual bonus earned varies greatly from one cutter to another, it averages about £4.3.0 for 30 days of work. The labourers work a six-day week, and the hours of work are not limited by law. For a month of twenty-five working days, the migrant labourer averages about £7.6.0. The field worker has no legal recourse of any sort in the form of minimum wage, maximum hours, etc. He is unorganized and tied down to his job for a six-month contract. Breach of contract is a criminal offence and deserters are prosecuted.

During the cutting season, the work is strenuous, and has to be done at a very fast pace to cut anything above the daily task. The work is supervised both by African *indunas* (otherwise called "boss-boys") and by European overseers on horseback. Corporal punishment through flogging was routine until the 1920's but has now been completely abolished. Describing conditions in the 1920's, Whitehead writes:

> Flogging . . . was still condoned on the Estate where it was accepted as the traditional and most effective method of getting work out of coolies and kaffirs and of maintaining plantation discipline. The overseer's badge of office was still the sjambok looped to his wrist. If he passed a day without beating somebody up he would be afraid that he was not doing his job or losing his nerve.

During the off-season of about four months, the work is lighter, but the labourer only receives his basic wage of £4.10.0 plus rations.

Likewise at the bottom of the wage hierarchy are the 750-odd casual workers, who are mostly women and children. The women are either Africans or destitute Indians. They are paid sixteen shillings a week plus half-rations. Children are employed from about the age of ten or eleven and are paid on a sliding scale by age in proportion to a woman's wage. Children usually do light work such as weeding, but women are put to quite strenuous tasks. One often sees gangs of Indian women working on road repairs, carrying heavy logs, or weeding artificial lakes waist-deep in dirty, stagnant water. Few African women are employed by the Company because the mass of the Pondo migrant workers come without their families. Furthermore, many of the settled African women supplement their earnings through the brewing of beer which they illegally sell to the migrant workers. This source of income does not exist for Indian women.

Non-White factory workers are somewhat better off than the field workers. They receive better housing, their wages are higher (and subject to a legal minimum), and they receive a cost-of-living allowance in lieu of a ration in kind. Through a "gentlemen's agreement" between the sugar mills, however, the minimum wage rates laid down for non-White employees are treated as if they were *maximum* wages. Table V shows the number of CSC employees in each racial group falling in various monthly wage brackets. For the non-White workers, only the (better-paid) factory workers are included, and for the European workers, the top executives are excluded. The table, thus, underestimates the racial differential in wages.

Quite apart from the mass of African field workers, the modal wage bracket for non-Whites is £15 to £19.19.11 and for Whites £80 to £89.19.11, a ratio of about one to five. If

TABLE V
Number of CSC Employees in Various Total Cash Wage Categories (1959–1960)*
(Percentages in Parentheses)

£ per month	Africans	Indians	Europeans	Total
10– 14.19.11	79 (36.4)	24 (11.4)	0 (0.0)	103 (17.9)
15– 19.19.11	137 (63.3)	142 (67.6)	0 (0.0)	279 (48.5)
20– 24.19.11	0 (0.0)	10 (4.8)	0 (0.0)	10 (1.7)
25– 29.19.11	1 (0.5)	19 (9.0)	0 (0.0)	20 (3.5)
30– 34.19.11	0 (0.0)	13 (6.2)	0 (0.0)	13 (2.3)
35– 39.19.11	0 (0.0)	0 (0.0)	0 (0.0)	0 (0.0)
40– 44.19.11	0 (0.0)	2 (1.0)	0 (0.0)	2 (0.3)
45– 49.19.11	0 (0.0)	0 (0.0)	0 (0.0)	0 (0.0)
50– 59.19.11	0 (0.0)	0 (0.0)	23 (15.5)	23 (4.0)
60– 69.19.11	0 (0.0)	0 (0.0)	1 (0.7)	1 (0.2)
70– 79.19.11	0 (0.0)	0 (0.0)	12 (8.1)	12 (2.1)
80– 89.19.11	0 (0.0)	0 (0.0)	72 (48.6)	72 (12.5)
90– 99.19.11	0 (0.0)	0 (0.0)	0 (0.0)	0 (0.0)
100–109.19.11	0 (0.0)	0 (0.0)	33 (22.3)	33 (5.7)
110–119.19.11	0 (0.0)	0 (0.0)	7 (4.7)	7 (1.2)
TOTAL	217 (100.2)**	210 (100.0)	148 (99.9)**	575 (99.9)**

* For Africans and Indians, only factory workers are included. The European employees exclude the executive level, whose salaries are confidential. For all three racial groups, the income brackets are for *total* cash wages inclusive of bonuses and cost-of-living allowance.

** Because of rounding, percentages do not add up exactly to one hundred.

the modal White wage is compared to that of all non-Europeans including the field workers, then the ratio becomes about ten to one. Nearly 90 per cent of the non-White factory workers earn less than £20 a month, and over two-thirds of the Whites earn £80 or more. Top executives earn up to £250 a month, plus luxurious housing, and free servants. The lowest-paid young White field overseer without any particular qualifications gets £12 more than the most qualified non-White worker. Not only is the gap very great, but it has widened over the last ten years. During that period, European wages have increased by about 75 per cent while non-White wages have increased in a lesser proportion.

A closer examination of Table V reveals that, besides the large White–non-White gap, there is a smaller but significant difference in the earnings of Indians and Africans. Virtually all (forty-four of the forty-five) of the better-paid non-European jobs in the factory are held by Indians. Furthermore, three times as many Africans as Indians are found in the lowest pay category. Indians, then, while much closer to the Africans than to the Europeans in their wage scale, are nevertheless significantly better off than the Africans. This Indian-African difference is partly accounted for by the higher level of education and Westernization of the Indian worker, but is also partly the result of informal discrimination on the part of the CSC. No job categories are specifically reserved for either Africans or Indians, but Indians as a group are held to be "more intelligent" than Africans. The latter have the reputation that they cannot be trusted with machinery. Machines, when handled by Africans must be, according to the local phrase, "Pondo-proof." Africans are well aware of the preference given to Indians for semi-skilled or minor clerical jobs, and this discrimination is one of the major sources of anti-Indian feelings among Africans.

This secondary discrimination between Indians and Africans is, however, overshadowed by the blatant White–non-White discrimination. According to the South African principle, the European must always be *baas* in the work situation. No White wants to do what he calls "kaffir work." Conversely, no non-White, no matter how qualified, is given a "White" job, except surreptitiously in a few instances, as we shall see later. The principle of economic discrimination on colour lines extends from wages to the whole scale of material facilities. The "model" house for a non-European family costs about £400, while houses for Whites are worth from £2,000 to £4,000. All employees are given free medical care, but only Whites get dental care, and, when hospitalized, Whites get much better food, service, and quarters than do non-European patients. Sports facilities are similarly down-graded. The Whites have a spacious club-house, a bowling green, a golf course, a swimming pool, and four tennis courts, while the Indians have soccer and cricket grounds and two tennis courts, and the Africans a recently completed soccer field and one tennis court. The Indians and Africans each have a club-house which by comparison with the European club can only be described as primitive. The same down-grading of facilities applies to schools, a subject that we shall examine in greater detail since schools determine to a large extent opportunities for occupational training.

Local Whites, with very few exceptions, view economic discrimination on the basis of colour in the same light as they view any other form of discrimination. It is taken completely for granted as the normal and desirable state of affairs. I must, once more, say that non-White facilities in Caneville are much better than in the other sugar estates, but that changes nothing regarding the principle of discrimination. The fact that facilities are better than elsewhere is taken by the Whites as a good reason for self-complacency. Whatever is given to the non-Whites is viewed by the CSC management as a proof of its liberalism and generosity under the motto: "Look what we have done for the Natives and Indians." The hidden premise of that philosophy is that the non-Whites have really no *right* to anything at all.

Let us look at the school situation in greater detail. The schools have nothing to do with the Company, except insofar as the CSC has often contributed money to them. There is complete three-way racial segregation in the entire school system, and the quality of schooling follows the colour hierarchy. European and Indian schools are administered by the Province of Natal and the African schools by the central government. The European primary school is in a spacious building and provides for the first eight years of schooling. Classes are small (thirteen to twenty-three pupils), and rooms well-furnished and pleasantly decorated. The teachers are well-qualified and relatively well paid. The principal gets an annual salary of about £1,700. The children all get free books, and are driven to and from school in a bus. Parents send their children away to boarding schools when they reach high-school age. Virtually every European child who is not a moron completes his Junior Certificate after ten years of school. Education for Europeans is compulsory; for non-Europeans it is not.

Indian school buildings range from excellent to totally decayed wood and iron buildings and make-shift accommodations. Three of the seven Indian schools in the area were built on a pound-for-pound basis by the Indian community and the Province of Natal. The other four schools are entirely government-built institutions. The Indian community was forced to contribute to the erection of schools, because the Province would not have provided sufficient accommodations. Due to this remarkable community effort, a much higher proportion of Indian children attend school in Caneville than in neighbouring towns. Ample facilities are provided for the well-to-do European children at no direct cost to the parents, but not so with the non-European schools. In all Indian schools except the upper grades of the high school, there is overcrowding. Classes average from forty to fifty pupils. No transport is provided for the children, some of whom have to walk up to five or six miles each way often on empty stomachs. Indian teachers are paid from 20 to 30 per cent less than equally qualified White teachers. On the whole, teachers are reasonably well qualified and classroom furniture, while inferior to that of the European school, is still adequate. Whereas European children get free books, Indian children have to prove indigence to get them, and then they are only eligible for free books in the government schools. The vast majority of Indian children complete four years of school. Some two-thirds complete eight years, but only about one-third complete their Junior Certificate, and less than 5 per cent complete high school and get their Matriculation Certificate.

There are two African primary schools in Caneville. Both are controlled by the Bantu Education Department; but one is owned and operated by the Catholic Church, while the other is a government school. In the last six years since the central government has taken over "Bantu education," the standard of instruction has greatly dropped. The Government clearly intends that the African masses should only get a smattering of primary education, barely sufficient to make them useful helots.[1] Both schools are appallingly overcrowded. The Government school crams 560 pupils into seven classrooms, and still has to turn away about 100 children for lack of room. Furniture is barely adequate in the Catholic school, but practically non-existent in the Government school where most children squat on the floor. The principal does not even

[1] For evidence on this statement see Horrell, A Survey of Race Relations in South Africa, 1958–59, pp. 260–261.

have a regular chair to sit on in his office; he only has a primitive stool. His salary is £36 a month. One woman teacher earns only £6 a month, less than the wages of a domestic servant in Durban. Teachers are poorly qualified (most do not even have their Junior Certificate), constantly harassed by restrictive Government regulations, and overloaded with pupils and work. The children are given no transport, and there is no provision at all for free books, no matter how poor the parents. The vast majority of children can afford no books at all. Finally, local African residents have to pay a school tax of 6 shillings a year. Only about one child in three finishes as little as four years of education. Only one in seven finishes eight years. Virtually none go on to high school.

I have briefly described the school situation because it illustrates the effect of economic and other forms of racial discrimination, and because schools are at the root of the self-perpetuating vicious cycle of poverty and ignorance. If anything, I have understated the abysmal condition of the African Government school, which would require much space to describe fully. Schools, as everything else in Caneville, follow the general South African principle of separate and *unequal* facilities.

Returning to the general economic organization of Caneville, the malfunctions of the system must be obvious to anyone familiar with the most elementary principles of economics. Again, Caneville illustrates the situation in the rest of South Africa all the more forcefully because in many respects Caneville is "better" than other towns. In the field of industrial organization, the CSC has unquestionably been the leader in the sugar industry. (For example, the use of motorized trailers for the transport of cane instead of the antiquated narrow-gauge railway cars created a minor revolution in the South African sugar industry.) Yet, in spite of its relatively progressive outlook, the CSC suffers from the economic mal-functions of racial discrimination.

Admittedly the economic effects of colour discrimination are not all unfavourable to the CSC. The system ensures for the Company an almost unlimited reservoir of cheap labour and an amount of general control that would be unthinkable under a democratic government. It is an open question whether these advantages (from the point of view of the CSC) outweigh the malfunctions of the system, but the exist-ence of such malfunctions cannot be disregarded. There is, of course, the obvious cost of triplicating public facilities to satisfy the mania for segregation; but here, one can also argue that, since the vast majority are given *inferior* facilities, the minority actually saves over what it would cost to give *everybody* adequate ones. The saving to the ruling group be-comes even greater when destitute groups are made to pay "for their own race," as the Africans are through beer-hall profits.

Whatever the economic apologists of White domination might say, racial discrimination is responsible for at least two staggering material malfunctions in the system as a whole:

1. The lost purchasing and saving power that results from keeping the majority of the population poor.

2. The under-utilization and waste of the productive potential of the labour force.

CSC officials realize these negative factors, and would like to counteract them without endangering the "positive" aspects of the system. Therein lies one of the basic differences between the outlook of the Nationalist government, which is apt to ignore the economic consequences of apartheid, and the English capitalists, who are not. Obviously, if the earnings of the non-Whites were raised, sugar consumption in South Africa would greatly increase and make the industry less dependent on the precarious overseas market. Yet, at the same time, the CSC is reluctant to raise wages unilaterally, for such an increase would put the Company under a competitive disadvantage in the industry.

The position in relation to the second factor is similar. The CSC knows, as does any industrial concern in South Africa, that the migratory labour system is wasteful, but over the years the Company has grown so dependent on it, and the initial capital outlay to eliminate it would be so great, that the system perpetuates itself. Through various methods, the Company has endeavoured to reduce progressively non-European labour turnover, to retain trained personnel, to increase the productivity of labour, and to reduce the number of workers by introducing mechanization. These efforts have had limited success, but they have not struck at the root of the problem, namely that any "cheap," unskilled, and migrant labour force is always relatively unproductive and incompatible with a high degree of industrialization. Once a vicious circle is established, however, it is difficult to reverse the trend without initially costly readjustments. So long as labour is migratory it does not pay to train it, and so long as labour is untrained it does not pay to try to stabilize it. But any procrastination in reversing the vicious circle increases the initial difficulty and cost of changing the policy.

Another aspect of the economic malfunction of discrimination in employment is the rigidity it imposes on the utilization of labour. In any advanced free economy, wages tend to equal productivity. Yet, in South Africa, through customary and legal interference with free employment, the gap between White and non-White wages is much wider than the gap in productivity. In other words, many Whites are overpaid and non-Whites are underpaid. Consequently, it would be profitable for any industry to replace White with non-White labour, by paying the latter wages intermediate between the present rates for Whites and non-Whites. When the gold mines attempted to do this, the White workers rebelled and the Government passed legislation establishing an industrial colour bar in mining. So far, there is no "job reservation" in the sugar industry, but the fear of action on the part of the White trade unions prevents the CSC from introducing any drastic up-grading of its non-White labour, much as it would like to do so for self-interested motives.

In two minor, surreptitious ways the Company has, however, broken the industrial colour bar. In one case it has resisted pressure to exclude the creole Mauritians from White jobs, because it could not dispense with the valuable skills of these artisans. For fear of government interference, however, the CSC maintains a conspiracy of silence about its Mauritian artisans and refrains from hiring new ones. As one high official put it to me: "We don't want to aggravate the problem." The other non-White inroad into a previously all-White job is in the chemical testing department of the mill. Indian "chemists" (actually, testing technicians) have gradually replaced White chemists. Now, White and Indian chemists perform identical tasks, but at greatly different rates of pay, and at opposite sides of the factory.

Donald Sherwood speaks about establishing a field section directed entirely by non-Europeans, but no concrete attempt has yet been made in that direction. In spite of protective affirmations from the Whites that their skills are still irreplaceable, most job categories in the CSC could be taken over by non-White workers, after a short on-the-job training, without any reduction in efficiency. If that happened, however, the Government would probably step in to introduce further restrictive legislation, as it has so often done in the past.

In this chapter I have analysed the economic structure of Caneville with its giant (by local standards) industry overshadowing the economic as well as the political life of the town and the district. We have seen how dependence on the monoculture of sugar cane renders the local economy vulnerable to cyclical changes. We then turned to examine how the South African colour prejudice finds its economic expression in a large gap between White and non-White standards of living. Finally, we briefly surveyed the economic malfunctions of colour discrimination. In the next chapter, I intend to analyse the status or the prestige dimension of Caneville's social structure.

Chapter VI _____

THE STATUS SYSTEM

As ONE may expect in a heterogeneous
population, the social stratification of Caneville is highly complex. The status or prestige system can certainly not be described as a simple hierarchy of social classes in the Warner
sense, or as a uni-dimensional continuum from high to low
status. Similarly, the Marxian schema of class as determined
by the relationship to the means of production would lead to
a gross distortion of reality. A political view of class as a
distinction between the rulers and the ruled, such as Mosca
advanced, would likewise be an oversimplification of the
situation.

The "caste and class" approach used by Warner, Dollard,
Myrdal, and others in describing the United States is a closer
approximation to the Caneville or the general South African
situation.[1] If one adopts a minimum definition of caste as an
endogamous, ascribed group into which one is born, out of
which one cannot move (except by surreptitious "passing"),
and which is ranked in relation to other similar groups, it is
clear that the "racial" groups in South Africa and the United
States are castes. Each of these colour castes is internally
stratified into relatively permeable social classes, so that the

_____
[1] Cf. G. Myrdal, *An American Dilemma;* J. Dollard, *Caste and
Class in a Southern Town.*

stratification system can be described as a dual hierarchy of closed castes sub-divided into open classes.

The use of the term "caste" in this context has been criticized by Cox and others, and it is not my intention here to reopen that debate.[2] I accept the minimum definition of caste as a useful analytical tool. This does not mean, of course, that the racial situation in the United States or South Africa is identical or even similar in all major respects to the classical Hindu caste system. Since, in Caneville, both the Hindu and the racial variety of caste are found, I shall distinguish them by calling the Hindu variety simply "caste," and the racial variety "colour caste."

For broad descriptive purposes, I shall follow the "caste and class" schema in dealing with Caneville. However, the "fit" with reality is still imperfect, so that I accept the schema only with one important reservation, which I must spell out before proceeding. In the case of Whites and Negroes in the United States one deals with a culturally homogeneous society sharing the same basic values and accepting to a large degree the same criteria of social stratification. If the South African population consisted only of Whites and Coloureds, then the parallel with White-Negro relations in the United States would be very close indeed. The fact, however, that the Africans and Indians in South Africa are still incompletely Westernized complicates the situation. South African society is integrated economically by common participation in a White-dominated economy and is held together politically by repressive force. In most other respects, South Africa consists of four "racial" and many more cultural groups living mistrustfully side by side in a highly unstable and explosive symbiosis. There certainly exists no consensus in South Africa at the broad level that Parsons calls the "value system," much

---

[2] Cf. O. C. Cox, *Caste, Class and Race*.

less at more specific levels such as political aims or criteria of stratification.

Returning to our immediate problem of the social stratification of Caneville, there does not exist the broad basis of agreement that Warner found in Yankee City or Jonesville, whereby different people rank each other much in the same order. In Caneville, the criteria for ranking people are not only numerous, but they vary and they have different relative weights in the various racial and cultural groups. In short, Caneville is a culturally pluralistic society with several status ladders that can be compared to one another only imperfectly. Our task in this chapter is to analyse this complex stratification system and to see what Caneville can contribute to the study of stratification in pluralistic societies.

We have already seen how race in Caneville determines one's position in the political and economic systems. In the status system also, race is by far the most important criterion. This overriding factor is of such importance that the next chapter will be entirely reserved to the effect of race in day-to-day relations. At this point, I only want to sketch the general lines of the colour-caste system and then proceed to the finer status distinctions within the colour castes.

The overriding distinction between Whites and non-Whites is largely imposed by the dominant European group in the country as a whole, and in Caneville in particular. The colour consciousness with which at least 95 per cent of the White population are imbued ranges from the crude use of abusive terms to more "sophisticated" conceit and more or less genuine concern for the welfare of the "less fortunate members of the community." The extent to which White colour prejudices are entrenched in the economic and political systems has already been shown. The details of segregation and other discriminatory practices will be studied in the next chapter. Of the non-European groups, Africans have the lowest caste status, while Indians and Coloureds are accorded a somewhat higher status. The status gap between Whites and non-Whites is, however, much greater than that between any of the non-European groups. No amount of education and Westernization can give any non-European access to the dominant group. The criterion of racial membership is completely rigid and ascribed.

Admittedly a minority of the more educated local Whites claim allegiance to the Progressive Party and advocate "civilisation" as the criterion of acceptance into the dominant group. Among the more sophisticated English Whites, this "progressive" outlook has lately become fashionable, as it sets one apart from the "uncouth, raw Afrikaners," but, *not a single local White* practises to the full extent the implications of that position. Pressure from other Whites is given as the excuse for not associating socially with non-Whites on terms of equality. A non-White cannot escape the stigma of colour, except if he looks White and is not known to be Coloured. "Passing" is the exception that proves the rule.

The non-Europeans (with the exception of a few accommodated "Uncle Toms" who have come to interiorize their inferiority feelings) reject this European-imposed "albinocracy," but they are not entirely devoid of racialism themselves. Among Africans there probably is a recent rise in Black counter-racialism as a reaction to White racialism. While many Indians look down on Africans, their ground for doing so is cultural rather than racial. As a group, the Indians are probably the least racialistic, and the Whites and Coloureds are the most colour-conscious.

As we shall see in detail later, the three main racial groups in Caneville constitute colour castes. The groups are hierarchized, completely rigid and endogamous. This albinocracy is fully accepted by the Whites and imposed by both legal and customary discrimination. Where the law does not already define the disabilities of a racial group, private White prejudice steps in to maintain the rigidity of the colour-caste hierarchy. The non-Whites deeply resent this racial caste system, but they outwardly appear to tolerate it because the penalties for rejecting the subservient role are heavier than for pretending to accept it.

Laying the relations between Indians, Africans, and Europeans aside until the next chapter, we shall now turn to the internal stratification of the three colour castes. The European group is perhaps the simplest to describe as its class system follows the well-known Western pattern. But, even here, the Mauritians introduce a complication. The twenty-five–odd Mauritian families who live in and around Caneville all hold "White" jobs, live in "White" houses and are officially treated as Whites by the CSC which, for reasons already mentioned, maintains a discreet silence about them. Of these families, all but half a dozen, which have one or more members whose skins are a shade darker, are also treated socially as Whites and intermingle freely in the European community. None of the White Mauritians holds high status in the CSC at present, but the father of one of the private planters had a high position in the older days of the Company.

The few creole Mauritian families are socially ostracized and keep themselves apart for fear of discrimination from the Europeans. They do patronize the European cinema in the CSC club-house, the men attend the yearly drinking party given by the Company at the end of the crushing season for the European employees, and the children go to the Company-sponsored Christmas party for the European children. Although they used to be concentrated in a small area just outside Town limits, several of them now live in Sugartown among the European employees. Yet, they are clearly not considered to be White and they constitute a colour sub-caste on the fringe of the dominant European group. They are not members of the European sports club, they do not use the club premises or the sport facilities, and they are not invited to the homes of either Mauritian or English Whites. In the Catholic parish, they sit among Europeans at Mass, they share with the White Mauritians the conduct of parish affairs, and they freely chat (often in French) with the White Mauritians; but social contacts do not extent beyond the church.

Creole Mauritians talk freely with White artisans in the mill, but friendships are confined to the work situation. As one English-speaking White phrased it, "We talk to each other on the job, but afterward we each stick to our own colour." When one of the families attempted to send its children to the European school in Sugartown, an anonymous protest was made, and the children had to be withdrawn and sent to a Coloured school. Some of the creole Mauritians successfully pass for White in Durban, where their families are not known, but this is impossible in Caneville. As may be expected, all Mauritians are extremely sensitive to colour, more so than the English Whites. Among non-Europeans, they have a reputation for harshness against Africans and Indians. I have heard several Mauritians refer to Africans as "kaffirs" (or "caffres" in French), a term that is no longer used in "polite" English society. When colour is mentioned, White Mauritians hasten to say that only ignorant South Africans believe that all Mauritians are Coloured. This, one informant defensively advanced as proof of the stupidity of White South Africans.

Yet, the position of the creole Mauritians is quite different from that of the Indians and the Africans. They enjoy most of the material benefits of Whites, and their status is closer to that of the Whites than to that of the Indians and Africans. But their position is ambiguous, insecure, and marginal. The Company adopts a conspiracy of silence about them for fear of government intervention, and the English Whites exhibit a large amount of guilt concerning them. While discrimination against Africans and Indians is taken completely for granted, the English are extremely uneasy about the Mauritians whom they see as being "just like us, except for colour." The topic of the Mauritians is avoided as far as possible, and when it is mentioned, it always elicits embarrassment. The creole Mauritians are referred to by the English as "a lost people" and "a tragedy" in a way in which the Indians and the Africans are never talked about, much more debased though their position is.

In short, the creole Mauritians are the only group about whom the dominant English Whites feel *guilty*. The reason is clear. With regard to Indians and Africans, the Whites have acquired a protective callousness that allows them to discriminate with a clear conscience. Africans and Indians are held to be an entirely "different" and inferior sort of *Untermensch* whom it is "natural" to treat badly. For example, when I asked a European woman living near the beach whether she had any neighbours, she replied, "No, no one lives near here, only Indians." This double standard becomes so deeply internalized that guilt is effectively warded off. Not so with the Mauritians. In this case, daily egalitarian contact on the job leads to bonds of friendship and makes it impossible to maintain the fiction that "they are different." Yet, strong social pressures from the White community (which often take the hysterical form of the miscegenation bogey) make it difficult to break down the colour barrier off the job without encurring the threat of ostracism. English Whites cannot escape the conclusion that the creole Mauritians are "just like us," and, hence, they feel guilty about discriminating against them.

The theoretical implications of the Mauritian situation in Caneville are interesting. The "Law of Contact" states that equal status contact not involving the threat of competition breaks down group thinking along stereotypical lines.[3] Cane-

---

[3] Cf. G. W. Allport, *The Nature of Prejudice*, pp. 261–282.

ville confirms this generalization, but it also shows that, if the dominant social system firmly supports racial prejudice, the resulting "change of heart" is not translated into good human relations but into guilt.

Aside from the Mauritian complication, the White system of stratification in Caneville follows general Western lines, except for the absence of a real proletariat. The highly privileged position of the White artisans makes them identify with the dominant group to which they, in fact, belong. While Caneville White society is internally stratified, the social pyramid is top-heavy. In terms of a normal Western European country, local White class differences only range from upper class to petty bourgeoisie (or to Warner's lower middle class).

There is yet another minor respect in which the White group differs from a Western European class system. In the quasi-colonial situation of the local White group, there is a tendency at the verbal level to deny class differences and to present a united White front against the "sea of colour." This factor is probably more pronounced in Caneville than in the rest of South Africa, and certainly more than in Durban, which has a reputation for class snobbery among the English. This verbal egalitarianism within the dominant group has the effect of de-emphasizing the manual–non-manual distinction, and of facilitating social mobility. Until the relatively recent past, it was for example possible for any gifted European to rise to the top of the CSC hierarchy without higher education. With increasing demand for highly specialized skills, however, the rate of upward mobility is rapidly declining. A generation ago, only two of the top executives were university graduates. Today, thirteen of the top employees hold degrees; i.e., all but three or four of the people at the executive level. University graduates are now hired at the junior executive level, and employees without degrees have but slim chances of promotion to the top.

Although it is considered in bad taste to make class-conscious remarks, in practice, minute distinctions of status are made, and the White status system is largely determined by position in the Company hierarchy. In the past, these distinctions were not so much based on class but rather on position in an open hierarchy where promotion to the top was realistically possible. The White employees were, to use a military analogy, in the position of officers from lieutenant to general who in spite of rank differences are social equals. Today, the ideology of what may be called "*Herrenvolk* egalitarianism" is still present, but the reality has largely disappeared. The ideology may *retard* the crystallization of social class among Whites, but it has not prevented it.

The yearly ritual of the beer-drinking party for White male employees at the end of the crushing season is revealing in this respect. At the party I attended there was, early in the evening, a rigid hierarchical arrangement. In the cinema hall where the function was held, a long polished wooden main table, with polished wooden armchairs, dominated the scene. Reginald Sherwood sat at the center of this table, his father being absent. To his right and left, the present top executives, plus two distinguished retired executives, sat in descending order of seniority. Nearby, to one side, was a smaller table at which sat the junior executives of just below main-table rank. (This was also the table where, as a guest, I was invited to sit.) The rest of the employees sat at long tables placed at right angles to the main table. There, a horizontal "aggregation" of workers took place with the field, factory, and office sections of the Company concentrated at their respective tables.

All furniture, except the main table and chairs, was of the functional cafeteria type, such as is regularly used in the clubhouse. A number of special delicacies such as whisky, olives, anchovies, and the like were only found at the main table, while the other employees were provided with cheese and ham sandwiches, peanuts and potato chips. After formal speeches were delivered by "Mr. Reg" and by Hancock, and as gradual intoxication began to take effect, the main table executives slowly dispersed among the rest of the employees and jovially fraternized with them in a slightly contrived atmosphere of good fellowship, off-colour jokes, and choral singing in back-slapping circles. As a high executive later said to me, "This is a good way for Management to show its appreciation to the workers." This annual ritual illustrates both the stratification within the White group and the conscious attempt to preserve the diminishing spirit of *Herrenvolk* egalitarianism.

Let us describe in greater detail the distribution of status within the European group. Besides Company employees, local White society also comprises a group of government workers employed by the police, the post office, and the railways. These civil servants are almost all Afrikaners of low education and qualifications, and they are accorded low status by the Company people. They are allowed to use the European Company cinema and club facilities, and the police sergeant, the stationmaster, and the postmaster are invited to the annual drinking feast. But they are distinctly looked down upon by the top English Company executives, who have a low opinion of Afrikaners in general and of the Government and its civil servants in particular.[4] These civil servants are tolerated on the bottom fringe of White society, and enjoy a status that is only a shade higher than that of the creole Mauritians.

Class status in the large group of White Company em-

---

[4] This low opinion of civil servants is easily understandable in South Africa. I have personally met postal clerks, for example, whose intelligence could be only charitably described as "borderline," and who, without my assistance, could never have mailed overseas packages and registered letters.

ployees is closely correlated with position in the CSC, and position in the Company is closely related to education and other class characteristics. Before we turn to this vertical segmentation, I must briefly describe the horizontal division into the field, factory, and office sections of the Company. This division cuts across the hierarchy and links all White workers from high to low in a sectional *esprit de corps*. The "field" people are on the whole more permanent and claim greater loyalty to the Company. The office and factory people are more highly trained and take pride in their technical competence. But there is no consensus that one section is better than the others. In the past, the field section enjoyed perhaps a slightly higher status as it constituted the main stream of promotion to the top, but today the highest executives are increasingly recruited from the office staff. The mutual attitudes of the field as opposed to the other two sections take roughly the form of a mild tug-of-war between "country rednecks" and "city slickers."

Vertically, the White Company employees can roughly be divided into an upper class and a middle class with still finer gradations within these two groups. The upper class consists of the top executive families, most of whom are university educated and steeped in the highly respectable, conservative English Natalian way of life. They all live in large comfortable houses, perched on isolated hills in the pleasant rolling countryside of the sugar-cane fields. Officials of equivalent rank have their houses on neighbouring hills where they try to emulate on a reduced scale the style of life of Donald Sherwood. All executive mansions are surrounded by large, immaculately kept gardens that remind one in varying degrees of the "royal park" with its palm-tree alley, its water-lily ponds, its private tennis court and its swimming pool. These little private domains are kept up by a staff of five or six servants and guarded by one or two large watchdogs. As one woman put it, "The dogs are very friendly but if a Native came on the property they would tear him to bits. It's amazing how they know. Indians they would only push around a bit but not seriously wound."

A university education is an important prestige symbol in the upper class and conversational references are made to which university people attended. Of highest prestige value is a British university education at Cambridge or Oxford, a distinction that only Reginald Sherwood has achieved. Everything British, from tea services and monarchy to clothing (but excluding liberalism), is praised in the typical more-British-than-the-British attitude of the Natal English upper class. A South African accent, whether Afrikaans or lower-class English, is considered a colonial stigma. Houses are luxuriously but discreetly furnished with a studious avoidance of "knick-knacks" that could be considered in bad taste. Travel ranks among the most important status symbols. Typically, the top executive takes his family for a long leave "home" (i.e., Britain), followed by a quicker grand tour of the Continent, and spends much time exchanging travel memories and exclaiming on the cultural resources of London with other top executives. Travel by ship is more valued than travel by air, as the ability to spend three weeks at sea each way indicates conspicuous leisure and distinguishes holiday trips from utilitarian business journeys by aeroplane. Departure of prominent people by ship is featured in the "social" page of Durban newspapers. Politically, the traditional upper-class outlook is that of the United Party, though, more recently, it has become fashionable to claim allegiance to the somewhat less conservative Progressive Party, and to be willing to shake hands and drink tea with "clean Natives" at charity bazaars. This willingness coupled with a claim to treat their servants well is advanced by such people as proof of their "non-racialism." In its religion, the upper class is mostly Anglican, but rarely appears in church except at Christmas and Easter. The women refrain from participation in the women's organizations, which they leave to the middle class. ("Not that we don't mix with the people—we do," added a woman defensively.)

On the job, the top executives generally wear a white shirt and a tie, but Donald Sherwood sports an open-collared safari jacket, and the field manager, in keeping with the *esprit de corps* of the field staff, wears the khaki shorts and shirt that are the uniform of field duty. The top executives all drive grey Mercedes motorcars (or are driven in them by chauffeurs), and there is a further minute status distinction between two models of Mercedes. At the main office of the Company, the parking spots nearest the entrance are by tacit rule reserved for the fleet of executive Mercedeses. Office size and furnishings are likewise subtly graded from the small functional offices of the minor executives with their chart-covered walls to the elegant period-furniture office of the president where paintings on the walls suggest serene dedication to the finer things of life and freedom from down-to-earth worries.[5] All top executives address and refer to one another by abbreviated Christian names or surnames except for "The President."

The European middle class, consisting of artisans, field supervisors, and clerks, lives mostly in Sugartown in standardized houses (coming in two sizes), or in dispersed houses in the field sections where their duty calls them. Their houses are spacious and comfortable by comparison with "model" non-

---

[5] At the height of the anti-Indian riots of 1949, Whitehead hastily returned from his vacation to see whether the unrest had affected Caneville. He describes his meeting with Donald Sherwood on that day in the following words:

"A clock slowly ticked, magnifying the utterness of the silence. A figure stirred in the depths of one of the library chairs. It was Donald, and he was deeply engrossed in a treatise on Chinese ceramics. Faintly startled, he looked up and put down his book. 'What the hell are you doing here?' he demanded."

European houses, but modest by comparison with the executive mansions. Around the houses are well-kept little gardens. Middle-class families all have one to three African or Indian servants and a small-to-medium motorcar. Living rooms are comfortably furnished with factory-made pieces, conspicuous among which is a large mahogany radio. The living room is often decorated with small ornaments such as porcelain animals and miniature liquor bottles that would be considered tasteless by the Caneville upper class.

The men, on the average, have had from eight to ten years of schooling, plus some technical training in the case of artisans. Middle-class families cannot afford overseas trips and usually spend their vacations in South African mountain or seaside resorts. They speak with unashamedly South African accents. They attend church more regularly than the upper class, belong largely to the Catholic, Methodist, and Dutch Reformed Churches. They take a more active part in club activities, and are politically divided between a United Party majority and a Nationalist minority. They attend the Company-sponsored New Year's Eve dance which "top" people do not attend. On the job, the men wear either overalls or field khakis. (The White artisans' overalls are distinguished from those of the non-European workers in that only the latter, are labeled on the back with the red letters "C. S. C.") Only those who need motorized transport for their jobs are provided with Company cars—Land Rovers, Austin pick-ups, or Ford Zephyrs—which they drive themselves and park on either side of the executive Mercedeses at the main office. White employees address the executives with "Mr." and surname, except for Reginald Sherwood who is affectionately known as "Mr. Reg."

The above description is, of course, only a general characterization which obscures minor individual variations and minor subdistinctions within these two broad classes. There is no definite barrier between the two classes. Though class mobility is becoming more difficult, several of the present or retired top executives started at the bottom and have adopted upper-class mores with varying degrees of success only in middle age. Some of the "top" people have militantly refused to accept the dominant English model. For example, the ex-Company physician, Dr. du Plessis, an ardent Afrikaner Nationalist, has furnished his house with Great Trek relics from the Bible to the muzzle-loading rifle. The general picture, however, is much as I described it.

The stratification of the Indian community is much more complex than that of the White group. Great religious and linguistic differences account for part of the complexity; the Hindu caste system introduces a further complication; finally, the relative strength of traditional as opposed to Western criteria of status makes a simple description in terms of Western classes difficult. This is not to say that Western class criteria are not operative among Indians. They are becoming increasingly important, but they do not exhaust the Indian status system.

Whatever degree of cohesion exists in the Indian group is largely a creation of European discrimination. Indians are lumped together by the dominant Europeans into one racial group with a somewhat higher status than the Africans. After a century of common discriminatory treatment, Muslims and Hindus (not to mention the linguistic sub-groups) have to some extent acquired a feeling of separate group membership in relation to Europeans, Coloured, and Africans. Proof of that can be found in the two major political bodies claiming to represent the Indian people of Natal, namely, the Natal Indian Congress and the Natal Indian Organization. Both organizations cut across religious and linguistic barriers (though Muslims tend to be over-represented in the more conservative Natal Indian Organization). For most purposes, however, religious and linguistic segmentation within the Indian race remains quite important.[6] While these distinctions are not the basis of a hierarchy of groups that is recognized by all Indians, some of these cleavages have a hierarchical aspect, as we shall see presently.

The deepest cleavage in the Indian community is between Muslims and Hindus. Intermarriage is strongly discouraged on both sides, even if conversion takes place. While there are a few cases of concubinage between Muslims and Hindus, I was told of only one mixed marriage. Muslim and Hindu children attend the same public schools, but go to separate mother-tongue schools in the afternoon. Commensality between Muslims and Hindus is rare, as most Muslims strictly observe the dietary rules of Islam. Muslims and Hindus likewise do not invite one another to weddings and funerals as these events are religious. Intervisiting is also rare. In a sample of 243 high-school children (23 of whom are Muslims and 5 Christians), 75 per cent of the parents exchange visits *only* with people of the same religion and only 10 per cent of the 1,101 home visitors listed by the pupils belong to a religion other than that of the hosts. In employment, Muslim merchants prefer to hire co-religionists, though this is not so much the case among Hindus. The women's clubs, student organizations, welfare societies, and taxpayers' associations cut across religious lines, although there has existed a now-defunct social club restricted to Muslim young men. Voluntary associations are, then, the main link between the two groups, but, through the numerical preponderance of Hindus in the town, all these associations are predominantly Hindu.

---

[6] For greater detail on Hindu caste and religious and linguistic segmentation in Caneville, see van den Berghe and Miller, "Some Factors Affecting Social Relations in a Natal North Coast Community"; and Rambiritch and van den Berghe, "Caste in a Natal Hindu Community."

On the whole, Muslims have stronger prejudices against Hindus than Hindus have against Muslims, and the lack of relations between the two groups except at the casual, superficial level, is largely (but not solely) the result of Muslim exclusiveness. Muslims, particularly the more conservative older people, view Hinduism with distaste as an idolatrous religion. The Westernized Hindus, on the other hand, consider Muslims clannish, intolerant in religious matters, and too conservative and unprogressive. Though Muslims are wealthier than Hindus on the average, and are proportionally over-represented in the merchant class, there is no consensus that Muslims have higher status than Hindus. In fact, the latter are over-represented in the high-status professional group.

Christian Indians number only about twenty families. They are generally accepted by and interact freely with the Hindus, but not with the Muslims. A prominent Christian teacher married a Hindu woman, and the daughter of a Christian couple married a Hindu youth in a Hindu ceremony. Christians are invited to attend Hindu weddings, exchange Christmas cards with Hindus (a practice that is widespread in the Hindu middle class), visit and entertain Hindus. The free interaction of Hindus and Christians is further evidence that the relative lack of intercourse between Hindus and Muslims is largely the result of Muslim rejection of other religions. It is also true that most Christians are converts from Hinduism, not from Islam, and that they retain their kinship ties after conversion. I do not think, however, that this fact invalidates the argument about Muslim religious "exclusiveness" as compared to the Hindu. Though Muslim prejudice against Christianity is not as great as that against Hinduism, Christian and Muslim Indians do not interact any more than Muslims and Hindus. A conservative Muslim summed up his view of Christianity in the following terms: "Islam and Christianity are sister religions. We accept Jesus as a prophet. The only difference is that you believe in three gods and we only believe in one. Also we don't have idols in our mosques."

Much of what was said about the religious cleavage in the Indian group applies to a lesser extent to the linguistic distinctions. Like the religious groups, the language groups are not hierarchized, except among Muslims. On the whole, language cleavages, while still strong, are not as strong as religious ones. With the exception of the small Gujarati group that cuts across the Muslim-Hindu barrier, all other five Indian languages spoken in Caneville follow religious lines. The Muslims are sub-divided between the Memon-, Gujarati-, and Urdu-speaking people, and the Hindus include the Hindi (or Hindustani), Gujarati, Tamil, and Telugu language groups. Numerically, the Tamil constitute about 40 per cent of Caneville's Indian population, the Hindi about 35 per cent, the Telugu and the Urdu about 10 per cent each, and the Gujarati and Memon some 5 per cent together. Memon is actually a spoken dialect closely akin to Gujarati, and is not generally classified as a separate language, but in Caneville the Memon families distinguish themselves clearly from the Gujarati-speaking Muslims, and say that they speak "Memon."

Among Muslims, the language distinctions follow class lines rather closely, but not rigidly. The Memon and Gujarati population constitute a minority of merchant families and consider themselves "better" than the Urdu-speaking Muslims. At the verbal level, this hierarchy is denied because it contravenes the principle of the equality and brotherhood of all followers of the Prophet. In practice, however, the linguistic distinctions take the form of a barrier to intermarriage and a mild snobbery on the part of the Memon and Gujarati. There is no formal rule of endogamy, but marriages are arranged by the parents within the linguistic group (and often, according to Islamic custom, with the father's brother's daughter). There is less resistance to hypergamous marriages (i.e., to

Urdu girls marrying "higher-class" Memon or Gujarati boys)
than to hypogamous ones (where girls marry into a lower
class), but both types are rare.

Although all Muslims can go to the mosque of their choice,
there is a tendency for the Memon to go to one mosque and
the Urdu to go to the other; and there is a perceptible difference in the economic positions of the congregations. This
arrangement is by no means rigid, and some people go
alternatively to both mosques. Moreover, the Imams at both
mosques are Urdu-speaking. Nevertheless, there is a distinct
linguistic and class polarization between the two places of
worship. One of the Imams characterized his mosque as "the
poor people's mosque." The linguistic distinction in attendance
is generally explained on grounds of proximity. While it is
true that the Memon merchant families live near one mosque
and several Urdu families somewhat nearer the other, the
argument is not very convincing as the two places of worship
are only five hundred yards apart.

Professions of equality within Islam serve to de-emphasize
class distinctions and to maintain an amount of fluidity which
might otherwise not exist. Muslims of the various language
groups attend one another's weddings and associate socially.
One of the Urdu families is quite well-to-do, and the few
Muslim professional men are predominantly Urdu, so that
the economic distinction between the language groups is not
clear-cut. None of the Memon is really poor, but quite a few
of the Urdu are well-off. The Urdu are, on the whole, darker-
skinned than the Gujarati and Memon, and this distinction
is recognized by all groups, but skin colour is largely insignifi-
cant as a status symbol among Indians, whether Muslims or
Hindus. Occasionally one hears of rejection of a prospective
spouse on the ground that his or her colour is too dark, and
there might be a slight aesthetic preference for light com-
plexions. But by comparison with the European group, skin

colour among Indians is of minor importance. The origin of
the snobbery against the Urdu is mostly religious. Many of
the Urdu are known to be relatively recent lower-caste Hindu
converts to Islam, as opposed to older-stock Muslims of the
Memon and Gujarati groups. Yet, at the same time, the latter
groups feel guilty about their snobbery, which conflicts with
the basic principle that conversion confers total equality.

Among Hindus, linguistic distinctions are not as hierarchical as among Muslims, but language is somewhat correlated
with economic condition. The Gujarati Hindus are a small
group, composed chiefly of well-to-do merchants, with very
few professional people. The Hindi are second to the Gujarati
in economic position and they include quite a few professional
persons, but the mass of the Hindi-speaking people is poor.
The Tamil are the poorest group of all. Of the 200-odd Indian
workers at the factory, all but a dozen are Tamil, while the
Tamil only comprise some 40 per cent of the Indian population
of Caneville. Only a few small merchants are Tamil-speaking,
though a number of the schoolteachers belong to that group.
In spite of this objective correlation between wealth and
language, the linguistic groups are not ranked by the people
into an agreed-upon hierarchy. The Gujarati are lighter in
skin colour than the other groups, but again, although that
fact is recognized, it is of little social significance.

As a form of horizontal segmentation, mother tongue is
still an important barrier among Hindus. The language groups
are almost entirely endogamous except for the Tamil and
Telugu, who are culturally quite close and who both come
from the Madras area in South India. Tamil and Telugu are
often collectively called "Madrassi." In the sample of 243
school children, only 6 per cent of the parents belong to
different language groups. Ten of the fourteen cases of linguistic exogamy occurred between Tamil and Telugu, but even
in these two groups, 91 per cent marry endogamously. To

a lesser extent, linguistic differences determine other social relationships such as commensality and visiting, but not nearly as much as religion does. Two of the main Hindu temples have a predominantly Hindi attendance while the other two are almost exclusively Tamil and Telugu. This cleavage corresponds to great cultural and religious differences between northern and southern India.[7] The reformed Hindu movement known as the Divine Life Society, which is quite influential in Caneville, is however trying to break down this sectionalism. To a considerable extent, Hindus of the various language groups attend one another's weddings, and all the voluntary associations (except for the temple committees) cut across linguistic lines.

While language barriers are not vertical among the Hindus, caste, in the classical Hindu sense, is hierarchical, insofar as it still operates. Elsewhere,[8] I have already treated in detail the subject of caste in Caneville, and here, I shall only give a brief description of the local remnants of the Hindu caste system, assuming knowledge of the latter in its classical form. As a system of occupational specialization, caste has disappeared in Caneville, except in a few instances such as the Nao (barbers) and the Maistry (washermen). Clearly, most traditional caste occupations have become redundant in the Western economy of South Africa. Furthermore, local White employers have paid no attention to caste occupations. The concept of untouchability was quickly abandoned in South Africa where the rules of defilement could not be maintained in the promiscuity of the sugar-estate barracks. Although a caste council (*panchayat*) existed in Caneville until the 1930's, it fell into decay as the South African courts did not recognize its authority. Regulations against breaking caste rules could thus not be enforced.

---

[7] Cf. Kuper, *Indian People in Natal.*
[8] Cf. Rambiritch and van den Berghe, *op. cit.*

A number of people still use caste names as surnames, a practice that is almost entirely confined to the "twice-born" upper three *varnas* (Brahmin, Kshatriya, and Vaisya). The "once-born" Sudras sought to escape the stigma of low caste by dropping their caste names, or usurping upper-caste names. Except among old, uneducated, and very conservative Hindus, caste is no longer a barrier to social relationships, but caste and *varna* endogamy are still practiced. In a sample of 312 cases, the rule of *varna* endogamy is broken only 25 times; caste endogamy, however, is no longer as rigidly followed. It is broken in 80 cases in the sample. While caste is still one of the factors taken into account by the parents in arranging marriages, it is no longer the major one. Religion, "race," and language group are more important.

To summarize a complex situation in a few sentences, it may be said that Hindu caste in Caneville is moribund, as it is in the rest of South Africa. Very few people indeed are still aware of all the intricacies of the classical caste system. The latter subsists only as a vague dichotomy between the "high" caste (twice-born) and the "low" caste (once-born). Except among the older and less educated Hindus, caste is no longer operative in anything but marriage. Even here, caste is only one of the factors that determine the suitability of a marriage and not the most important one. Younger people openly joke about caste and ridicule the more conservative for attaching any importance to a relic of the past. Religious sanctions for caste have disappeared, references to caste in the Gita and other sacred writings are explained away, and reform movements such as the Divine Life Society openly attack any form of caste discrimination. Yet caste still lingers on in the private prejudices of the conservative older people.

So far, I have dealt only with the traditional factors of social stratification and segmentation among the Caneville Indians, i.e., those factors that are traced back to Hindu and

Islamic culture. But, to the extent that the Indian population has become Westernized, these traditional factors no longer give a full nor even an approximate idea of social status in the community. One of the other distinctions which must be mentioned is that between "passenger" and "indentured" Indians. The former, mostly Muslim and Hindu Gujarati, came from India as clerks or merchants, paying their fare on the ships, whereas the latter arrived as indentured labourers to work on the sugar estates. The distinction was then perpetuated by the South African government, in that the two groups were dealt with through separate agencies. Although most Gujarati, and more Muslims than Hindus, are of "passenger" stock, the dichotomy cuts across religious and linguistic lines. Until about a generation ago the distinction was a hierarchical one, but now (except, again, among a few old people) the matter is considered to be of only historical interest.

The ordinary Western criteria of status are rapidly gaining importance among Indians, more particularly among Hindus. Of these criteria, wealth, education, and occupation are the principal ones. In Western class terms, the Indian population can be broadly divided into five groups: merchants, professionals, petty bourgeoisie, farmers, and proletarians. The last group is also the largest and can be further subdivided into the semi-skilled and the unskilled. For the most part, the Indian working class still speaks Indian languages at home, and is poorly educated. All but one of twenty-three workers interviewed at the factory speak exclusively Indian tongues at home, though the majority (seventeen) also speak fluent if limited English. They average 3.4 years of English education, and six of them have no formal Western schooling at all. Of a sample of indigent Indian applicants for state support, 90 out of 101 women and 20 out of 35 men could not sign their names in Roman script, though a few of them may have been literate in Indian tongues. However, as the vast majority of Indian children now attend school for at least a few years, the younger generation is predominantly literate, even in the working class.

Working-class families are overwhelmingly Hindu and predominantly Tamil, with a good sprinkling of Hindi and Telugu. As may be judged from the wage statistics given earlier, poverty is general and malnutrition common. Large families aggravate the low wage problem. The workers interviewed at the factory average 5.5 children, not to mention other dependents. Most manual workers in Caneville are housed in small four-room cottages, which compare favourably with the usual one-room, windowless shack that is still common on the other sugar estates. Furniture, particularly in the parlour, is an important status symbol. In the upper reaches of the working class, the parlour is often crowded with a table, chairs, armchairs, and sofas and the walls are covered with family photographs, images of Hindu deities, calendars, and the like.

Farmers are mostly Hindi- or Urdu-speaking and range widely in social status. A dozen large cane farmers belong to the élite of the community and take active part in school committees and voluntary associations. Some of these big farmers combine farming with teaching or business. They live in comfortable, well-furnished houses and they own small motorcars. The mass of the Indian farmers, however, barely subsist on very small holdings growing either cane or vegetables. They live for the most part in corrugated iron dwellings, some of which can only be described as hovels.

The petty bourgeoisie or white-collar class consists mostly of shop assistants and clerks. The mass of small shopkeepers could also be classified in this category, but through their more conservative and less Westernized outlook they belong more in the merchant group. This class is, of course, better educated and more Westernized than most manual workers and farmers. The men average from six to ten years of education, and are all fluently literate, though many of the women of middle age and older are less well educated or even completely illiterate. This class speaks fluent English, and the middle-age generation is mostly bilingual at home (i.e., speaks both English and Indian tongues). Numerically, this class is fairly small, consisting of perhaps 10 per cent of the Indian population. People in this group are paid relatively low wages, but are securely above starvation level. Those who are privately housed have no better and in many cases worse housing than the manual workers housed by the Company, but in their furnishing they emulate the Indian professional class. Modest radios begin to appear in their parlours, and the cheaper decorations such as calendars are not found as much as in lower-class homes.

Apart from the few well-to-do farmers, the Indian élite of Caneville consists of two clearly distinct groups, the merchants and the professionals. The outlook of the two groups is antithetical. The professionals (who number about 120 families, 90 per cent of them teachers' families and the remainder physicians, nurses, midwives, etc.) are highly Westernized. With the exception of the older generation, they speak only English at home, listen to popular and classical Western music, have a high degree of political consciousness, and are much more conversant in Shakespeare than in the Bhagavad-Gita. This professional class is, with few exceptions, Hindu and non-Gujarati; i.e., it tends to be recruited from the groups that are *not* represented in business. Except for the few Muslims among them, the professionals are quite secular and in some cases distinctly anti-clerical in outlook. They have comfortable incomes and live in houses that are similar in size and quality to those of the European middle class, but they generally can afford only one servant (usually African), and, as often as not, they cannot afford a motorcar. Houses are furnished in much the same taste as middle-class European houses with artificial flowers and paintings (or prints thereof) replacing the family photographs and the calendars on the walls. The mahogany radio cabinet and the upholstered furniture are important status symbols.

Education rather than material symbols determines status in the professional class (though furniture and cars play their role). Important though education is in the European community, it is even more strongly stressed among Indians. The holder of a doctorate is viewed with a sentiment approaching veneration, and the title is constantly used in conversation, even when talking about relatives. Thus a man will refer to his physician brother as "the doctor." University degrees in general have high prestige value, and framed diplomas often adorn living-room walls. Several degree holders conspicuously wear university blazers complete with coat of arms and necktie. The degree letters (B.A., B.Ed., B.Sc., M.A., etc.) are popularly known as "the handle" which one adds to one's name. Matriculation (i.e., a complete secondary education) is the minimum educational qualification for men in this class. While wives of professionals have, as a rule, less education than their husbands, few have had less than eight years of school and a great number are themselves nurses or teachers. The twenty-odd Indian university graduates in Caneville are all men.

In contrast to the professionals, the merchant class is conservative, less well educated and recruited mostly from the Gujarati and Memon, with a few Hindi, and an over-representation of Muslims. Muslim merchants as a rule are particularly conservative, speak only the vernacular at home, and have attended only primary school. They rigorously observe the rules of Islam, and the *Hadj* (pilgrimage) to Mecca is an important mark of status symbolized by adding the title

"Hadji" to one's name. (There are about twenty hadjis in Caneville). Though the men all speak English and can read and write fluently in that tongue, some of the women in the wealthiest Muslim families are still completely illiterate in English, and barely able to express themselves in that language. The Hindu Gujarati merchants are also quite traditional in outlook, and observe caste endogamy more closely than the other Hindu groups. Half a dozen of the richest merchant families exceed the income of the average teacher, and, as may be expected, wealth rather than education is the major prestige symbol in the merchant class. But, contrary to the European stereotype of the "flashy" Indian merchant, Indian businessmen make a much less conspicuous display of their wealth than Europeans in a similar position. Of their motorcars, only one late-model yellow Ford could be described as "flashy" (and then only by South African, not by American standards).

Foreign travel is a symbol of status shared by the business and the intellectual élites, but travel does not have the conspicuous leisure undertones that are found among the Europeans. The Muslim derives religious prestige from the *Hadj*. The Gujarati merchant goes to India for business and marriage purposes, not strictly speaking on vacation as the English who go "home." Overseas study, a distinction achieved only by a couple of young professionals, is considered the acme of academic accomplishments, as among Europeans.

Both Muslim and Hindu merchants lead a rather austere life that one associates with the "Protestant Ethic." Homes are comfortably furnished but without extravagant luxury. By European standards, the Indian merchants live below their income. The only clear case of conspicuous consumption is the wearing of expensive silk saris by Hindu women at weddings. The sari worn on such an occasion is not supposed to have been seen by anybody before. A good Benares sari costs up to £40 or £50, though very nice saris can be found at prices from £10 to £20.

Donations to charity, much more than conspicuous consumption, are a source of prestige in the merchant class. Collectors for charity go down the list of merchants in order of wealth, and the first person sets the standard of donation for the rest of the community. In his autobiography, Mahatma Gandhi mentions how, in 1894, organizers of the newly founded Natal Indian Congress realized the importance of that fact. When collecting funds in Caneville, they spent the whole night trying to convince their host, a well-to-do merchant, to contribute £6, instead of the £3 he was prepared to donate. If they had accepted £3, it would have jeopardized the entire collection as other merchants would have followed suit, writes Gandhi. At dawn, the Congress organizers finally broke down their host's resistance, and sat down with him for dinner.[9] Plaques in Whitehead Stadium, tell the visitor how many stadium seats were donated by the town's leading businessmen. Engraved trophies given at school sporting events remind the public of one's generosity and make good publicity at the same time. With one outstanding exception, the business élite stays away from politics and plays the expedient game of guarded co-operation with the local and national government, following the well-proven principle that it pays to be "in" with those in power.

Membership in voluntary associations also underlies the professional-merchant split. The business people contribute generously to charitable institutions, but the organization and the "foot work" is largely done by professionals, and, to a lesser extent, by the white-collar class. The periodic blood-bank drive in Caneville is a case in point. Caneville justly takes

---

[9] Cf. M. K. Gandhi, *An Autobiography: The Story of my Experiences with Truth,* Part II, Chap. XIX.

pride in being the town in Natal with the highest per capita donation rate, and the mobile blood unit collects four hundred to five hundred pints on each visit there. While blood donations come from all segments of the Indian community, the enthusiasm for the drive is largely whipped up by a group of teachers, mostly from the high school.

The Happy Girls Club, a group of about twenty unmarried girls, typifies the professional as opposed to the business outlook. Most of the members are former high school students and many are themselves school teachers. To be sure, the club includes a Muslim girl from a merchant family, but she was admitted only after attending literacy classes. As a Hindu teacher in the club phrased it, "She became so good [in learning to read English] that she could join the club." The club members are undoubtedly the most Westernized and emancipated group of girls in Caneville. They speak only English, wear saris only on formal occasions such as weddings, and listen ecstatically to rock-and-roll music. This Happy Girls Club has its counterpart for married women in the Friendly Women's Guild.

Both clubs are social pace-setters in the Hindu community and important agencies of Westernization. Members of the Happy Girls Club are active in spreading literacy among the Muslim women of the merchant class, and actively encourage their emancipation. Only in recent years have Muslim women begun to serve customers at shop counters, and, for the first time in 1960, a number of Muslim women attended a baby show organized by the Friendly Women's Guild. Previously the Muslim women stayed away from such public events. Another instance of the Westernizing influence of the Happy Girls Club is in the introduction of the Western type of dancing in Caneville within the last couple of years. In 1960, despite considerable parental opposition, the girls for the first time took the initiative in organizing the New Year's Eve dance and in inviting the predominantly male high school alumni. The event was strictly middle-class and largely confined to the educated youth (with a cluster of lower-class spectators wistfully looking in through the windows). After an initial period of uneasiness on both sides, the dancing became quite uninhibited. The girls all remained in the dance hall under the eyes of a married woman, however, and there was no petting.[10]

These two élite groups, the merchants and the professionals, are clearly distinct and mildly antagonistic (or, at least, antithetical) groups with few common interests and radically opposed outlooks. The political implications of this situation must be emphasized again. The business group is largely apolitical because activity in that field would endanger its interests. The professional group, consisting mostly of teachers, on the other hand, is politically conscious to a high degree, but specifically debarred by statute from taking part in politics. As a result, the rule of the CSC remains unchallenged by those who would normally have been the leaders of the Indian community.

To review briefly the stratification system of the Indian group, I have shown that it is determined by two superimposed and complementary sets of criteria. On the one hand, the complex, rigid, ascriptive, traditional system of stratification is slowly receding in importance. On the other hand, the Western, open-class system gains in importance as more and more Indians become Westernized. The two systems combine (quite differently in various segments of the Indian

---

[10] Standards of sexual morality are very strict among Indians. The girl should be a virgin at marriage, and "dating" is still strongly taboo, though practiced surreptitiously. Most of the complaints of parents at the high school concern the breaking by girls of rules of sexual propriety. The teachers are often accused of being too lax and of condoning romance among their pupils.

group) to make the internal structure of that group one of bewildering complexity. Finally, the Indian group is itself a colour caste of intermediate status in the rigid South African albinocracy imposed by the dominant White group.

The last major task in this chapter is the analysis of the African status system, which is not so complex as that within the Indian group. The Africans share with the Indians the fact that they are segmented into language groups, and that both traditional and Western criteria combine to determine status, but the general picture is somewhat simpler.

Linguistic segmentation among Africans is not recognized by the people as forming any strict hierarchy, yet certain language groups claim and are generally granted a mild and ill-defined superiority over others. A distinction is first made between the "foreigners" and the Africans coming from within the Union. The foreigners come mostly from Mozambique, a few from Nyasaland and Rhodesia; they can be easily identified in that their Zulu is often far from flawless, and almost always retains the trace of a foreign accent. Foreigners are looked upon as more backward than Union Africans and the general attitude towards them is one of condescension. To escape this mild stigma of foreignness, Shangaan and others often speak Zulu among themselves.

Union Africans are further subdivided by the location inhabitants into two large groups (Zulu and Pondo) and several smaller groups (Sotho, Ndebele, Xhosa, etc.). Most of the Union Africans either speak languages that are closely related to Zulu or have been in contact with Zulus for a long time. Consequently, in most instances, they speak Zulu quite fluently. There nevertheless exists a prestige ranking between these language groups. The Zulu consider themselves as *the* people, and they are culturally dominant, as I have indicated earlier. Their military fame is still a source of pride among Zulu who (in common with the French and the Spanish) like to recapture nostalgically their hour of historical glory. This "Ex-great Nation Complex" in relation to other African groups, is accompanied among the Zulu by "cultural shame" in rela-tion to European culture as I have already stressed in Chap-ter III. Occupationally, the Zulu hold twenty-four of the thirty non-manual jobs in Dube Village where they constitute less than half of the population. Nearly 40 per cent of the Zulu speak English, compared to 10 per cent of the other groups. The Zulu also tend to have been settled in Dube Village longer than the other groups. Their socio-economic status is clearly superior to that of the other groups, and reinforces their high traditional status.

Pondo on the other hand are regarded as backward and unintelligent. These anti-Pondo stereotypes have a factual basis. The wages paid to migrant workers on the sugar es-tates are (together with those paid in the mines) among the lowest in South Africa. Consequently the more Westernized and the more intelligent Pondo find employment in other sectors of industries, and the migrant Pondo workers who find their way to the sugar estates are, on the whole, at the bottom of the labour-force barrel. It must be emphasized, however, that none of these ethnic distinctions constitutes a rigid system of stratification. The various ethnic groups simply follow a loose hierarchy similar, for example, to that of various European immigrant groups in the United States.

Apart from ethnic or linguistic differences, other traditional criteria of status are of rapidly diminishing importance in the semi-urban environment of Caneville. Cattle ownership, which in traditional Southern African culture is perhaps the most important single yardstick of status, becomes impossible in the urban environment. While many migrant Pondo own cattle, very few of the residents of Dube Village do. Similarly, polyg-yny which in rural society is an economic asset, becomes a liability in the town. The spread of Christianity has also contributed to the disappearance of polygyny. Though there are many instances of concubinage among Caneville Africans, polygyny is virtually non-existent. The concubine simply replaces a legitimate wife who has been left home in the reserve or who has deserted.

Positions that in tribal society were the object of respect (such as herbalists and chiefs) and of fear (such as witches) have lost their function in town. Two or three herbalists do a fairly brisk trade in Caneville, but draw their clientele largely from the more rural Pondo and Shangaan. Chiefs are no longer looked upon with respect because of Westernization on the one hand, and because of the prostitution of the traditional system of chieftainship to suit the government scheme of apartheid and "Bantustans" on the other hand. Most chiefs are now looked upon as mere puppets of the Government, except by the very old and conservative people.

The traditional structural backbone of most South African tribal societies, namely the patrilocal extended family based on the patrilineal rule of descent, has been shattered both by the migratory labour policy and by urbanization. With it, the importance of a large number of descendants to a man's status has also decreased. Clearly, with the amount of geographical mobility found among Africans, and with the restrictive influx-control legislation that takes little account of family units, the extended patrilocal family has become a phenomenon of the past in Caneville. Family housing in Dube Village is allocated to married couples as vacancies occur in the small four-room cottages. Obviously, a four-room cottage is incompatible with an extended family. Nearly 60 per cent of the Dube Village families are nuclear, and those that include relatives other than spouses and children are not traditional patrilocal families. They simply include one or two other relatives such as an old parent, a younger brother, or a nephew.

The factor of "cultural shame" that I have mentioned

earlier accelerates the decrease in importance of rural status criteria and emphasizes Western, "civilized" criteria of class stratification. Everything tribal is looked down upon as "backward" by the urbanized inhabitants of the location, and Western status symbols are sought-after. One of the most superficial symbols of Western status, but also one of the most important, is clothing. Tribal dress and body marks (such as pierced earlobes) which the Europeans find colourful, are viewed as primitive by educated Africans. In Dube Village, only a few of the women still dress in the tribal fashion. Even the migrant Pondo men are almost all dressed in ragged remains of European clothing, although most Pondo women still wear traditional dress.

The settled urban African tries to emulate the European middle class in clothing to the extent that his means permit it. White shirts, ties, jackets, shoes, and hats are the indispensable marks of bourgeois respectability for men. For women the use of Western cosmetics, cotton dresses, high-heeled shoes, nylon stockings, handbags, and hats spells solid middle-class status. Subtle distinctions are made among women, between, for example, wearing a hat to church and wearing a cheaper and more plebeian beret or scarf. In this emphasis on bourgeois sartorial respectability (which only the small professional and white-collar group can achieve), the Africans tend to dress *more* formally than middle- or upper-class Europeans. For example, hats, which have become a rarity among Whites, are worn by many middle-class Africans.

Formal Western education is of great status value among Africans and a B.A. is taken as *prima facie* evidence of profound erudition and wisdom. Only one local African is a university graduate. Matriculation (or a complete secondary education), and to a lesser extent the Junior Certificate, are still rare enough to be considered major educational accomplishments. At a lower level, the ability to speak English (which only about 25 per cent of the Dube Village men and fewer of the women do with any fluency) and a reasonable degree of literacy in the vernacular (achieved by about 40 per cent of the adults) are the minimum educational standards of solid, petty bourgeois respectability. (This African literacy estimate of 40 per cent of the adults does not include the largely illiterate field workers. The 1951 census lists 32.5 per cent of the Africans in the entire country as literate in some language.)[11] As in the Indian community, the stress on education is quite strong, but the scale of evaluation is lower and related to the level of achievement among Africans.

Religious affiliation is also closely related to social status. The Methodist denomination ranks highest and includes most of the small middle-class group. Next in status come the Anglicans, Presbyterians, Catholics, and the smaller established churches. The numerous small African separatist churches are considered to be of distinctly lower status than the recognized churches. These churches are collectively referred to as "Zionist" by some people, but others make a further fine distinction between the respectable sects and the fringe groups. The latter are viewed with contempt by the established churches. They are said to be "half-heathen" and to engage in strange backward practices such as "speaking with tongues," dancing, and beating drums. As the Anglican clergyman spoke of them, "They go out dressed gaudily. They have one foot in heathenism. These people aren't far from the witch-doctor stage." These "Zionist" denominations have strong revivalistic undertones and draw none of the educated people. Anybody who claims to have received the "call" can become a minister and found a sect of his own. None of the Zionist sects is recognized by the Town Council and all are denied access to the interdenominational chapel in Dube Village. Lowest of all are the

---

[11] See Horrell, *A Survey of Race Relations in South Africa, 1959–60*, p. 240.

people who do not belong to any Christian group at all. These people, mostly migrant Pondo, are viewed by the urbanized Christians as backward heathens, altogether beyond the pale of respectability.

The idea of respectability is a vague but nevertheless quite important status criterion among Africans in Caneville. In its Victorian emphasis on morality and conventional behaviour, it has a close counterpart in the upper fringes of the American or Western European working class. As we have just seen, this respectability finds an expression in church membership and in standards of dress. Respectability is not incompatible with poverty but it implies moral stamina. To illustrate it crudely, one's clothes may be poor, but they must at least be clean and neatly ironed, thereby proving one's industriousness. A similar distinction is found in sexual morality. Pre-marital pregnancy is common among the lower class, but is considered a disgrace in the middle class. Extra-marital unions are common, but are incompatible with solid bourgeois status. Illegitimate children, however, suffer from no social ostracism, and the distinction between legitimacy and illegitimacy is not a clear-cut one, as a stable common-law union is regarded in much the same light as a formal marriage. It is not quite as respectable, but it is accepted.

Wealth does not play a prominent role as a status criterion in the African community, for the simple reason that most people are poor, that nobody could be called well-to-do, and that the range in income is a relatively small one. The income differences that exist find their expression in clothing, which is *the* most visible material symbol of status. But restrictive legislation and low wages make the accumulation and investment of capital among Africans very difficult. Even school teachers, nurses, health assistants, and similar professionals or semi-professionals receive incomes that, while securely above starvation level, allow for no luxuries and for very little comfort. All Africans have to live in standard "model" municipal housing, or in tin squatters' shanties on somebody else's land.

The tenants in Dube Village whose total family income exceeds £15 a month, include three clergymen, eight teachers, five nurses and health educators. These persons constitute the African occupational élite. In the same income category, but in jobs commanding lower prestige, are found four small retail merchants (including two herbalists), three clerks, five policemen, and six semi-skilled workers. Over two-thirds of the Dube Village adult males (not to mention the migrant field workers) are unskilled labourers.

Everybody from unskilled worker to minister, nurse, or school teacher lives in substantially the same type of house. Few people can afford expensive furniture, though a strong effort is made to have at least a table and a few chairs in the living room and to sleep in beds. Luxuries like radios are quite rare and only a couple of people can afford to drive antique, rattling motorcars. (One of them is rumoured to be able to afford a car only through illicit sources of income from beer.) This general poverty is somewhat relieved by the fact that the mean number of children per African family (3.7 in Dube Village) is lower than for Indians, but this lower number of children is largely the result, not of a lower birth rate, but of a higher infant mortality rate: 127.5 per 1,000 for Africans; 47 for Indians. (These figures are the average number of infant deaths per 1,000 recorded live births within the municipality of Caneville from 1943 to 1953. As the Health Centre no longer keeps such statistics, more recent figures are not available.) Thus the smaller African family is itself an index of poverty, malnutrition, and poor hygiene.

One point must be stressed again. Although the vast majority of the Africans try to emulate (against overwhelming odds) the Western standard of living, *they are not trying to be White*, in the way that many Coloureds or American

Negroes are. Colour is of little, if any, consequence within the African community. This is not because they are all black. In fact, there is a wide range of skin colour among Africans from middle brown to almost black. This colour range is due to an admixture of Hottentots, Bushmen, and Whites; and, as mentioned earlier, a few people who are distinctly Coloured live among the Africans in Caneville. Yet this colour range has not become the basis of a status scale among either Africans or Indians as it has, for example, among American Negroes or South African Coloureds. A few of the fashionable African women in large cities use bleaching face creams, but the practice is limited and has not reached Caneville. Hair-straightening is even rarer.

In short, then, the African community is stratified largely according to Western criteria, but poverty and the systematic withholding of opportunity by the Whites prevent the Africans from even approximating the European middle-class way of life. A small minority of about 10 per cent of the settled African population constitutes a middle class by African standards, but lives on a standard that among Europeans would be called "poor White." Below this *Lumpenbourgeoisie* comes a stratum that is perhaps twice or three times as large. These are people with a minimum of primary education, bare literacy, a stable family life, membership in an established Christian denomination, and an income sufficient to ward off hunger. The majority of the Africans fall below even this extremely modest standard, and have virtually no prospect of improving their lot.

The frustration that such a situation brings about should be obvious. Yet the vast majority of Europeans are firmly convinced that "our workers are happy" and that "the Natives are a very contented lot." The more "enlightened" minority of the Whites acknowledge poverty, but believe that a few material palliatives would remedy the situation on the assumption that all the "Natives" really want is "food, family life, and freedom from fear."

The amount of social mobility is an important dimension of any stratification system. Before concluding this chapter we must briefly examine that topic. The four South African racial groups are rigid and allow for practically no mobility, except insofar as some light Coloureds pass as Whites. In a small town such as Caneville, the creole Mauritians cannot easily pass since they are known to everybody to have "a touch of the tar brush." One family attempted to escape Coloured status by emigrating to Australia, but experienced difficulty in settling there and returned to South Africa. Some members of creole Mauritian families attend White schools outside Caneville or pass as White for employment purposes in Durban. One might expect light-skinned Africans to try to pass as Coloureds, but there are no such cases in Caneville. On the contrary, a few families that could obtain Coloured identity cards associate with Africans. The few children of African-Indian unions, though legally Coloureds, are generally absorbed into the Indian group. For all practical purposes, however, the racial groups are completely impermeable.

Within each of the colour groups class mobility is possible, mostly through the acquisition of education and wealth. Education is probably the principal avenue of class mobility within all three of the main racial groups in Caneville. At the same time, the prospects of upward mobility without education are declining. As we have seen, this is particularly true of the Whites for whom executive positions are becoming increasingly dependent on University degrees. Within the White hierarchy, promotion to the next-to-the-top level is still possible, however, but the distinction between the White upper class and middle class is becoming more rigid.

Among non-Europeans, education is also the major avenue of class mobility. In a sample of forty-three Indian school teachers, three had fathers in the professional group, four in the merchant group, six in the clerical or sales category, twelve in farming, and eighteen in manual occupations. Eight teachers' fathers had no formal education at all, and only five went beyond primary school. Clearly, the Indian professional class is overwhelmingly upwardly mobile through education. In a sample of 243 Indian high-school children, 42 per cent of the fathers are in manual occupations, 21 per cent are farmers (mostly small cane farmers), 11 per cent are in clerical occupations, 11 per cent are professionals, and 15 per cent are businessmen (largely small retail merchants). Among Africans, the few local teachers and health assistants are also for the most part first-generation professionals. The importance of education among Indians and Africans is widely recognized, and most parents make the greatest sacrifices to educate at least one son, and if possible all sons in the family. The biggest local success story is that of a market gardener's son who recently received his Ph.D.

Wealth in the Indian community is not such an important avenue of mobility. With one exception, all the bigger merchants in town inherited their wealth. The same applies to most farmers. Admittedly, many smaller shopkeepers start new businesses, but they rarely prosper and their shops are often too ephemeral to be passed on to the next generation. Among the wealthier merchants money is rarely invested in higher education, as sons are expected to operate the family business rather than to enter the professions. Only about 11 per cent of the local teachers come from commercial families, although the merchant class is, by far, in the best position to finance the education of its children.

Important though education is as a method of upward mobility among Africans and Indians, the colour bar greatly restricts the scope of achievement and the avenues of employment open to non-Europeans. Certain outlets such as architecture or engineering are entirely closed. Medicine, nursing, teaching, and law are open, but only within narrow racial limits. An Indian teacher can only teach in Indian schools, an African physician can only practice in a non-European hospital, etc. To make matters worse, the Government is now systematically curtailing the opportunities for any non-White student to receive a higher education worthy of the name. Each "race" is now forced to attend segregated and inferior colleges under government control. These restrictions affect Africans even more severely than Indians because their entire school system, from primary school onwards, is rapidly deteriorating under the Bantu Education programme.

Discriminatory legislation restricts opportunities for the economic mobility of non-Whites even more drastically than in the educational field. Africans are debarred from freehold rights to either land or buildings in virtually the whole of South Africa, and can only trade in African areas and on rented premises. There is practically no outlet for African economic mobility, as I have stressed earlier. Indians, who have gained a precarious foothold in retail trade and who have acquired some freehold land, are now being systematically ruined and uprooted by the Group Areas Act.

Certain traditional criteria of status, notably caste among the Hindus, are no longer serious obstacles to upward mobility. Not only has caste become of vanishing importance, but one can escape low-caste status altogether by dropping caste names, as most Sudras have done in Caneville, and by conversion to Islam or to Christianity. Assuming a high-caste name (such as Naidoo) is another common procedure of caste mobility.

In short, the three main racial groups in Caneville are rigidly ascribed. Social mobility is only possible within the racial group, but for non-Europeans that mobility is even further circumscribed by many statutory restrictions, and customary ceilings and colour bars. There is, however, another side to these restrictions on non-European mobility. The level of achievement required for prestige and recognition within the racial group is lowest among Africans, second lowest among Indians, and highest among Europeans. Matriculation is considered a signal educational achievement among Africans, for example, whereas among Whites it is viewed as a minimum passport to a decent clerical job. Similarly, if the poorly qualified African teachers had to compete with their European colleagues, most of them would be unemployed. (Such factors are used by the government to "prove" that discrimination and segregation actually protect the "weaker races" and are in their best interest. It is true that any system of oppression leads to the development of vested interests on the part of *some* members of the subjugated group. The tribal chiefs would be a good example in South Africa.) Nursing and teaching enjoy much higher prestige in the African community than among Europeans. Not only does education have a greater scarcity value among non-Whites, but any given level of objective achievement is, in fact, a greater mark of merit among non-Whites than among Whites because of the obstacles that an African or an Indian has had to surmount. In economic terms the African "bourgeois" would be considered a "poor White" among Europeans, and the wealthiest Indian merchant is a petty capitalist by comparison with the CSC.

Because of this racial differential, objective criteria of class status are meaningful only within each of the three colour-castes. More abstractly, straight convertibility of class status from one racial group to another is not possible, because the racial groups themselves are hierarchized.

The complexity of Caneville's status system surpasses, I believe, that of any community described in the sociological literature. Indeed, the Hindu caste system, which is famous for its intricacy, is only a system-within-a-system in Caneville. In short, Caneville consists of three hierarchized colour-castes, each of which is further segmented horizontally and vertically according to a multiplicity of criteria that overlap only partly from one group to another. The general tendency is for the African and the Indian to develop an internal class system along Western lines and to discard traditional criteria of status. This tendency is part of the broader process of acculturation that I have described earlier. The end result of the process will presumably be a situation similar to the "caste and class" system of the United States described by Myrdal, Dollard, Warner, and others. To a certain extent, I have followed that "caste and class" schema, but I have also shown that, in the present state of cultural heterogeneity in Caneville, that schema oversimplifies reality.

I am myself guilty of oversimplification in dealing with Caneville. For example, I have deliberately left out the complication of the status of women in relation to men, which varies greatly from one group to the other. My description then follows the general male bias of sociological and anthropological literature. Clearly sex is an important determinant of status in any society, but as the importance of sex status is largely restricted to the micro-structure of the family, and as I have already arbitrarily excluded that topic from the present study, I felt justified in not needlessly overburdening an already bewildering picture. For similar reasons, I have excluded age from the description, except insofar as age affected the outlook towards other status criteria. Let me only note in a gross way, requiring many qualifications, that the status of women is relatively highest among the Europeans and lowest among the Indians (particularly among the Muslims), with the African women in an intermediate position. The reverse applies to old age which is most revered among Indians and least among Europeans.

Before finishing this chapter, I want to draw a few general conclusions. One of the most salient conclusions is the contrast between the simple, monolithic politico-economic structure of Caneville and its complex cultural and status system. I have already referred to the phenomenon of atomization in the political context. It is clear that cultural heterogeneity and fragmentation of the population of Caneville fostered political atomization, and helped to maintain the local brand of benevolent autocracy. Drawing from the history of Western colonialism, it is generally true that colonial regimes have maintained themselves longer where they could rule over an already divided and heterogeneous population, and have met most opposition where they encountered a homogeneous culture.

Caneville's status system also shows how closely that system is linked to acculturation in a pluralistic society. To the extent that Indians and Africans become Westernized, they discard traditional status symbols and move towards a Western type of open-class system. Normally, this process would lead to a fairly unitary class system, but in South Africa with its rigid hierarchy of colour-castes, each colour-caste reproduces its internal class system on a scale that is down-graded in rough proportion to the position of each colour-caste. Even taking for granted the colour prejudices of Whites, the long-range tendency in a free-enterprise economy would be for the status range within the colour-castes to increase, and for the gap between the colour-castes to narrow. But the whole political system of Nationalist oppression prevents that development.

We have also noted that colour in Caneville is an important status criterion only among Whites and Coloureds. This is not to say that the Indians and Africans do not have a great deal of group consciousness and many prejudices against the other groups. But among Indians and Africans, group consciousness does not take a specifically racial form, or if it does, it is only in reaction to White racialism. Within the European group, minute differences of pigmentation have an enormous influence in determining status as shown in the case of the creole Mauritians. Racialist legislation that constantly threatens doubtful "Whites" with reclassification as Coloureds heightens this colour sensitivity in the dominant group. This is not true among Africans and Indians, although the range of pigmentation in these two groups is greater than among the Whites. The creole Mauritians, on the whole, have internalized the White colour prejudices, seek acceptance into the White group, and reject the Indians and Africans all the more vigorously in an attempt to validate their own claim to White status. The Indians and Africans reject the notion that colour is important. They strive toward Westernization but they do not try to be *White*. The African has accepted the European's claim to cultural superiority but not to racial superiority.

Finally, two minor points are worth stressing because they corroborate social class findings in other countries. They concern the relative importance of respectability and of education. The drive towards respectability, which is so strong among Africans, seems to be a widespread phenomenon of economically deprived groups in many societies. Not being able to compete economically, they keep morally up with the Joneses. This leads to a subdivision of the working class into the "poor but respectable," and the plain poor, such as has been found in some American studies.[12] Returning to Caneville, we see that among Africans the top people are on the whole pillars of the church, whereas the top White executives generally go to church only on high holidays, leaving it to the middle class to be the church pillars. This finding confirms impressionistic evidence from other Western societies that respectability is a bourgeois phenomenon, and that the extremes of the social hierarchy meet in rejecting or disregarding

---

[12] See, for example, West, *Plainville, U.S.A.*

(though probably for different reasons) the conventional middle-class notions of morality. Altogether, the dimension of morality in stratification has been seriously neglected in sociology.

The point concerning education is akin to the one on respectability. We have seen that education is stressed more strongly among Indians and Africans than among Europeans. Whites also attach importance to education, but not as much and not in the same way. Among Whites, it is more the social polish, the manners, the speech and accent resulting from a university education that matter (hence the importance of attending Oxford rather than the University of Natal). Among Indians and Africans the degree itself is the status symbol. Again, we may advance that, where status competition in other fields is closed or restricted, education takes on greater relative importance. The parallel with American Negroes, where education is also highly stressed, would tend to support this hypothesis. One could, of course, also argue that education among non-Whites has a greater scarcity value than among Whites; but university degrees are nearly as rare among local Caneville Whites as among Indians, and yet the latter emphasize education much more strongly.

In the next chapter, we shall analyse in greater detail the *modus vivendi* between the three large colour-castes in Caneville, the mutual stereotypes that these colour-castes hold of one another, and the minutiae of their daily interaction.

Chapter VII

RACE RELATIONS

T HE overriding importance of colour in Caneville, as in the rest of South Africa, makes it necessary to devote a special chapter to what is usually known as "race relations." In doing so, I hope to describe in some detail the effect of a policy variously called aggregation, segregation, apartheid, or separate development. Much of the description of race relations in Caneville can be extrapolated to the rest of South Africa, bearing in mind that Caneville, in many respects, shows South Africa at its best. This chapter also aims to contribute to certain hitherto neglected aspects of race relations in South Africa, notably attitudes and mechanisms of interaction such as etiquette.[1] We shall first turn to a detailed description of the extent of physical segregation and of the few points of contact between members of different "races." We shall then try to describe the reciprocal attitudes that people hold of one another. Finally, the minutiae of racial interaction will be examined.

Broadly speaking, most facilities in Caneville are segregated on a three-way, or sometimes on a two-way, basis. We have already seen that this segregation is not only the "natural" result of private prejudices, but also the deliberate aim of the Caneville Experiment. Facilities are not only segregated but

---

[1] See also my studies: "Distance Mechanisms of Social Control"; "Race Attitudes in Durban, South Africa."

they are markedly unequal. Perhaps the most basic form of segregation is in housing, since physical proximity of homes establishes a whole network of relationships.[2] Rigid though racial segregation is in Caneville, there are some exceptions to the general "aggregatory" pattern.

Generally, Whites live in the Company village of Sugartown or in isolated houses in the canefields. The vast majority of Africans live either in the single men's compounds in the fields, or in Dube Village (otherwise known as "the location"). Indians live mostly in the remaining areas of Caneville, in the small Company villages in the fields, and on small scattered farms. The Caneville River has been proposed to the Group Areas Board by the CSC as the boundary between European and non-European housing areas, and, on the whole, the river already divides the majority of Whites living to the north from the majority of non-Whites living south of the stream. The scheme still contains many "flaws," however, but these flaws are being gradually eliminated by the Company under the prompting of the central government. While the CSC firmly believes in residential aggregation, it would not go quite as far as the Government in creating buffer zones between the various racial areas as the Government insists it should. For example, unlike most "Native locations" in South Africa which are situated miles outside the centre of town, Dube Village is contiguous to the Indian part of Caneville.

The European village of Sugartown includes some creole Mauritian families, but these are officially considered as White by the Company. No non-Europeans reside there except servants. The European area (including the golf course) is surrounded by a screen of several rows of eucalyptus trees

---

[2] See the results of the American studies on mixed Negro-White housing: Deutsch and Collins, *Interracial Housing*; and Wilner, Walkley and Cook, "Residential Proximity and Intergroup Relations in Public Housing Projects."

that isolate it from the neighbouring non-White areas. By expropriating the Indians in Fairwind the Company hopes to eliminate two "flaws" in the scheme. First, Fairwind, being north of the river, should be a "White" area; second, the few Whites now living in the centre of Caneville would be spared the "indignity" of living among Indians. No Indians live in Dube Village (though a few Coloureds do), but a sprinkling of Africans lives among Indians. These Africans are either lodgers or servants. The former have to get a special permit from the Town Secretary, and the permit is only granted because of accommodation shortage in Dube Village. This shortage will be overcome, the Company hopes, when the present construction programme is completed. The CSC has itself, in a few instances, housed Indians and Africans next door to one another, not as a matter of policy but when the available housing space made it convenient. Again, under prompting from the Group Areas Board, the CSC is separating Africans from Indians in the few compounds where they are mixed.

It must be noted that servants are exempted from residential segregation. Servants (all of whom are Africans or Indians) are generally housed in out-buildings in back yards. It is convenient to have servants nearby, but that is not the main reason for this exception to apartheid. The crux of the matter is that Whites reject non-Whites only as *equals*. So long as the non-Europeans remain in a subservient position, they are tolerated. This feeling is epitomized in the White South African phrase: "The Kaffir is all right so long as he stays in his place." The same Whites who complain about Africans and Indians being "smelly," "dirty," etc. express no distaste at all at having non-White servants cook their food, iron their washing, bathe, dress, and feed their children.[3] The explana-

---

[3] For a theoretical explanation of this phenomenon, see my "Distance Mechanisms of Social Control."

tion given for this apparent inconsistency is that "my girl is
different, I know her. She is clean." Yet these same Whites
would be furious if they found out that their servant had taken
a bath in their tub. (I have actually seen non-White "nannies"
enter the water at a White children's public swimming pool
in Cape Town. As they were in servile dress, none of the
Whites present minded in the least. Had these servants been
in bathing costumes, there would have been an outcry.) The
fact that servants are allowed to live in "White" areas clearly
points to the aim of apartheid which is not to segregate as
such, but *to prevent egalitarian contact between the "races,"
and, by doing so, to keep the non-Whites down.* Any other
reason given for apartheid or aggregation is either a deliberate lie or a self-deceiving rationalization.

Sports are likewise almost completely segregated. Until
recently the segregation was two-fold (Whites and non-
Whites), but the recent opening of a stadium in Dube Village
now makes for triplicated facilities on a down-graded scale.
At the administrative level, the separation is still only two-fold
as we have seen earlier, but both sports clubs are controlled
by the CSC. Whites and non-Whites never belong to the same
team nor play together except on very special occasions. A
number of predominantly Indian soccer teams have, however,
a few African players, while some teams are entirely African and
others entirely Indian. On the whole, Indians have welcomed
Africans to their teams, but many Africans are apprehensive
and critical of the Indians whom they accuse of wanting to
dominate Africans. Other sports, such as cricket, are not
played by Africans. Non-Europeans go entirely without facilities for certain sports such as swimming, bowling, golf, etc.,
for which the Whites are amply provided.

On great occasions, the CSC organizes an interracial sports
event to lend a special luster to the celebration. When the
Indian athletic field was opened, a European cricket team

played against an Indian team, and the occasion is still remembered as *the* case in Caneville where Whites and non-Whites played against one another. Similarly, when the African stadium was to be opened, an African-Indian soccer game was planned. Except for these rare events and for the sprinkling of Africans on some of the Indian soccer teams, sports in Caneville have been segregated and facilities unequal.

The project for a swimming pool for Africans in Dube Village will illustrate the Company philosophy of providing separate facilities. When Thomas Whitehead introduced the plan in the Town Council and in the Bantu Consultative Council he pointedly emphasized that the pool would have exactly the same dimensions as the European pool (disregarding the enormous disproportion in the size of these two groups). He justified the building of the African pool before the Indian pool on the grounds that African facilities had lagged behind Indian ones in the past, and that it was time to re-establish the balance (disregarding the fact that Europeans, whose facilities have always been far superior, have had a swimming pool for many years). The possibility that Africans and Indians (the majority of whom would not mind in the least sharing the same pool with anybody including Europeans) could use the same bath apparently never occurred to any CSC or Town Council official. People, according to the CSC, "want to be aggregated." Also, the notion that non-Whites might use the European pool (even on different hours or days) would meet with a storm of White objections rationalized on hygienic grounds.

Other forms of entertainment follow the general segregation pattern. Non-Whites are excluded from the Company's only cinema in the club-house. In town, there is an Indian-owned non-European cinema to which both Africans and Indians are freely admitted. In the past, African patrons have been segregated in a side-section of the theatre, but this form of discrimination has been eliminated, largely as a result of pressure from educated young Indians. Ironically, the non-White cinema is also patronized by a few Whites who live in the centre of Caneville, including the Afrikaner policemen and Post Office employees. These people are given seats in the first row of the balcony, and two seats are left vacant on either side of them. The taboo on interracial dancing is, of course, one of the strongest, and the mere suggestion of it would be viewed with horror by most Whites. To the best of my knowledge, there has never been any White–non-White dancing in Caneville, except when my wife and I attended an Indian dance. We were fully accepted by our Indian friends, showing, once more, that the colour bar is overwhelmingly a White invention, and that non-Whites welcome "disaggregation."

The hierarchical factor is important here. Subordinated groups do not object to contact with members of the dominant group nearly to the same extent as the other way around. While most Indians do not object to social intercourse with Whites, many Indians would reject intimate forms of contact with Africans, though not nearly to the extent that Europeans reject Africans. Africans, on the other hand, insofar as they avoid contact with Europeans and Indians, do so mostly out of fear of being insulted, dominated, and oppressed. If it were not, however, for the White encouragement and promotion of racialism, there would be no reason to expect South Africa to be any more racialistic than many other culturally pluralistic societies.

The Caneville Post Office has two entrances, labeled respectively "Europeans" and "Non-Europeans," but all people are served by the same White employees though on different sides of the counter. The few public benches in Caneville are *not*, contrary to general South African practice, labeled "Europeans Only," and are freely used by Indians and Africans.

Public toilets in the back of the Town Hall are unlabeled, but are used only by non-Europeans. Inside the Town Hall, there are four toilet doors, all unlabeled but segregated by sex and race by "voluntary" agreement. These toilets are for the use of people working in the building. As a further precaution, the two White women who use the facilities keep the key to "their" toilet in the office where they work. The two "White" toilets are clean and equipped with towels and soap, whereas the two non-White toilets are dirty and devoid of these facilities. The interracial use of toilets is also quite high on the European scale of colour phobias.

Barber shops are rigidly segregated and constitute the clearest instance of discrimination initiated by Indians in Caneville. There is no local European barber. An itinerant Indian barber cuts the hair of most Whites at their homes or offices. An African barber, catering only to Africans, exercises his trade in the Dube Village Community Centre. Of the three main Indian hairdressers' shops in town, two have different chairs and sets of instruments for Africans and Indians, and do not normally cater to European customers. I was, however, attended to in the "Indian" chairs in both shops. The third establishment, which is the best equipped and the most modern, displays a three-way segregation of chairs and instruments for Whites, Indians, and Africans. In all cases, the "African" facilities are inferior, but Africans pay only one shilling for a haircut, compared to three shillings charged other customers. A rationalization sometimes offered by Indian barbers for the segregation of Africans is that African hair is different. While it is true that the cutting of kinky hair requires special skills, it certainly does not require different instruments or chairs. When I patronized the modern barber shop, the owner firmly led me to the "European" chair and, in an attempt to ingratiate me, told me that his shop was the only clean one in town: "I keep a special set of instruments for you."

Perhaps the most amusingly inane instance of segregation in Caneville concerns the telephone. When an Indian professional man applied for a line to his beach cottage, he was told that he must pay £1,000 for the service. While he had several European neighbours with whom he could have shared a party line, he was told that it was against the policy of the Post Office to put Whites and non-Whites on the same party line, and hence, that he must pay for an individual line to his cottage.

In the same general spirit, locker-room facilities at the factory as well as the soft-drinks canteen are likewise aggregated. The two entrances to the canteen are also unlabeled, but there is no possibility of confusion: the European side is spacious and the non-European side is narrow. Excepting barber shops, all Indian businesses in town are unsegregated, but the Company store has a front entrance for Europeans and a back entrance for non-Whites. Inside, the Europeans are served at a long counter that occupies three-fourths of the store, and the Africans and the Indians have to stand in a queue at a short counter. Furthermore, the non-White counter is "protected" by an iron rail three feet in front of it "to prevent theft," while the European counter is unprotected. It must be emphasized that the Company trading store is run on a non-profit basis for all employees regardless of race. However, the store is not a co-operative venture, as its control resides in the Company, not in the purchasers. The store exemplifies again both the paternalism and the benevolence of the Company. The latter could use the store to exploit its workers, as do so many industrial concerns, but benevolence is once more accompanied by racial discrimination.

All three of Caneville's hotels are managed by Europeans, but one accepts only non-European guests, while the other two are for Europeans. Both White hotels, however, have a segregated non-White bar where Indians and Coloureds are allowed to drink, but not Africans who, until 1962, were entirely debarred by law from all alcoholic beverages except "kaffir beer." The bus and train services in Caneville are likewise segregated. At the main office of the Company, non-White employees who come on business are usually taken care of through small office hatches that communicate with an outside verandah, so that non-Whites do not have to enter the building. When White employees come, they enter the building and conduct their business inside the various offices. A number of office messengers run errands and serve tea inside the building, however, showing, once more, that contact is accepted so long as it is on a master-servant basis.

At the health clinic, the patients (who are all non-Europeans) are provided with rough wooden benches, and enter the building through a side entrance. The main entrance, dominated by oil portraits of Donald Sherwood and his father, has two more comfortable antique seats, which, under special instructions from Swanepoel, are reserved for Europeans. The Company hospital has a loose ward segregation between Indian and African men, but the White–non-White segregation is rigid. A spacious room with two beds is exclusively reserved for the occasional White patients. (At least six beds would be found in the room if it were occupied by non-Whites). Indian and African patients are served a standard meal that is mass-cooked in the hospital kitchen, while European patients are asked daily what they would like to eat, and an Indian orderly goes to town to buy the requested food.

All voluntary associations are also segregated by race, on a three-way basis. This applies to charitable organizations, social clubs, church guilds, and the like. The non-White groups, on the whole, do not have a colour bar in their constitution and would welcome sympathetic Europeans, but, with one single exception, no Whites are willing to join non-White clubs. White clubs, on the other hand, would never accept non-White members. The one exception to club segregation that I just mentioned concerns a European who is the chairwoman of the otherwise Indian, middle-class Friendly Women's Guild. That woman is largely snubbed by Whites for her liberalism.

Except for the Catholic Church, all religious services are completely segregated, but Europeans are entirely welcome at non-European services, whereas, once more, the reverse would not be true. The few Zanzibaree Muslims freely attend the two mosques, but otherwise there is no African-Indian mixture (excepting again at the Catholic services). The reason for this lack of African-Indian contact is simply that the two groups (with the few exceptions mentioned) belong to different religions or denominations. The segregation between Whites and Africans is, however, entirely a question of colour since many members of both groups belong to the same denominations (e.g., Anglican and Methodist). African services are held in the Dube Village chapel where all are welcome, and where I have always been given a cordial reception. No non-European would be welcome to attend the White services in the Sugartown church.

The Catholic services are mixed, but only partially so. There is an 8:00 A.M. Sunday Mass with a sermon in English which is attended mostly by Whites (including the creole Mauritians), but also by a number of Africans and by a few Indians. By tacit arrangement the non-Whites (with the exception of the creole Mauritians) sit in the back of the church, but as the church becomes crowded this seating segregation does not remain rigid. At this early Mass, the altar boys and the man who takes the collection are White. A second mass at 9:30 A.M. has a Zulu sermon and is attended principally by Africans, but a number of Whites and a few Indian latecomers also attend. The altar boys are all Africans, and so are the choir members and the man who takes the collection.

At the late Mass also, the Whites sit in front, but the priest, in an apparently deliberate attempt to combat this practice, seats the pupils from the adjacent African primary school in the first two rows of pews. The Whites sit just behind the African children, while the Africans and Indians sit behind the Whites. At this Mass too, the segregation becomes less rigid as the church fills up. Of all the local Christian denominations, the Catholic Church has been the only one to make a deliberate effort to break down segregation and to preach anti-apartheid sermons, largely under the initiative of Archbishop Hurley in Durban. After Mass, there is no social contact between the parishioners across the colour line. The Whites drive back to Sugartown in their cars and the Africans walk back in groups towards Dube Village. Parish affairs are entirely run by the White priest and an all-White (*cum* Mauritian) committee. While the priest keeps a list of all his White and Mauritian parishioners, he keeps no record of his African members and could only give me a rough estimate of their number. The "liberal" wife of a White Mauritian justified the European control of parish affairs in the following terms: "Africans and Indians are not in it [i.e., the parish committee] because they would have nothing to offer, just as some Whites would be useless on the committee."

In all these aggregatory practices, Caneville is typical of though probably "better" than most South African towns. This is not to say that, in practice, segregation is less rigid in Caneville than elsewhere, but rather that fewer "Europeans Only" signs hit one in the face. Caneville also has a few apartheid signs. At the entrance of the Community Centre of Dube Village a large sign proclaims that admission is for "Natives Only." On the whole, the Company prefers to avoid apartheid signs, first for aesthetic reasons as they would mar the beauty of the town, but mostly because it allows the Company to maintain the fiction that segregation is "voluntary" while in no way endangering the practise of it. Not all aspects of segregation that I have mentioned are the making of the Company. Some segregation such as the separate locker-room facilities in the factory are the object of apartheid legislation. Other practices such as the separate Post Office entrances are under the control of the central government, not of the local authorities. The fact, however, that the Company has deliberately enforced segregation where no laws existed, and anticipated in practice many of the Nationalist laws, shows that the Company and the central government are in agreement as to the principle of racial discrimination. The difference between the two is one of method. As far as possible, the Company wants to discriminate by persuasion and "consultation" rather than by naked coercion.

Most local Whites sincerely and firmly believe that aggregation in Caneville is a voluntary process. One cannot dismiss this White belief as an expression of hypocrisy. For one thing, the myth of voluntary aggregation has become a Company slogan, and like all slogans, people finally believe it, if it is repeated often enough. But, more importantly, *segregation from the White point of view is indeed voluntary.* The dominant White group could abolish it at the polls if it cared to do so. Quite apart from repealing the apartheid legislation, each local White knows that he would receive courteous treatment if he cared to attend functions that are non-White only because the Europeans refrain from attending them. The Europeans are indeed free to aggregate or not to aggregate as they choose. The non-Europeans are *not* free to attend White functions where they would definitely be snubbed, denied admission, or thrown out. For the non-Whites there is no such thing as voluntary aggregation. There is only *baasskap apartheid.* Segregation of racial groups can never be equal, because the very intent of segregation is to maintain inequality.

If the aims of apartheid are inequality and domination, it

follows that attitudes towards segregation vary with a person's position in the racial hierarchy. Generally speaking, the Whites are in favour of apartheid because they want to retain their supremacy and privileges, and the non-Whites are opposed to it because they seek equality. This general statement requires some qualifications and refinements. The lower-class, uneducated Whites are particularly vocal and crude in their expression of racialism because their privileged position would be specially vulnerable in a freely competitive society. Most Coloureds identify with the Whites with whom they seek assimilation, and they do not share many of the disabilities of Africans. They have so far sided with the Whites for the most part, and shared White colour prejudices. Recently, however, since their hope of assimilation to the Whites has been extinguished by ever increased oppression under the Nationalist government, some Coloureds have begun to identify with the Africans. In a much milder form than the Coloureds, many Indians object to intimate forms of contact with Africans, not because they seek assimilation to the Whites, but because of a feeling of *cultural* superiority over the Africans. Neither Coloureds nor Indians, on the whole, object to contact with Europeans. Many Africans reject and avoid members of other racial groups, not because "they want to be aggregated," but because they do not want to be insulted, dominated, and exploited. Since contact with Whites often brings unpleasant consequences, many Africans develop an avoidance or withdrawal reflex against Europeans. When a White person proves his willingness to associate with Africans on the basis of complete equality and without paternalism, he is generally accepted. Non-White racialism is thus largely a reaction to White racialism. The basic South African problem is not a non-White one. It consists in curing the White population of prejudice. The solution, I fear, will only come *after* the Whites lose their privileges, not before.

Racial attitudes are difficult to assess except at a relatively superficial level by means of questionnaires. In the present study, I shall rely partly on questionnaires (given to an Indian student sample), but mostly on interview material, on casual remarks, and on observation at meetings.[4] The most important single component of racial attitudes in South Africa is the extent of "racialism" which we may define in simple terms as feelings of group superiority based on unchangeable, innate physical characteristics. I distinguish racialism from ethnocentrism, which is based on feelings of *cultural* superiority. We have already given evidence to show that racialism is much stronger among Whites than among non-Whites, but this statement is only a first approximation to a more complex reality.

Let us start with the attitudes held by Europeans about Indians and Africans. With a few exceptions, these attitudes are fairly uniform and widely held, though the words in which they are expressed vary from the cruder to the more "sophisticated." The vast majority of Whites look down on Africans and Indians because of their physical characteristics, mostly their skin colour. Their physical traits are assumed to be correlated with a whole set of other attributes, mostly negative ones, in a way which allows for few exceptions. No matter how educated and Westernized a non-White is, he remains forever an Indian or an African (or a "coolie" or a "kaffir," as the crude Whites say) because of his skin colour. Whites judge other Europeans on the basis of individual merit and qualities, but automatically lump all Indians and Africans into two racial groups supposedly endowed with indelible, uniform characteristics. To be sure, prolonged contact with non-White individuals leads to a reluctant admission that "my boy is an exception," but the general stereotype remains intact.

---

[4] The main studies on racial attitudes in South Africa are: MacCrone, *Race Attitudes in South Africa*; Pettigrew, "Social Distance Attitudes of South African Students"; and van den Berghe, "Race Attitudes in Durban, South Africa."

Europeans view Indians as a distinct threat to themselves, and anti-Indian stereotypes are quite similar to anti-Semitism in Western Europe. Indians are assumed to be economically powerful, whereas, in fact, only a tiny merchant class has made a very modest inroad in certain segments of the retail trade. Not only are they thought to be rich, but also to be dishonest, to engage in underhanded, sly practices that put European businesses at a disadvantage: "Those cunning, money-grabbing Indians are out to drive us out and to exploit the Natives." When an Indian family moves into a new area, Whites raise an outcry about "Asiatic invasion." In spite of the fact that Indians have been in Natal nearly as long as Europeans, and that Indian leaders have repeatedly affirmed their loyalty to South Africa, the Whites view the Indians as an alien group which should be sent back to "their country." The rapid rate of population increase among Indians is perceived as a threat to the Europeans who believe that they will be "swamped." "You know how fast they reproduce," a high Company official told me as a justification for denial of political rights. (The European population increase is welcomed as an asset to the country.) Indians are also believed to be naturally dirty and smelly, and to relish living under slum conditions. The argument offered against Indian "invasion" is that, once the Indians move in, the area deteriorates and is spoiled forever. Indians have a peculiar acquisitive instinct for land, Whites allege. One high Company executive told me: "Indians instinctively stick to an empty plot of land." (When a White buys an empty plot he makes a "wise investment.") In short, Europeans, on the whole, view Indians as sly, underhanded, disloyal people who try to "swamp" the Europeans. The "Asiatics" are supposed to be particularly dangerous because they are intelligent and hard-working—qualities which evoke praise when found in Whites but fear when found among Indians. In their crudest expression, these anti-Indian feelings lead to statements such as that the "coolies" should all be sent back to India. Polite, upper-class Caneville Englishmen "only" advocate (with one or two exceptions) rigid segregation, and restrictive measures to contain the Indians.

The White attitudes towards Africans are quite different, though fully as derogatory. Although the Africans are viewed as inferior to the Indians, feelings towards the traditional rural African are more benevolent and paternalistic, so long as he stays "in his place." The "raw kaffir" (i.e., the unsophisticated, illiterate, rural African) is treated as a rather stupid child who cannot be given any responsibility, who is not able to understand any but the simplest repetitive tasks, but who is a happy, contented, good-natured creature full of laughter and humor. In short, the rural African is viewed as a simple-minded but lovable grown-up child. He cannot be trusted with complicated machinery which he is sure to wreck, but he is very good at monotonous labour requiring muscles. He loves his music and dancing, which show how happy he is. He loves discipline and routine, because he is incapable of initiative. Like Indians, Africans are supposed to be dirty, smelly, and unhygienic. (Ten minutes after expressing that stereotype, a White overseer pointed out to me how many of the "Native boys" use the showers in the Company compounds, and how much they complain when the hot water runs out. When I pointed out the contradiction to him, he reluctantly admitted, "Well, of course, if you give them a chance they like to wash just like we do." A few minutes later, he thought that hot water showers were "spoiling the Natives," then guiltily corrected himself, adding, "I should not say that".) "Native" culture is backward and primitive and the "Native" is bloodthirsty by nature, but he has the redeeming qualities of being "unspoiled," honest, hard-working, and respectful of his White *baas*. In a way, he even deserves respect because of his simple tribal pride which must not be offended because, if you do, "he will never forgive you." These are the views of the Europeans who take great pride in "knowing the Native."

Under the impact of the events of the last decade or so, this paternalistic view of the rural African is beginning to change, though not nearly as fast as one might expect. Waves of demonstrations, mass protests, and concerted African political action are interpreted as the work of a few Communist agitators. Simple children of nature that the "Natives" are, they are, of course, easily swayed by "demagogues who stand on boxes." However, the emergence of a "new Native" is slowly being recognized. He is the "detribalized scum" of the towns, the cheeky, arrogant "Native" (or "baboon," or "kaffir," or "nigger," depending on the degree of education of the White speaker), who has lost all his good tribal qualities. He is spoiled, shiftless, lazy, and prone to violence and crime. Because he has a thin veneer of White civilisation (from which he only slavishly "apes" the worst aspects), he believes that he is civilized, he does not stay in his place, he demands a vote (which he is utterly incapable of understanding), and he does not respect his *baas* any longer. In the words of a Company official, "detribalization is the worst thing that can happen to a Native."

Any description involves a certain amount of oversimplification. I am not suggesting that all Whites have an identical view of Indians and Africans. I simply have tried to give a composite picture of the views held by the vast majority of Europeans. The more "progressive" Whites from the upper class would of course express their opinions in a more sophisticated manner (e.g., "The democratic principle is equally foreign to the mind of the Bantu male. . . . When the Native tries to conceive the idea of an election his tribal mind thinks of some form of mortal combat between the candidates."). A few Whites would even concede that the Africans have some legitimate grievances that could be satisfied by minor concessions. On the whole, however, the description I have given of White racial attitudes would undoubtedly be endorsed by the majority of Caneville Whites as a good summary of their feelings.

To some extent White racialism has proven infectious and has spread to Africans and Indians, though in a milder and less crude fashion. The Africans are probably more racialistic than the Indians, though much less so than the Europeans. Africans express many anti-White and anti-Indian attitudes and stereotypes, and are developing a black counter-nationalism with many racialistic undertones. At the verbal level, educated African leaders whether they belong to the African National Congress or the Pan-African Congress, deny any racialism and say that by "African" they mean any person who identifies with the liberatory struggle, regardless of skin colour. Nevertheless, the vast majority of Africans in Caneville, as in the rest of South Africa, express anti-White and anti-Indian attitudes. Oppressed as they are, it would be extraordinary if they did not. There is an important difference, however, between African attitudes towards Whites and White attitudes towards Africans. The Africans do not make any claim to superiority, either on cultural or on racial grounds. In that sense, they are not racialistic. They accept Western culture and, in fact, often have an inferiority complex about African tribal culture. They are not ashamed of being black, but neither have I ever heard an African, in Caneville or elsewhere, declare that the black "race" is destined to rule because of innate superiority. Claims to ruling South Africa are generally based on the principle of majority rule. If many would exclude Whites from the government, it is mostly because of fear of continued oppression, or because of a desire for revenge for past and present oppression.

From the above it is clear that the vast majority of Africans in Caneville have strong anti-White feelings. Most Africans dichotomize between the English and the Afrikaners. The latter are probably most bitterly hated because they are associated with the repressive policies of the Nationalist Government, but the English do not fare much better in public estimation. The Afrikaners are said to be crude and blunt. They openly say that they consider Africans inferior and want to keep them down. To be sure, the gross insults that several Afrikaners in Caneville use in daily conversation with Africans are bitterly resented, but at least the Afrikaners (or the "Boers," or the "Dutchmen" as some of the older Africans still refer to them) are credited with the saving grace of honesty in their bigotry.

Africans view the English Whites as basically much like the Afrikaners, only more subtle, more openly polite and superficially conciliatory, more hypocritical and two-faced in their dealings. Educated Africans point to the local policy of the CSC as a typical example of the United Party approach. The English are said to want segregation and White domination just as much as the Nationalists, and to have shown the Nationalists a blueprint for apartheid long before the "Nats" came into power. As evidence of the desire of the English to keep the Africans down, an intelligent and articulate school teacher told me: "The English didn't want the Africans to learn English, so they invented Fanagalo." Most Africans resent being addressed in Fanagalo or "kitchen Zulu," which they consider a degrading pidgin tongue. Educated Africans particularly resent the Europeans, whether Afrikaners or English, who claim to "know the Natives." The English are viewed as more dangerous than the Afrikaners because they are much more astute and cunning in their means of deceiving the Africans. In short, the general African attitude toward the Whites could be best summarized as that of the citizens of an occupied country towards an enemy army of occupation. Most Africans willingly concede that there are a few "good" Whites, but believe that no White man can be trusted until he has proven himself to be "on our side." The Progressive Party approach is rejected by all but a tiny conservative minority, and even the Liberal Party, which stands for complete equality and universal franchise, is viewed with great suspicion as dominated by White paternalists.

African attitudes towards the Indians are also predominantly negative, though not as strongly so as anti-White attitudes. No serious incidents of violence have taken place in Caneville between Indians and Africans. Caneville was spared the horrors of the 1949 riots, a fact which the Company uses to prove the success of its policy of aggregation. But latent anti-Indian hostility exists among the Africans, and, if fanned by politicians, could easily erupt into violence. Like the Jews of Europe, the Indians in South Africa are a small, powerless minority and, as such, a safe scapegoat to attack. African grievances against Indians take four principal forms. First, the Indians are accused of not siding with the Africans in the political struggle, but of "sitting on the fence." This argument is commonly heard among Africans. Second, the Indian merchants are accused of cheating and exploiting uneducated Africans in shops. Third, Indians are said to monopolize all the better-paid non-European jobs, leaving only unskilled work to the Africans. And fourth, Indians are accused of wanting to dominate non-European organizations such as the sports clubs.

The third grievance clearly illustrates the scape-goating mechanism. It is true that Indians almost entirely monopolize the semi-skilled positions in the CSC, but the fault lies in the prejudices of the European employers. Yet the hostility is deflected toward the Indians. In the non-European sports club (sponsored and controlled by the Company), the Indians are accused of wanting more than their share of the club's funds. It is true, on the whole, that the Indians are interested in a greater range of sports than the Africans, and hence are more heavily represented on the sports committee. But the Indian teams for the most part welcome African members, and much of the segregation in sports is initiated by the CSC. A few Indian merchants do cheat uneducated African customers, but they also cheat uneducated Indians, so that they are non-racial in their dishonesty. Furthermore, business dishonesty is not widespread.

It is probably in sports that African antagonism against Indians is most marked. On the rare occasions when Africans play against Indians, the spectators are all mixed, but they tend to support the team of "their own race." When an African-Indian game was suggested by the Town Council for the opening of the Dube Village stadium, African players were generally adverse to the idea for fear that the Indian team would be stronger and would beat them. A suggestion that two selected mixed African-Indian teams play against one another was emphatically rejected by the African players. The game had to be postponed because the African stadium, built at a cost of several thousand pounds from the beer profits, was seriously damaged by rain as a result of lack of adequate drainage provisions and the fact that the stadium was built in the path of a stream.

While the CSC and the Town Council aim to maintain good African-Indian relations, the implementation of policies by Mr. Swanepoel certainly has the effect of inciting Africans against Indians, as for example when he ordered Africans to expel Indians from Dube Village Community Centre. To suggest that two sports teams segregated along racial lines should play against one another must also have the effect of heightening racial consciousness and competition. In addition, Swanepoel threatened repeatedly that severe reprisals would be taken if there were any trouble between Africans and Indians at the game, thereby suggesting that it was normal to expect trouble.

The Indians are probably the least racialistic of the three groups. Whatever racial consciousness exists among Indians has been forced upon them by the system of White domination. Whatever loyalty some Indians may still feel towards India is largely a reaction to White rejection. The loyalty of the overwhelming majority of Indians is with South Africa. At the celebration for the centenary of the arrival of the first Indians in South Africa, the school children read the following pledge: "I am a South African like all the young people of this country of every race and colour. This is my country, too, my native land. . . . I know no loyalty to any other homeland." Yet the highly precarious position of the Indian group in South Africa as a rejected minority makes for considerable fear.

The average Indian attitude towards the Europeans is one of surprising tolerance. While the vast majority of Indians abhor and emphatically reject segregation and discrimination, antagonism is largely restricted to the Government (whether it be Nationalist or United Party). Unlike with many Africans, these feelings have not generalized to a blanket of rejection of Whites as a group. I have never experienced the slightest reticence or suspicion on the part of Indians in Caneville, but on several occasions I have had to overcome considerable initial suspicion among Africans, just because of the colour of my skin. This tolerance towards Europeans as individuals is probably one of the factors that opens the Indians to the accusation of "fence-sitting" by Africans. A considerable segment of the conservative merchant class, of course, still believes in co-operation with the more "progressive" Whites in order to attain minor concessions. Distinctly anti-White stereotypes are rarely expressed by Indians, except for accusations of colour consciousness, snobbery, etc. Specific policies are of course under constant fire, and the alleged duplicity of the United Party and of the CSC is a recurrent theme among educated Caneville Indians. A rather conservative middle-class man said to me, "The Nats didn't start this apartheid business; the English did, right here on the sugar belt."

Indian attitudes towards Africans are also largely non-racial. Educated Africans are accepted in professional Indian circles in all but the most intimate forms of contact such as intermarriage. Many Indians look down on Africans, but not for racial reasons as the Whites do. With their sense of belonging to an ancient culture, many Indians regard the mass of the Africans as backward, primitive, superstitious, dirty, and violent. In spite of this feeling of cultural superiority, Indians, unlike Europeans, are willing to accept educated Africans in their homes, in their sports clubs, and so forth. On the whole, Indians are probably more willing to accept Africans than Africans are to accept Indians. In both cases, grounds for rejection are not strictly racial, and Africans and Indians rarely assert a feeling of racial superiority comparable to that of the Whites. (It may be argued that many Whites also do not discriminate strictly on racial grounds. Among educated Whites, expressions of crude racialism have lately become unfashionable and prejudice is rationalized on cultural grounds; but even in those circles it is not difficult to elicit claims to racial superiority.) It remains true, however, that both Africans and Indians hold derogatory views of one another based on faulty generalizations.

Fear is perhaps the most important component of Indian attitudes towards Africans. Most Indians are acutely aware of their position as a small minority group in South Africa, and they know that they are used as a scapegoat by most Europeans and Africans. While they resent White domination, most educated Indians now begin to realize that European supremacy is only temporary and that the future belongs to the Africans. The memory of the 1949 riots where Zulu attacked Indians in Durban and other Natal towns is still very vivid, although Caneville itself was spared. One informant recollects a frightening experience where his life was threatened: "I was at the mercy of them [i.e., the Africans]. Nobody was there to protect me." An Indian school teacher expressed the fear that "if the Africans get the opportunity they'll knock us down" while he was telling about incidents of African-Indian hostility during mixed soccer games. The ever-present fear of a repetition of the 1949 anti-Indian pogrom, and the expectation of continued, and perhaps worsened anti-Indian discrimination, if a militant African nationalist government takes over, inevitably colours Indian attitudes towards Africans. This overriding fear prevents the more conservative business class from identifying with Africans in the liberatory struggle. Much as they resent the present discrimination to which they are subject, they are wary of exchanging it for possibly intensified oppression under a black government. At the other end of the Indian political spectrum, the Westernized intelligentsia and some of the proletariat firmly believe that their only salvation lies in complete political identification with the Africans in the struggle for freedom in a non-racial society. The latter point of view is that of the Natal Indian Congress, the most influential of the Indian political movements.

Another interesting phenomenon found among some Indians is a form of group self-criticism akin to Jewish anti-Semitism. This phenomenon is not found at all prominently among either Africans or Europeans. In the Indian professional class many people express considerable guilt over the treatment of Africans by Indians and readily admit that some Indian merchants cheat and exploit the Africans. These self-criticisms in the professional class are undoubtedly motivated in part by fear of Africans and the knowledge that the political future belongs to the Africans. Yet another phenomenon worth mentioning is the compulsive over-reaction against certain stereotypes that Europeans hold of Indians. Educated Indians are very sensitive, for example, to the European stereotype that Indian functions never start on time. Most Indian functions which I attended started very punctually, and when they did not, it usually was because European guests of honour arrived late. When a prominent White arrived fifteen minutes late at a high school function, for example, one of the teachers gleefully remarked to me: "Look who is late now. *They* [the Europeans] always say that *we* [Indians] don't start on time." This finding is probably unique to Caneville, for at Indian functions elsewhere I heard jocular references to lack of punctuality among Indians.

We come now to the final topic of this chapter, namely the detailed analysis of interracial behaviour. Clearly, as a result of physical segregation imposed by the White group and the negative attitudes that the various groups hold of one another, interracial contact is largely limited to fairly superficial, casual, fleeting relationships in the business or occupational spheres. Intermarriage between Whites and non-Whites is forbidden under the Prohibition of Mixed Marriages Act of 1949. Some thirty years ago, before the act was passed, there were two cases of Indian men married to European women and one case of an Indian woman who had married a White man, but all three couples have left Caneville. African-Indian unions are not forbidden, but I know of only one case: a Zulu woman who converted to Islam when she married a Muslim. One Indian businessman is married to a Coloured woman who is completely accepted in the Indian community. The Zanzibaree, who technically are classified as Coloureds, have as a rule married Zulu women.

Extra-marital relations between Whites and non-Whites are a criminal offence in South Africa under the Immorality Act, which provides for penalties of up to seven years in gaol. Some surreptitious unions do take place, however. Two White farmers (one of them a Mauritian) are rumoured to have had affairs with Indian women. One African and two Indian house-maids are suspected of having had children by their European employers. Some Afrikaner railway employees are also ru-moured to have sexual relations with non-European prostitutes. A tragic case occured of an Indian youth falling in love with a White girl from outside Caneville. When the parents of the girl found out about the relationship, they prosecuted the boy for rape, and the youth got a three-year prison term. African-Indian sexual relations are not forbidden, but the cases are quite rare. I only know of three cases of Hindu Indian women who lived with Africans and had children by them. These women are looked down upon in the Indian community more because they had children out of wedlock than because they had relations with Africans. The children attend Indian schools, are brought up as Indians, and suffer from no ostra-cism in the Indian community.

Excepting these few cases, the racial groups are endog-amous, and contrary to White racial mythology, non-Whites are no more eager to marry Whites than the other way around. The stigma attached to intermarriage among non-Whites is, however, much milder than among Whites where the fear of "bastardization" has become a pathological mania.[5] Whites often use the miscegenation bogey as a last-ditch rationali-zation for segregation. Donald Sherwood writes, for example: "We want racial purity and to ensure this we must have social segregation of all races." Most Indians, while generally dis-couraging and disapproving of intermarriage, consider it, in last analysis, as a matter of individual choice. Among most Africans, intermarriage is a matter of indifference, though a minority may oppose miscegenation and a few may favour it as a solution to racial problems. It is interesting to note that, although the Immorality Act and the Prohibition of Mixed Marriages Act constitute glaring denials of private liberty,

---

[5] Cf. Alan Paton's masterful novel, *Too Late the Phalarope*.

these acts are not given nearly the same prominence in non-White opposition speeches and pamphlets as are other pieces of discriminatory legislation. Extra-marital unions are fairly rare, though undoubtedly more numerous than the cases I have mentioned. Such unions are strongly condemned by Whites, but, in spite of heavy legal penalties under the Immorality Act, they take place in a clandestine fashion. Africans sometimes accuse Indians of sexual exploitation of African girls, but I could not confirm a single case in Caneville. This African stereotype of Indians arises from a cultural difference in the position of women in the two groups. Indian women, being closely kept at home, are not nearly as available to African men as the more emancipated urban African women are to Indian men. Hence the frequent charge by African men that Indians "take our women but won't let us touch theirs."

After miscegenation, other forms of intimate egalitarian contact across racial lines are high in the White scale of rejection. I have already spoken about the strong taboo on interracial dancing, because of the sexual undertones of this form of entertainment. Commensality is probably next in the scale of taboos, with a further fine gradation between having a regular meal at table, having a cup of tea sitting down, or drinking a cup of tea standing at a public function. To the best of my knowledge, Mr. Whitehead is the only local White to invite non-Europeans to his home, though not at regular parties where they might meet other Whites. Though he is considered an "extreme liberal" among Caneville Whites, he escapes ostracism because of his high position. One European man, who died recently, accepted cups of tea from one of his Indian neighbours, but his wife did not, and he never returned the invitation. Another liberal European couple in Sugartown is very friendly with a middle-class Indian family at whose home they often eat, but their Indian friends do not dare to visit them in Sugartown for fear of being snubbed by White neighbours. This White couple is socially ostracized in Sugartown for associating with Indians.

In commensality as in other things, it is the Whites who withdraw from interaction and not the non-Whites. Throughout the period of my study, I was most graciously entertained by many non-European families. The White taboo is so strong that, one day, when I invited an Indian Town Council employee to sit down at table with me in the office and share my sandwich lunch, he embarrassedly refused for fear of being seen by other Whites in my company. Europeans patronize the milk bar next to the market side by side with non-Whites, but they usually only stay for a couple of minutes to drink a cold beverage. I have never seen any Whites and non-Whites sit down together in the other tearooms in town, excepting in cases where I was directly involved. On one such occasion I had to prompt an African school teacher to join me for a cold drink, and he made a half-jocular remark about the South African police not liking it. All of what applies to commensality also holds for social calls and home visiting.

Intervisiting and commensality are also rare between Indians and Africans. Most Africans, because of extreme poverty, are in no position to entertain guests. Residential segregation is also a barrier to African-Indian relations, and so are dietary differences and religious prohibitions. But neither among Africans nor among Indians is "race" the reason for lack of contact. There is no taboo against interdining and visiting, and, in fact, in the professional class such contacts do occur. At a tea party organized by Indian teachers for example, the African teachers from a neighbouring school were invited and fully accepted as equals.

Generally speaking, however, all forms of intimate, equal contact between the three racial groups are rare. This is particularly true between the Whites and non-Whites where the strong European prejudices prevent such contacts. Other barriers that I have just mentioned also limit Indian-African interaction, though not quite to the same extent as White–non-White contacts. The result of such artificial restrictions on interaction is an almost total rupture of communication between Whites and non-Whites. The complete inadequacy of the official "consultation" channels has already been shown in the political chapter. CSC and Town Council officials are only told what they like to hear, and I have witnessed non-White "representatives" utter complete falsehoods to Whites with a perfectly straight face. They do not lie because they want to lie, but because they know that the truth is unpalatable to the White governing group. A large gulf exists between the political opinions of the most progressive Europeans and the most conservative non-Europeans, so that a person like Whitehead is described as an "extreme liberal" by Whites and as a "conservative" by moderate non-Whites.[6]

Whites are completely unaware of the feelings of the non-Europeans, and the more they claim to know the Natives, the greater their blindness. Persons assumed by the Whites to be leaders in the African and Indian communities are almost invariably unpopular or devoid of any influence, and the influential persons are dismissed as extremists and agitators, or are entirely unknown to the local authorities. Fear and unwillingness to talk on the part of the non-Whites are not the only reasons for this rupture of communication. The Whites themselves vaguely perceive that reality is unpalatable, and

---

[6] There are a few South African Whites in the country as a whole whose opinions coincide roughly with those of non-European political movements, but none of them lives in Caneville. Of some three million South African Whites, about 2,000 belong to the Liberal Party and some 200 to the (largely Communist) Congress of Democrats. The Progressive Party has many more White members, but very few non-White members. The Progressive Party platform is inacceptable to all but a handful of conservative non-European leaders.

withdraw into a fool's paradise, reassuring themselves that all is basically right and that unrest is the work of a few agitators. It is also interesting to note that the breakdown in communication is *unidirectional*. Most non-Whites have a clear perception of the major aims and policies of the White government whether local or central.

The remaining contacts between Whites and non-Whites are almost all at the superficial, transitory, and strictly utilitarian level. Furthermore, such contacts, as I shall analyse presently, are mostly of a master-servant nature, and follow a highly stereotyped etiquette that precludes any candidness. This etiquette is subject to much ambiguity because, under present conditions, the traditional master-servant relationship is becoming increasingly challenged. Depending on the social class of the non-Whites and the Whites involved, the etiquette may be modified. I shall therefore start by describing the most common and expected type of relationship between European master and non-White servants, and introduce the necessary qualifications later.[7]

In shops, European customers expect to be served first, no matter how many non-White customers are already waiting. Furthermore, they expect a humble, deferential attention from Indian shop attendants, and they receive altogether better service than the Indian and African customers. Whites get their heavy purchases carried for them to their cars, for example. They expect to be granted credit as a matter of course in Indian shops, and some less scrupulous Europeans never settle their debts because they know that most Indian merchants dare not insist on payment or start legal proceedings.

Another form of superficial White–non-White contact is

---

[7] Most of the information regarding etiquette was obtained by direct observation rather than by asking informants. Interviews were used only to corroborate observation.

through formal functions. Frequently, prominent Whites, who are known to be somewhat more liberal and sympathetically inclined, or who are powerful and useful to ingratiate, are invited as guests of honour to non-White functions. They are always given front-row seats and are often called upon to open meetings, to distribute prizes, etc. They are treated with respect but without subservience by the non-Europeans. Mr. Whitehead and the Catholic priest, for example, were invited to speak at the ceremony for the centenary of the arrival of the first Indian immigrants in Natal. They spoke from a common platform together with Mr. Sham, a high school teacher, and Reverend Mvusi. "Mr. Reg" is also a frequent guest at such functions. These Europeans never reciprocate by inviting prominent non-Whites to European functions.

When English is spoken, Europeans expect to be addressed as "Sir" or "Madam" by non-Europeans. By their own servants, they are often called "Master" and "Mistress." The Afrikaans word *baas* ("master"), which is common elsewhere in South Africa, even in the speaking of English, is rarely used in Caneville except in addressing an Afrikaner policeman. When Zulu is spoken, Africans are expected to address Whites as *Nkosi* ("king" or "chief"). Conversely, Whites address and refer to non-Europeans as "boys" and "girls" regardless of age, if they do not know their names. If the European knows the name of an African he uses the first name only. In the case of Indians, Whites usually address them by last name only, without title. Sometimes, when the White does not know a non-White's name, he uses a standard fictitious first name: usually "John" for African men, and "Sammy" and "Mary" for Indians.

The terms "kaffir," "coolie," "coon," "nigger," and "monkey" are known by all Whites to be highly insulting, but are nevertheless in common use among many Afrikaners, Mauritians, and some of the working-class English. In polite upper-class English circles these words are considered crude and in bad taste.

The terms "Native," "Bantu," "Asiatic," and "Mohammedan," though not directly insulting, are resented by the majority of the groups to which they refer. This fact is unknown to all but a small minority of the Whites who constantly use these terms, even in the English upper class. (The only terms acceptable to the various groups of non-Whites are "African," "Indian," and "Muslim" or "Moslem"). When a European uses the words "people" or "South African," he almost invariably refers only to Whites. The concept of citizenship is implicitly denied to non-Europeans. When Whites relate an incident involving other Whites, they rarely use a racial label, whereas they almost always refer to non-Europeans by a racial term. Thus, when a White says, "I met somebody this morning," he most probably means a European. If he had met an African, he would say: "I saw a Native this morning."

A non-European meeting a White is expected to initiate the greeting. Apart from this, he must wait until he is spoken to. If a non-White comes into a room on an errand and finds Europeans in conversation, he must stand aside silently until his presence is acknowledged by one of the Whites. When a non-European has to come to a White home on business, he must come to the back door, never to the front door. He must remove his hat, keep his head slightly bowed, and be generally subservient. Above all, he must remain standing. Once, when I was preparing to interview Indian factory workers and was fetching a chair for the interviewees to sit on, a White employee told me: "I wouldn't invite them to sit down." When I asked him why not, he replied, "Oh, you know, it might embarrass them." In office transactions, the same rules apply. A White subordinate is asked to sit down, offered a cigarette and a cup of tea, and introduced to strangers, whereas a non-White subordinate must remain standing, call the White "Sir" repeatedly, and be generally servile. Never, in my entire period of field work, has a non-European employee been formally introduced to me by a White employee, while White employees have always been introduced or have introduced themselves. When a White employee called an Indian clerk into his office to help me with something, for example, the introduction was replaced by an order: "Naidoo, do that for the gentleman."

The vast majority of Caneville Whites never use any courtesy titles (such as "Mr.," "Mrs.," "Dr.," etc.) when speaking to non-Europeans and never shake hands with them. Most Whites resent other Whites observing elementary courtesy with non-Whites; being polite to non-Whites brings on one the stigma of "liberalism" (a term of contempt in White South Africa). There are some exceptions to that general rule, however. The high-ranking CSC officials such as Hancock, Whitehead and Sherwood always call prominent non-Whites "Mister," "Doctor," or "Reverend." Swanepoel does so only in the presence of Whitehead and Sherwood. At the other end of the scale, a few Whites, mostly Afrikaners, go out of their way to be offensive to Africans and Indians by openly using the insulting terms mentioned earlier. Deliberately making non-Whites wait is another harassing technique used by the White Post Office employees. There exists a whole number of more or less subtle vexations to which non-Whites are subjected by some Whites, but these practices are not general. The majority of Whites show callous indifference to the self-respect of non-Europeans, but do not go out of their way to be offensive, except when they feel that their superior status is threatened by "cheeky" Africans or Indians.

The choice of language spoken by Europeans in addressing Africans is a question of considerable importance. Fanagalo or "kitchen Zulu" is deeply resented by Africans if they can express themselves reasonably fluently in English. Even the use of proper Zulu by Whites when speaking to educated Africans is resented by the latter, because they know that some Whites often speak Zulu as a subtle way of showing that they do not differentiate between an educated and an uneducated African.

Most uneducated Whites in Caneville resent educated non-Europeans, whom they perceive as a threat to their status. This type of interaction is the one that is most laden with hostility on both sides. On the one hand, the educated non-White emphatically rejects the degrading, subservient role, while, on the other hand, the uneducated White keeps forcing the relationship back into the traditional master-servant mould. Such Whites are often good Zulu linguists who claim to "know the Natives," who have been brought up on farms with rural Africans, and who can only conceive of a rigid, paternalistic relationship with Africans. When an African makes any show of asserting his dignity, he immediately becomes a "cheeky kaffir."

Let us try to analyse in greater depth this paternalistic model of master-servant relations between Africans and Europeans and the mechanisms used on both sides to make the relationship "work." On the White side, the argument runs something as follows: The "Native" is a dull-witted, but good-natured, grown-up child and must be treated as such, i.e., kindly but sternly, as a good father would do to his own children. As a child he requires both guidance and protection (from "agitators," "liberals," "money-grabbing Indians," and a host of other imaginary enemies). The "Native," on his side, must show his gratitude for all that is done for him and must respect his Great White Father. One White field employee of the Company, the ex-sergeant who so deplores detribalization, expresses this condescending benevolence rather vividly:

> You must never hit a Native or shout at him because it lowers the boy's dignity. You lower yourself lower than a Native if you hit him. You have got to show the boys

that you care for them. It's the little personal things that count. That's what makes for good human relations here in Caneville. For example, when a boy cuts himself you have to see that he gets proper medical treatment. He respects you for it. He is going to remember it all his life and will tell his children and grandchildren about it. At the same time, you must not let matters with Natives get personal. You must keep distance otherwise they don't respect you. The most important thing in handling the Natives is to give every man a hearing. You must listen to what he has to say. A fellow with a grudge can spoil the happiness of a whole compound.

The White paternalist forces his relations with Africans into this rigid, stereotyped mould with its whole etiquette of debasing subservience and benevolent *hauteur.* This artificial and superficial relation (which virtually all younger Africans, whether educated or not, reject and resent) becomes the basis of the paternalist's much-vaunted knowledge of the "Natives" and qualifies him for a job in the field section of the Company.

The African on the other hand devises a whole series of mechanisms to deal with the Whites. For every White who "knows how to handle the Natives," there are a dozen Africans who know how to behave in front of these Whites. The safest solution for an African is to play the role that the Whites ascribe to him, i.e., to be submissive; to say *"Ya baas";* and to pretend to be a happy, dull-witted child by bursting out laughing at the White man's jokes, by clowning in his presence, by affecting a misunderstanding of simple tasks, etc. This "playing it dumb" can, of course, be an effective weapon of passive resistance, output restriction, and even minor sabotage of machinery. The self-debasing use of clowning in the presence of Europeans is one of the most effective means of ingratiating them, because it reaffirms the notion that "the Natives are happy." Conversely, a certain type of heavy, homely humour is effectively used by some Europeans to reaffirm their superiority, while at the same time convincing themselves that they are in close touch with non-Europeans.

Some examples will illustrate the point. A White Town Council official supervises the cleaning of a public fountain by two Indian workers. The fountain is full of tadpoles. The White turns to an Indian worker and asks, "Pillay, don't you Indians eat tadpoles?" The Indian answers non-commitally, "No Sir." The European then insists, "Haven't you tried to curry them?" and receives the same negative answer. He then concludes, "Well, that would be the only thing you don't eat." The same person, when receiving a complaint about the quality of the African beer, jocularly dismissed it by saying, "These monkeys can drink anything." Sarcastic praise is also used to reaffirm White superiority. A White Mauritian, for example, addressed an Indian waiter at the Company club-house in the following terms: "You are the best boy in Caneville. I see a great future for you here."

Virtually all African workers, even rural ones, bitterly resent the servile role that most Whites ascribe to them, and more and more workers devise new methods to evade servility, rather than outwardly pretending to be satisfied with their humble lot. A relatively safe way of evading servility is to adopt an impassive, blank mask in the presence of Whites, to interrupt all conversation when a White approaches, and to reduce interaction to the bare minimum. This evasion of contact can be effectively combined with sullen, passive resistance through pretending incomprehension.

Deception of Whites is also a widespread device. Some of that deception is induced by the Whites themselves, who are only told what they like to hear. For example, I heard an African "leader" tell the Town Council with a perfectly straight face that the Africans are satisfied with the Bantu Consultative Council and consider it an honour to belong to it. Had he said the same thing in an African meeting, his comments would have provoked a wave of derisive hilarity, yet the Whites present gravely accepted the "information" as a true reflection of reality.

Besides this forced lying, however, Africans use deliberate deception with Whites, either with the object of gaining something through it, or with the intention of out-smarting the White man and making a fool out of him. The latter procedure is quite common, and is conceived of as a subtle, cunning game of wits where the powerless African takes his revenge by out-foxing the White lion. An African school teacher, for example, pasted on his wall a newspaper photograph of the Prime Minister near that of two orangoutangs. When a White civil servant noticed Dr. Verwoerd's picture, the teacher led him to believe that he was a firm supporter of the Nationalist government.

Apart from these subtle methods of rejecting the subordinate role assigned to him, the African increasingly resorts to concerted opposition. In Caneville this opposition came into the open when the 1960 Government census was boycotted by the largely illiterate Pondo field workers. The White field managers attributed the success of the boycott to intimidation by "agitators," and undoubtedly there was a great amount of pressure put on the workers by their leaders to co-operate with the protest movement. But widespread support for the boycott among the workers was subsequently shown when I tried to interview them. The interview schedule was thought to be a Government census and the boycott was immediately revived with nearly complete success.

I have tried to show that the retention by most Whites of the completely obsolete and artificial master-servant relationship has led to an utter rupture of communication between Africans and Whites. The same applies to a lesser extent to White-Indian relations. Most Whites still view the Africans as happy, retarded children, and most Africans view the majority of Europeans and certainly the representatives of authority as powerful oppressors. Such a state of affairs is one of the symptoms of a pre-revolutionary situation. Marie Antoinette's famous "Let them eat cake," if uttered, was probably a statement of ignorance rather than of cynicism. Its South African equivalent is: "I know the Natives. They are a happy lot."

There are very few cases in Caneville where the White–non-White master-servant relationship is reversed. In contrast to larger cities, there are few White shop assistants to serve non-Whites for example. In one case, however, the relationship, if not reversed, is at least ambiguous. This one case, which concerns White civil servants, deserves careful examination because it is one of the major sources of tension in Caneville, and because it will give us a deeper insight into the rigidity of race relations there. As the term indicates, the role of civil servants is socially defined as having to perform services for the taxpayers. In all countries, this subservient role is ambiguous and challenged by bureaucrats whose overbearing behaviour toward citizens is a common source of complaints. In a dictatorship or quasi-dictatorship, the ambiguity of the role is even greater, as the bureaucrat then becomes the representative of oppression. In a *racialist* quasi-dictatorship like South Africa, the role conflict reaches its acme of intensity because of the added complication of colour. The function of the South African Police, for example, is to maintain "law and order," but only for the benefit of the Whites whom they "protect" against the non-Whites. The Africans generally regard the police as a public enemy.

Let us return to the local situation. We have already seen how the local authorities attempt to keep the South African Police out of the African location. But constant friction persists between the non-White citizens and White officials, in particular Swanepoel and the postal employees. Swanepoel's dual role, as defined both by himself and by the Company, is that of a servant of the Company and of a police commander for the non-White inhabitants. In the presence of Whitehead, Sherwood, and Hancock, Swanepoel behaves subserviently, while with non-Whites he plays a domineering and autocratic role. Non-Whites resent his attitude because they as taxpayers define his role as that of *their* servant. While Whitehead insists that Swanepoel be polite with prominent non-Whites such as Goshalia, Swanepoel loses no opportunity to reassert his assumed superiority over other non-Whites who challenge what they consider an abuse and usurpation of authority.

The behaviour of White Post Office employees towards Indians and Africans likewise illustrates the role conflict. Here, the non-White customer is clearly defined by the State as inferior since he enters through a "non-European" door and is served at a segregated counter. But the White employees have to perform direct services for non-Europeans in a face-to-face situation. This they do only with great reluctance. Indians and Africans are deliberately kept waiting while the White employees leisurely drink tea or coffee; they are treated rudely, and they are harassed in a variety of ways such as through the refusal of "improperly packed" parcels. Non-Whites are constantly and pointedly shown who is boss, and they resent this treatment. Referring to an open quarrel he had with the postmaster, an African clerk told me: "When I go to the Post Office, I expect service and only service." A mild-mannered and sensitive Indian school teacher related how he dreaded and avoided going to the Post Office: "Each time I go there, it is an ordeal." A postal employee, on the other hand, crisply summarized his attitude when he told me at the beginning of the study: "You will find nothing interesting here, only a bunch of coolies." To make matters worse, state civil service in South Africa predominantly recruits those

Europeans who are least educated and intelligent, and who
are most rabidly prejudiced.

A final word must be said on Indian-African relations. We
have already seen that these relations are limited, though for
different reasons than White–non-White relations. In the educated professional class, African-Indian interaction is egalitarian, although sometimes poisoned by mutual fears and sus-
picions. Many Indians, however, look down on the mass of
Africans as savages and have adopted the same attitude of
condescension toward them that the Whites have. This
attitude is particularly prevalent among Indian merchants,
who for the most part still refer to Africans as "Natives" and
discriminate against them in employment and in business. In
most Indian businesses, Africans only perform heavy unskilled
labour, while all the better jobs such as those of shop at-
tendant, clerk, etc., are held by Indians. Most Indian merchants address Africans in Fanagalo without inquiring whether
they speak English. I have often heard Indians make fun of
the Africans' "simplicity." An Indian girl at a charity bazaar
told me, for example, about an African woman, who bought
clothes: "They [the Africans] are so simple that they buy
without knowing whether it is going to fit or not." At the
same time, however, she was encouraging the Africans to buy.
In shops, African customers generally get a more casual, perfunctory service than Indian customers. Whereas an unknown
Indian woman will be addressed with a respectful "Aunt" or
"Grandmother" depending on age, African women are called
by a more familiar "Mama." All these pin-pricks are a source
of resentment against Indians on the part of Africans.

Few Africans can afford to patronize the Indian cinema,
but those who do are not discriminated against. The condescending attitude of many Indians towards Africans unlike
that of some Whites, arises more from ignorance than from
design. Except for a couple of Indian children making fun of

an African girl, I have never witnessed any Indian being openly and deliberately offensive towards Africans. On the whole, African servants in Indian homes are treated as members of the family (though with a trace of paternalism), and Indian women often work side by side with their African servants and chat good-humouredly with them. This relationship is also found in some European homes, but, I think, not as frequently as in Indian homes.

Caneville illustrates certain theoretical principles in the study of prejudice and race relations. American studies have shown that equal contact across racial or ethnic lines fosters tolerance, provided there is no threat of competition.[8] The converse of that finding is shown in South Africa, namely that segregation which prevents equal status contact leads to intolerance and antagonism.[9] At the psychological level, segregation encourages people to think along racial lines, and facilitates the development of stereotypes through lack of free communication between members of racial groups. The phenomenon of the White who claims to "know the Native" epitomizes the process of stereotypy. Knowing the Native simply means lumping all members of a group into a preconceived simplistic mould that has little if any relationship to reality.

The sociological counterpart of prejudice is discrimination. Where the dominant society actively rewards discrimination and punishes tolerance, a vicious circle is established whereby discrimination reinforces prejudice and prejudice reinforces discrimination.[10] From the White point of view, the spectacle of non-Whites being treated as inferiors leads to the belief

---

[8] For a bibliography and a treatment of the subject, see G. W. Allport, *The Nature of Prejudice.*

[9] See Kuper, "The Heightening of Racial Tension."

[10] See Kuper, unpublished paper delivered at the Natal Convention, April, 1960.

that they are, in fact, inferior. Not only is discrimination customary, but the laws of South Africa make many forms of racial discrimination compulsory under the threat of severe penalties. Acts that are perfectly licit when performed within one's race (e.g., marriage) become criminal offences when they cut across racial lines. Discriminatory laws and customs breed prejudice. Conversely, the belief that non-Whites are inferior serves as a rationalization for inferior treatment and racialist laws. Belief in one's racial superiority allows one to discriminate with a clear conscience. From the non-White standpoint, discriminatory treatment obviously leads to the development of anti-White feelings, and these feelings in turn lead to the constantly fulfilled expectation of discrimination.

Caneville and South Africa show the operation of a vicious circle consisting of three mutually reinforcing elements: segregation, prejudice, and discrimination. Racial segregation always involves discrimination because the function of segregation is to maintain a racial hierarchy. The practice of segregation and discrimination fosters prejudice, and prejudice serves to rationalize segregation and discrimination.[11] The vicious circle can be attacked from any or all of the three factors. People's prejudices can be reduced through a variety of psycho- and socio-therapeutic techniques, but in a racialist society this approach is slow and ineffective so long as the state enforces discrimination. It is, I believe, unrealistic to expect a change of heart on the part of South African Whites so long as the present system of government is maintained. Furthermore, from a social point of view, what must be eliminated

---

[11] At the individual level, the relationship is more complex. In generally tolerant societies, many persons have a deeply internalized prejudice but do not discriminate because discrimination is discouraged or punished; and conversely, in racialist societies, many people who are no bigots at heart discriminate because the society encourages or forces it.

are not so much the private prejudices of people as the expressions of prejudice, namely segregation and discrimination. The most effective way of abolishing these is through state action. I fear only a revolution can bring about such a change in South Africa. Within certain limits, however, the vicious circle can be broken by vigorous action on the part of private concerns.

Let us examine again the case of the creole Mauritians in Caneville, because their position clearly demonstrates the principles that I have just enunciated. For reasons given before, the CSC has treated that small group as Whites in the areas of salary, housing, and employment. Private colour prejudices against them exist, to be sure, but in a milder form than against Indians or Africans. Through equal-status contact on the job, people get to know one another as individuals and prejudice recedes. This equal-status contact is made possible through the Company policy of non-discrimination towards creole Mauritians. To the extent that Whites still hold prejudices against them, the Whites feel guilty. As guilt is a heavy burden to bear, prejudice slowly recedes. Where the Company, on the other hand, sanctions, encourages, and consciously plans segregation and discrimination against Indians and Africans, White prejudices towards these groups are reinforced and rewarded. Whites are able to be bigoted and discriminatory without any feeling of guilt, and to accept the situation as "natural." There the vicious circle is in full operation.

In this chapter I have tried to show the effect of "aggregation" on human relationships across racial lines. The philosophy of segregation in South Africa as a whole, and in Caneville in particular, is rationalized on the grounds that:

1. apartheid prevents conflict and fosters good race relations by reducing contact;

2. apartheid is a voluntary process through which each group realizes its maximum potentialities; and
3. everybody wants to be aggregated.

The evidence clearly refutes all three of these rationalizations, either partly or *in toto*, and shows that the real intent of segregation is to maintain White supremacy. Whites don't object in the least to close physical contact with their non-European servants. They only want to prevent *egalitarian* contact because such contact threatens their supremacy. Racial segregation can never be equal, because its object is to perpetuate inequality. Only the Whites want to be aggregated, and only for them is the process voluntary. Most local Whites when they speak of "voluntary segregation" mean that the segregation is not imposed by law.

But whether segregation is forced on people by law, by economic measures, or by customary prejudices does not make much difference to the subjugated groups. Neither is it a notable achievement to forestall discriminatory legislation by discriminating privately. As to the state of race relations in Caneville, it can only be described as "good" if by "good" one means the absence (or postponement) of physical violence. In Caneville we have seen apartheid at its best, in a situation where its architects have been moved by a sincere desire to do good as well as to maintain themselves in power. I leave it to the reader to imagine the impact of apartheid on the lives of 80 per cent of the South African population at large.

Chapter VIII

CANEVILLE IN TRANSITION

So far my picture of Caneville has been fairly static. To be sure, I have made passing references to change, but my description must of necessity have given the impression of a much more stable community than Caneville in fact is. The reasons for this static emphasis are two-fold. The first is heuristic: Reality looked at statically is already complex enough without introducing simultaneously the complication of change. Second, social change is rarely fast enough for a perceptible amount of it to be encompassed in a few months of field work. Unless the social scientist has spent many years in the community, or unless he has visited the community at two widely separated times, his statements about change must be based largely on inferences or on the none-too-reliable memory of informants. Written documents rarely record enough material to enable the sociologist or anthropologist to reconstruct the detailed past social life of a small community.

Notwithstanding these difficulties, it would give a distorted picture of reality to conclude this study of Caneville without describing, at least broadly, the tempo and direction of the principal aspects of social change. By projecting or extrapolating from past change, one may even stick one's neck out in the field of prediction (or perhaps better, of prophecy).

The most general statement that can be made about change in Caneville also applies to the rest of South Africa. Caneville's rapid and accelerating pace of change in most fields is accompanied by rigidity in the political sphere. Historically this is the classical setting for a social revolution. Let us first analyse the broad trends in the various aspects of the social structure, then see how these trends interact, and finally draw the future implications of past change.

In Chapter III, I have attempted to convey the complexity of Caneville's cultural pluralism. A detailed anthropological description of the various cultures would have been entirely beyond the scope of this study. This deliberate omission accounts for the strong structural slant of the study. Over-riding this cultural pluralism, however, the trend of all the non-Western cultures toward Westernization is clear. The pace of acculturation has varied from one group to another. Various groups have selectively accepted different aspects of Western culture, but the general direction has been the same for all groups. The major agencies of acculturation have been the various Christian denominations, the Western school system, and participation in an increasingly industrialized and urban wage economy. These factors have in turn led to the internal development, within the African and Indian groups, of acculturative forces, notably the political liberatory movements. These movements are predominantly Western in their aims and values, though they also show a strong Gandhian influence.

The interdependence of various elements of culture makes for an accelerated chain-reaction effect, once acculturation has begun. For example, the breakdown of traditional African kinship ties has also contributed to the downfall of the tribal political structure. This is not to say that certain islands of resistance and cultural conservatism cannot resist the general process. The resilience of Hinduism and Islam among Indians, and of the *lobola* (bride-wealth) among Africans are cases in point. But such institutions or segments of culture can only survive the general trend if they are reinterpreted in a way which isolates them functionally from the traditional culture, and integrates them into the dominant culture. Using the same examples, the *lobola* now serves functions that are quite different from the traditional ones. Similarly Hinduism has been reinterpreted to make it fall in line with Western values as shown, for instance, in the identification of Christ and Krishna, and in the rise of reform movements such as the Divine Life and the Ramakrishna societies.

The fast tempo of acculturation can be illustrated by the fact that, during the short time covered by the present study, perceptible changes took place. These changes concerned the introduction of Western dancing among Indians and the attendance of unescorted Muslim women at public functions. Other changes took place in a somewhat longer period of about five years, for example, the spread of English and of literacy among Muslim women from merchant families, and the employment of Muslim women as sales personnel in shops.

The topic of acculturation raises an interesting theoretical problem. Parsons, Clyde and Florence Kluckhohn, Ruth Benedict, and others have argued with considerable cogency that the value system (or ethos, or *Weltanschauung*) of a culture constitutes the deepest and most significant core of that culture, and exerts a determining influence on other aspects of the same. Parsons has gone one step further by asserting that internalization of a common set of basic values by most members of a society is a pre-requisite to the existence of a society. Such a common set of values, argues Parsons, is not only the highest level at which a social system is integrated, but also a *sine qua non* of the existence of what he calls a society.

Such a concept of society excludes all culturally pluralistic systems (such as colonial societies). An easy way out of this difficulty is to accept Parson's definition as arbitrary but legitimate (as all definitions intrinsically are), and to give pluralistic systems another label. However, such a distinction between unitary and pluralistic societies (or whatever one would have to call the latter) is not particularly useful. Pluralistic societies, though not integrated at the value level, are nevertheless held together by other forces in such a way as to make their description as social systems meaningful.

Clearly, in Caneville as in the rest of South Africa, there is no broad consensus at the value level. Yet, Caneville does constitute a social system in the sense that it includes people who interact in a well structured, predictable fashion, and who are interdependent. Caneville is integrated at the economic level by common participation in a system of production from which the livelihood of all depends, and at the political level by common subjugation under a government that maintains itself by force (or the threat of force). By no means can the people of Caneville (or South Africa) be said to share a set of common values, however. This absence of value consensus does indeed contribute greatly to the total *malintegration* of Caneville, and will probably bring about the *disintegration* of the system in its present form. But Caneville also shows that societies can exist for a long time under conditions of acute malintegration. The functionalist position is only tenable, in my estimation, if phrased in a very cautious way; namely, that there is a limit to the amount of malintegration which a society can take without breaking down (or blowing up), and that, in the long run, the tendency is generally towards integration.

Lack of value consensus exists at two levels in Caneville and in South Africa as a whole. It arises first of all from cultural pluralism. This point is obvious and need not be belaboured; but lack of consensus also arises, paradoxically, from acculturation. Normally one would expect that, as Westernization gains in extent and in depth, the basis of value consensus would broaden. In certain respects this is the case; for example, in the increasing acceptance of material symbols of success among Hindus whose traditional values are certainly non-materialistic. But, in a very important way, Westernization does not bring about value consensus as one might predict. The crux of the paradox is that non-Europeans eagerly adopt Western values of democracy, individualism, achievement by merit, and universalism that the local White variant of Western culture has rejected.

In many other societies with a colonial history, for example in Latin America, acculturation to the Western way of life has entailed full social acceptance. In other words, these societies not only ceased to be culturally pluralistic, but became integrated replicas of open-class Western European societies. In South Africa, on the contrary, no amount of Westernization can gain one's acceptance into the dominant White group. The Westernized non-European thus finds himself in the frustrating position of relinquishing his traditional way of life because he has internalized Western values, and yet of being rejected by those people who claim allegiance to Western culture but who, in fact, are imbued with values that conflict with the whole Western tradition. Thus, the African is told that he is incapable of exercising a vote because he is a savage, but when he becomes educated he is told that he is "cheeky" and that "detribalization is the worst thing that can happen to a Native." Similarly, the Indian has discarded the Hindu caste system which, he has been told, is inhuman and degrading, but he is forced to live in a colour-caste society that reduces 80 per cent of the population to the role of helots.

This bitter and tragic paradox of South African society constitutes one of the most important sources of malintegration and potential disintegration of the system. As Westernization continues at a fast rate (in spite of futile government attempts to reverse the process through tribal authorities, Bantu Education, etc.), this malintegration must increase, barring the unlikely prospect of a White "change of heart," i.e., a rediscovery of Western values.

In economic change, Caneville again exhibits the same gross tendencies as the rest of South Africa. With the growth of the local sugar mill, the town's population increased and became more permanently urbanized. As technology became more complex, the demand for skills rose, while the demand for bulk labour diminished. All these trends, which are typical of developing economies, occurred in spite of legal and traditional impediments which run counter to all principles of economic rationality in a supposedly free-enterprise economy. Influx control did not stop the African from settling in Caneville. The wasteful migratory labour system continues, but on a reduced scale as workers are replaced by machines. In this respect, I have mentioned, for example, the introduction of motorized trailer transport of cane that has eliminated the need for much human labour.

Colour prejudice has prevented the rational utilization of labour on the basis of competence, but specialization of production has created a number of semi-skilled positions for non-Europeans. In several other respects, restrictions to free enterprise have prevented developments that would otherwise have taken place. Under normal conditions, wages would tend to equal productivity, with the result that White manual workers would receive lower wages and non-Whites higher wages than they now receive. Artificial protection of European artisans, and discrimination against non-White workers (through denial of the right to strike, for example) have maintained a gap between skilled and unskilled wages that is unparalleled in any other industrialized country. A rapid increase in European wages since World War II has, in fact, widened the already enormous wage gap. Had it not been for the opposition of the CSC to any other large industry settling in Caneville, the economy of the town might have been more diversified than it is.

In spite of all these restrictions, there has been a rapid increase in White living standards, and a much slower but steady rise in non-White standards. Recent events indicate, however, that the sugar industry and Caneville face a lean future after a comparatively prosperous recent past. This prognosis is based both on the threat of overproduction of sugar and on politically induced dangers of withdrawal of capital, depression, and social upheavals. From the above prediction, one may also assume that the rate of population growth will slow down.

In the field of social stratification, we have seen how the process of acculturation was accompanied by the development of a Western type of class system within each of the three colour-castes. Conversely, traditional criteria of status lose in importance. The virtual disappearance of the Hindu caste system is a case in point. Although the economic gap between Whites and non-Whites has probably increased in recent years, the educational gap tends to narrow as more non-Whites attain secondary and university education. The Government has, of course, attempted to reverse that trend by introducing tribal education to train obedient helots, and, from the Government point of view, the policy of Bantu Education begins to bear its fruits of obscurantism and indoctrination. On the whole, there is a tendency for class stratification within each of the three racial castes to increase both in range and in rigidity. The colour-caste system has also become more and more rigid since the Nationalists came into office, through a whole set of oppressive laws. At the same time, rejection of the White-imposed albinocracy has greatly increased among non-Europeans.

The political structure of South Africa has remained basically unchanged since the nineteenth century. Since the Nationalists came into power in 1948, the change that has taken place has been in a reactionary direction with a view to the re-establishment of the Golden Age of the Boer Republics of the second half of the nineteenth century.[1] Locally, through the appointment of Indian and African members on the Town Council, the fiction of representative government has been introduced without in any substantial way deviating from the general South African principle of White domination. Nor do the local authorities envisage any change that would bring about an approximation to democratic government. Even the relatively minor suggestion that Caneville's town secretary should be an Indian was emphatically rejected by Mr. Whitehead, the most "liberal" of the local officials, as "far too premature."

This political inflexibility of the dominant White group has been challenged for a number of years, but only in the last few years has the challenge become a direct threat. Mounting external and internal pressures have combined with the final collapse of colonialism in the rest of Africa to make for a realistic prospect of a drastic change in the near future. Political consciousness in the oppressed masses of the non-European population has mounted rapidly in the last few years, to a level that is unparalleled in any other part of Africa, except perhaps in Algeria.

So far, there is nothing to suggest the imminent collapse of the Caneville Experiment. No crack is yet visible in the elegant white-washed façade of the edifice. The casual visitor taken on a conducted tour of Caneville leaves with a very favourable impression. As late as 1958 or 1959, the average

---

[1] For an interpretation of the policy of apartheid, see my paper, "Apartheid, Fascism and the Golden Age."

European traveller in the Congo left in much the same spirit of admiration for "all of what they do for the Natives."

Quite apart from the ethical merits or demerits of the philosophy of paternalism, that policy contains the seeds of its own destruction in the twentieth century. The reason is very simple. Paternalism is a political fossil which can only survive in a relatively static agricultural society where the labour is furnished by a hereditary servile or quasi-servile class. A body politic like the old Belgian Congo or South Africa that is economically thriving but that has failed to grasp the lessons of the French Revolution is plainly unviable. The greater is the discrepancy between economic prosperity and development on the one hand and political archaism on the other hand, the more certain is the collapse of the entire system.

At the risk of belabouring the obvious, let me spell out some of the factors that make for the incompatibility of paternalism in an industrial context. A stable paternalistic master-servant relationship requires a number of conditions. There must be an intimate, face-to-face, affective bond between master and servant. Such a bond implies a small-sized organisation incompatible with large, impersonal, industrial concerns. Furthermore, the development of paternalistic bonds requires a long-standing relationship that cannot normally be established in a highly mobile industrial context, all the less so in one that perpetuates a migratory labour system. Paternalism also requires that the servant or slave internalize the feeling of his inferiority. In other words, he must believe that he is inferior, and be happy with his humble lot, for otherwise he inevitably challenges his subservient status. That condition can only be fulfilled in a relatively static, isolated society where the servile class can effectively be cut off from all currents of emancipatory ideas, and be kept in ignorance. Obviously, ignorance is incompatible with modern industry, which requires specialized skills on the part of the workers as well as a minimum of general education such as ability to read and to count. Furthermore, the bringing together of large masses of workers from widely separated areas makes for the exchange of ideas and the development of a class consciousness that transcends ethnic and local loyalties. That class consciousness then organizes in trade unions or, if unions are prohibited, in underground organisations (as demonstrated by the Pondo of Caneville).

What remains, then, of paternalism in an industrial and urban context such as that of Caneville is a one-sided relationship that calls for the development of an elaborate mythology. The dominant White group clings to the antiquated notions of how it should treat the subjugated non-Whites, but the non-Whites overwhelmingly reject the role of servant. The attachment of the ruling group to the obsolete ideology of paternalism is understandable. To one in a dominant position, paternalism is attractive for it appears to reconcile despotism with justice. But paternalism, in order to "work," implies *acceptance of inferior status by the servile group*. When that acceptance is absent as in Caneville, then self-deceiving fictions are created to make it possible to cling to the ideology: "Our workers are happy here," "People want to be aggregated," "We are one big happy family," etc. These myths must not be dismissed as cynical, Machiavellian deceptions for outside consumption. They are firmly believed in by the vast majority of local Whites, who are sincerely hurt when the "Natives" are not grateful for all that is done for them. If these fictions were a cynical smoke-screen, they would not be as effective as they are. Their efficacity resides in the fact that the Whites believe in them.

The dominant group has, of course, a vested interested in retaining the belief in paternalistic myths intact. These fictions are defence mechanisms; for if the myths are exposed, then the system of domination shows itself in its true colour, namely as government by force, not by consent or by "consultation." Evidence that threatens to expose the fictions is sub-consciously repressed and outwardly rejected by the development of new fictions (i.e., "It's all the work of a few Communist agitators") and the invention of imaginary enemies who subvert the happy, simple-minded Natives.

The analysis of paternalism in Caneville leads us, once more, to reject the Marxist, conspiratorial, and Machiavellian view of power. To be sure, the Marxist notion is not entirely false, but it is one-sided and it oversimplifies reality. Some people are Machiavellian. Entire systems such as the Nazi regime may even be predominantly so. But, as a generalization, the Marxist view cannot be accepted, because it fails to account for the role of ideas in human behaviour. If anything, Caneville shows a reversal of the Marxist slogan. Racialism and paternalism in Caneville are the opium of the ruling class, not the opium of the masses. They are not only consciously devised rationalizations of the ruling class to make the masses accept White domination; they are also self-deceiving defence mechanisms of the dominant group which allow that group to rule and to discriminate with a clear conscience. Myths are effective to the extent that they are believed in, not only by the masses for whom they are supposedly devised, but also by the ruling class that invents them.

We have studied Caneville at a crucial time in its history, when the social system of the town and of South Africa as a whole has probably reached its maximum of disequilibrium or malintegration. If it has not reached it yet, it is close to it. Caneville has undergone throughout its existence a process of cultural and economic change. On the cultural side, its inhabitants have become increasingly Westernized; on the economic side, Caneville grew and became an urban, semi-industrialized community. Both these change processes have been cumulative and their tempo has increased as each new change in turn has generated a wave of adjustive changes in other aspects of the social structure. In these respects Caneville has conformed to the classical model of a system in a state of dynamic equilibrium, and does not present any particular interest for the study of social change.

Caneville's (and South Africa's) contribution to the study of change comes in where change did *not* take place. The political and the stratification system failed to adjust to change in the cultural and economic fields, and, where they changed, it was in such a way as to increase *maladjustment.* In other words, the change was reactionary: political oppression increased and stratification rigidified. Caneville shows, as it were, an equilibrium system that has run amok. Instead of being a single unitary system, all the parts of which can be permeated by waves of change, the social system of Caneville (and South Africa) is compartmentalized. One-half of the system (the cultural and economic one) operates "normally," while the political and stratification half responds in a reactionary direction. The spread of education among non-Whites brings about the "threat" of egalitarian contact with Whites, so segregation is introduced to prevent such contact. Urbanization of the Africans undermines White supremacy in the European areas, so influx control steps in to send the people back to impoverished reserves. The tribal system collapses under the impact of industrialization, so tribal authorities and Bantustans are artificially established with the backing of armoured cars and machine guns.

Examples of political reaction could be multiplied. While it is true that Caneville escaped some of the insanity found elsewhere in South Africa, it has nevertheless been influenced by the larger system. By South African standards, Caneville's local government looks progressive. In fact, it has been simply *conservative* rather than *reactionary* as the central government has been. The short-run effect of political reaction is to contain and retard inevitable change in other parts of the system, though at ever rising cost in money, and more importantly, in suffering and frustration. The long-range consequence of such a policy is a cumulative cycle of ever deepening malfunction, of which we have analysed the symptoms earlier.

It follows from the above analysis that Caneville and South Africa are on the eve of a drastic political change to re-establish the balance. Rapidly mounting external pressures will precipitate the internal change, but the latter would take place in any case. To be sure, South Africa has shown that a social system can exist for a long time under conditions of acute disequilibrium, but there are limits to the amount of malfunction that a social system can take. I believe that, not only has the breaking point been almost reached, but that the possibility of an orderly, gradual reversal of the vicious circle has disappeared. Change will probably have to be revolutionary. The main questions are how bloody, long-drawn, and violent that revolution will be, and whether it will be liberal or socialist, racialist or non-racialist. The answers depend in part on how soon it will occur.

Chapter IX

CONCLUSIONS

IN THIS study I have tried to describe as succinctly as possible the social structure of a small South African community. Caneville was not chosen because it is a "typical" South African town. The cultural and "racial" composition of its population is certainly atypical. In most major respects, however, what applies to Caneville applies *mutatis mutandi* to the country as a whole. Although Caneville shows South Africa at its best, the basic ingredients of its social structure are much the same.

After placing Caneville in its larger context and describing its physical lay-out, I have shown how the many cultures present influence one another. Complex as this process of acculturation is in its details, the general trend towards Westernization is clear. Caneville and South Africa are unquestionably well on their way to becoming Western in every basic respect, and there is no reason to expect that the process will be reversed. The major practical implication of that fact is that it explodes the prevalent White South African myth that "White civilisation" is threatened. Caneville shows that Western civilisation has no skin colour. If anything, the non-Europeans have assimilated the fundamental values of the Western world better than the Whites have. White *domination* is doomed in South Africa, but the Western way of life is secure for any foreseeable future. Colour and culture are two entirely different phenomena.

Though the general trend toward Westernization is clear, acculturation is a selective process to which cultures react differently. We have seen, for example, that the strong cohesive force of Islam as opposed to Hinduism has retarded the Westernization of Muslims. Attitudes towards one's traditional culture also affect selectivity of cultural borrowing. We have contrasted the African's cultural shame with the Indian's cultural pride. Caneville confirms the generally known fact that acculturation takes place mostly from the technologically less advanced to the technologically more advanced culture, but it also shows that, when several cultures can be ranked on a scale of technological complexity, the borrowing process largely "skips" the intermediate levels. Hindu and Muslim cultures exerted no perceptible influence on the African population (except in politics through Mahatma Gandhi, but then, the African National Congress can hardly be called a product of traditional African culture). The rigid South African colour-caste system has in some respects retarded the process of Westernization, but it has certainly not prevented it. Indeed, at the level of basic values, racial discrimination has probably accelerated acculturation. The political credo of the French Revolution and the ethics of Christianity are better understood by many Africans than by most Whites who claim a monopoly of Western civilisation.

Dealing with the power system, we have seen how the large local industrial concern imposes its policy of paternalism on the town. The local power system is clearly autocratic and racialistic. In its racialism it follows (and in some respects anticipates) national policy, although the local implementation of racial discrimination and segregation is more benevolent than at the national level. We have analysed in detail the methods used by the local authorities to maintain their monopoly of power. To view these methods as the result of a conscious Machiavellian plan would be a distortion of reality. In many cases the techniques of domination have been empirically evolved without any malevolent intent.

The underlying philosophy of government in Caneville is that democracy cannot work except among the Anglo-Saxon "race," and that the mass of the people are incapable of governing themselves. In contrast to government in South Africa as a whole, where a semblance of democracy is maintained within the White ruling group, autocracy in Caneville applies to Whites as well as to non-Whites. As in the rest of South Africa, however, the Whites enjoy a standard of material rewards that is about five or six times higher, on the average, than that of non-Europeans. A rigid physical segregation is maintained on the assumption that contact between the races breeds conflict. We have shown, however, that no matter how racial segregation is rationalized it remains a technique to maintain White supremacy.

The consent of the people is assumed by the local authorities, but generally exists only among the Whites, and perhaps in a segment of the Indian merchant class. Opposition to the authorities has so far remained mostly latent and ineffectual, largely because the community is politically atomized. As opposed to democratic systems where public opinion organizes itself into groups competing for power, in the autocratic system of Caneville the alignment takes the form of the authorities *versus* the people. But conflicts of interest among the people militate against their taking a united, concerted stand against autocracy. Even if the popular opposition were organized and united, it could not unseat the authorities by constitutional means.

The economic structure of Caneville closely resembles the political structure. Indeed, the two are counterparts of each other. The local sugar company is by far the biggest concern in town. The economic life of the town is largely dominated by the sugar company. As any economy based on monoculture, Caneville is very sensitive to wide economic fluctuations. The retail trade is largely in the hands of Indian merchants. The rigid statutory and customary colour-caste system finds its material expression in large racial inequalities in living standards. While all Europeans live in comfort, the great majority of Africans and Indians live in poverty; in many cases, near starvation level. On the average, Indians are better off than Africans, but the difference between these two groups is much narrower than the wide gulf that separates Whites from non-Whites. This non-rational system of economic discrimination along racial lines makes not only for misery, but also for other malfunctions such as inefficiency and rigidity in the allocation of labour.

In contrast to the simple, monolithic politico-economic structure of the town, the stratification system is extremely complex. That complexity arises in great part from the cultural heterogeneity of the population, with the further complication of the White-imposed colour hierarchy. On the whole, the tendency is for each of the three main racial groups to develop an internal Western class system, but the process is far from complete. Many traditional criteria of status still retain some importance, as does the Hindu caste system, for example. Different criteria of status are differently weighted in various segments of the population. Some criteria, while not strictly hierarchical, are linked with objective socio-economic differences. The Indian community is the most complex in its stratification, but the Europeans and the Africans have by no means a simple system. Overriding all other distinctions of status, the three colour-castes are rigid, ascriptive groups, maintained by the whole repressive machinery of the South African state, and reinforced by private prejudice and discrimination.

In a special chapter on race relations, I have tried to analyse the *modus vivendi* of these three colour-castes. The major conclusions that emerge from the study are that racialism (in the sense of a belief in innate physical superiority) is predominantly a creation of the dominant White group, and is largely rejected by the Africans and Indians. Physical segregation, by whatever name it is called, is a clear-cut instrument of racial discrimination and of domination of the majority by a minority. This fact is widely recognized by the subjugated non-Whites, who, with few exceptions, find the system abhorrent. Unavoidably, such a system makes for a great deal of friction and antagonism in day-to-day relations. Anti-White feelings are strong among Africans. Indians serve as a scapegoat for both Africans and Europeans. There is an almost complete rupture of communication between Whites and Africans, because the former insist on maintaining the traditional master-servant relationship which the latter emphatically reject. Most Africans look on the White authorities and civil servants as enemies. Indian attitudes toward Africans are poisoned by fear. A vicious circle of prejudice, discrimination, and segregation leads to a continuous worsening of race relations.

Finally, by looking at Caneville from a dynamic point of view, I have pointed out the cumulative malfunction that an antiquated system of government and a rigidly ascribed stratification impose on an urban and industrial system of production. I have also shown how the colour hierarchy, coupled with the process of Westernization, makes for mounting tension. The resulting disequilibrium in the social structure is rapidly increasing in a way which, I believe, makes revolution unavoidable.

Inevitably my own value position must have been clear throughout this study. Because one's own values cannot be divorced from a study of this type, I stated my position at the beginning. The reader may dismiss my study as biased. This book is not anti-South African, nor anti-CSC, nor anti-White. It may have been written predominantly from what, in South Africa, would be called a "non-European point of view." In fact, I have tried to write from a universal viewpoint which, locally, happens to coincide more with non-European than with White attitudes. As stated at the beginning of the book, the object of this study is two-fold. First, I hope to have contributed to the scientific study of multi-racial and multi-cultural societies. Second, by showing the effects of segregation, discrimination, prejudice, and domination on the daily lives of human beings, I want to make a plea for sanity, tolerance, and non-racialism. For is not respectful tolerance of differences the ultimate test of civilisation?

BIBLIOGRAPHY

THIS bibliography does not purport to be complete. Of the many books on South Africa, only a few of the most basic and general works are listed here.

GORDON W. ALLPORT, *Personality and Social Encounter*, Boston, Beacon, 1960.

GORDON W. ALLPORT, *The Nature of Prejudice*, Cambridge, Addison-Wesley, 1954.

Anonymous, *African Taxation, Its Relation to African Social Services*, S. A. Institute of Race Relations Fact Paper, No. 4, 1960.

Anonymous, *South African Sugar Year Book*, Durban, 1960.

BURTON BENEDICT, *Indians in a Plural Society, A Report on Mauritius*, London, Colonial Research Studies, 1961.

BURTON BENEDICT, "The Plural Society of Mauritius," *Race*, 3, 1962, pp. 65–78.

BURTON BENEDICT, "Stratification in Plural Societies," *American Anthropologist*, 64, 1962, pp. 1235–1246.

G. H. CALPIN, *Indians in South Africa*, Pietermaritzburg, Shuter and Shooter, 1949.

G. M. CARTER, *The Politics of Inequality, South Africa since 1948*, New York, Praeger, 1958.

B. N. COLBY AND P. L. VAN DEN BERGHE, "Ethnic Relations in Southeastern Mexico," *American Anthropologist*, 63, 1961, pp. 772–792.

O. C. COX, *Caste, Class and Race*, Garden City, Doubleday, 1948.

A. W. DAVIS, B. B. GARDNER, AND M. R. GARDNER, *Deep South*, Chicago, University of Chicago Press, 1941.

C. W. DE KIEWIET, *A History of South Africa, Social and Economic,* Oxford, Clarendon, 1941.

M. DEUTSCH AND M. E. COLLINS, *Interracial Housing: A Psychological Evaluation of a Social Experiment,* Minneapolis, University of Minnesota Press, 1951.

JOHN DOLLARD, *Caste and Class in a Southern Town,* New Haven, Yale University Press, 1937.

EUGENE P. DVORIN, *Racial Separation in South Africa,* Chicago, University of Chicago Press, 1952.

N. N. FRANKLIN, *Economics in South Africa,* Cape Town, Oxford University Press, 1954.

MOHANDAS K. GANDHI, *An Autobiography: The Story of my Experiences with Truth,* Washington, Public Affairs Press, 1954.

ELLEN HELLMANN, ed., *Handbook of Race Relations in South Africa,* Cape Town, Oxford University Press, 1949.

MURIEL HORRELL, *A Survey of Race Relations in South Africa,* Johannesburg (yearly).

MONICA HUNTER, *Reaction to Conquest,* London, Oxford University Press, 1936.

N. HURWITZ, *Agriculture in Natal, 1860–1950,* Cape Town, Oxford University Press, 1957.

H. KUPER, *Indian People in Natal,* Durban, Natal University Press, 1960.

H. KUPER, *The Uniform of Colour,* Johannesburg, Witwatersrand University Press, 1947.

LEO KUPER, unpublished paper delivered at the Natal Convention, April, 1960.

LEO KUPER, *Passive Resistance in South Africa,* London, Jonathan Cape, 1956.

LEO KUPER, "The Heightening of Racial Tension," *Race,* 2, 1960, pp. 24–32.

I. D. MAC CRONE, *Race Attitudes in South Africa,* London, Oxford University Press, 1937.

J. S. MARAIS, *The Cape Coloured People, 1652–1937,* London, Longmans, Green, 1939.

LEO MARQUARD, *The Peoples and Policies of South Africa,* London, Oxford University Press, 1960.

ADRIAN C. MAYER, *Peasants in the Pacific, A Study of Fiji Indian Rural Society*, London, Routledge and Kegan Paul, 1961.

PHILIP MAYER, *Townsmen or Tribesmen*, Cape Town, Oxford University Press, 1961.

GUNNAR MYRDAL, *An American Dilemma*, New York, Harper, 1944.

TALCOTT PARSONS, *The Social System*, Glencoe, Free Press, 1951.

ALAN PATON, *Too Late the Phalarope*, New York, Scribner, 1953.

SHEILA PATTERSON, *Colour and Culture in South Africa*, London, Routledge and Kegan Paul, 1953.

T. F. PETTIGREW, "Social Distance Attitudes of South African Students," *Social Forces*, 38, 1959, pp. 246–253.

B. RAMBIRITCH AND PIERRE L. VAN DEN BERGHE, "Caste in a Natal Hindu Community," *African Studies*, 20, No. 4, 1961.

B. G. M. SUNDKLER, *Bantu Prophets in South Africa*, London, Lutterworth Press, 1948.

MELVIN TUMIN, *Caste in a Peasant Society*, Princeton, Princeton University Press, 1952.

PIERRE L. VAN DEN BERGHE, "Apartheid, Fascism and the Golden Age," *Cahiers d'Etudes Africaines*, 8, 1962, pp. 598–608.

PIERRE L. VAN DEN BERGHE, "Distance Mechanisms of Social Control," *Sociology and Social Research*, 44, 1960, pp. 155–165.

PIERRE L. VAN DEN BERGHE, "Race Attitudes in Durban, South Africa," *Journal of Social Psychology*, 57, 1962, pp. 55–72.

PIERRE L. VAN DEN BERGHE, *The Dynamics of Race Relations, An Ideal-Type Case Study of South Africa*, Ph.D. Dissertation, Harvard University, 1959.

PIERRE L. VAN DEN BERGHE, "The Dynamics of Racial Prejudice: An Ideal-Type Dichotomy," *Social Forces*, 37, 1958, pp. 138–141.

PIERRE L. VAN DEN BERGHE AND EDNA MILLER, "Some Factors Affecting Social Relations in a Natal North Coast Community," *Race Relations Journal*, 28, No. 2, 1961, pp. 24–31.

CHARLES WAGLEY, *Amazon Town*, New York, Macmillan, 1953.

CHARLES WAGLEY, ed., *Race and Class in Rural Brazil*, Paris, UNESCO, 1952.

MAX WEBER, *The Theory of Social and Economic Organization*, New York, Oxford University Press, 1947.

JAMES WEST, *Plainville, U.S.A.*, New York, Columbia University Press, 1948.

D. M. WILNER, R. P. WALKLEY AND S. W. COOK, "Residential Proximity and Intergroup Relations in Public Housing Projects," *Journal of Social Issues*, 8, 1952, pp. 45–69.

C. A. WOODS, *The Indian Community of Natal*, Cape Town, Oxford University Press, 1954.

INDEX

Acculturation, 6, 33, 34, 35, 39–64, 91, 142, 152, 165, 167, 174–175, 179–180, 182–184, 187–188, 193–195, 210, 212–213, 220, 230, 242–247, 254–255, 258

African National Congress, 48, 57, 82, 107, 110, 255

Africans, 3, 9, 11, 20, 30, 193; administration of, 83–85, 109, 183, 191; attitudes of, 49–50, 52, 60, 70, 82, 84, 86, 106–110, 122, 142, 154, 182, 185, 195, 209, 214–217, 225; attitudes towards, 54, 88, 90, 143, 157, 199–200, 210, 212–213, 219–220, 236; cultural tradition of, 31, 46–56, 61–62; disabilities of, 4, 48–50, 52, 56, 64, 66–67, 107–111, 130, 136–137, 157, 188, 190–192, 205, 214; economic position of, 128, 133–136, 186–188, 192, 246–247; education among, 49, 61, 138, 145–146, 184, 191–192, 219, 230; ethnic divisions among, 30, 54–55, 181–182; leadership among, 110–111, 225; occupations of, 11, 16–17, 20, 21, 49, 79, 84, 90, 96, 129, 133, 135–136, 139–143, 164, 183, 187; on Town Council, 80, 82, 83, 248; religion among, 30, 49–52, 54, 59, 110, 185–186, 195, 206–207; residential segregation of, 27, 71,

75–76, 100, 198–201; social stratification among, 49–50, 54, 96, 107, 181–192; status of, 153; Westernization of, 6, 33, 48–54, 64, 152, 182–184, 187–188, 194, 212–213, 230, 242–246

Afrikaans, 30, 48, 227

Afrikaners, 3, 4, 33, 34, 35, 58, 66, 69, 70, 78, 202, 227; attitudes of, 69, 70, 229; attitudes towards, 69, 154, 160, 215

Age as status criterion, 193

Aggregation, 75, 100, 112–113, 159, 197–209, 239–240, 250

Albinocracy, 154, 181, 247

Alcoholism, *see* Drinking

Algeria, 248

Allport, Gordon W., ix, 100, 157, 237n

Ancestor worship, 30

Anglo-Boer War, 3

Anti-Semitism, 211, 220

Apartheid (*see also* Aggregation, Segregation) 22, 63, 69, 75, 112, 115, 117, 121, 147, 183, 197–209, 219, 239–240

Arabic, 32, 36, 37, 81

Architecture, 31, 85, 116

Aristans, 129, 137

Asians, *see* Indians

Asiatics, use of term, 28, 228

Assimilation, *see* Acculturation, Miscegenation

Atomization, political, 100–102, 121, 194
Attitudes:
class, 160–161, 168, 170; ethnic, 182; political, 93, 100–102, 104–116; racial, 6, 9, 35, 45, 49–50, 52, 54, 60, 61, 62, 69, 70, 73–77, 81–84, 86–88, 90, 106–108, 142–143, 153, 154, 157, 199–200, 209–225; religious, 167, 185–186, 197; sexual, 180, 186, 222–223
Augustus, 74
Automobiles, see Motorcars
Authority, see Power
Autocracy, 104–105, 112, 118–120, 194, 256

Baas, use of term, 143, 212, 213, 227, 231
Baasskap, 208
Bakery, 126, 128
Bantu (see also Africans), use of term, 28, 61, 82, 213, 228
Bantu Administration, 67
Bantu Consultative Council (BCC), 54, 81, 83–84, 86, 98, 109, 110, 232
Bantu Education, 51, 67, 84, 85, 98, 145, 191, 246, 247
Bantu School Board, 84, 98
Bantustans, 53, 183, 252
Barbershops, segregation in, 203
Beauty, concern for, 31, 77, 85, 114, 116
Beer, 48, 67, 84, 89, 125; illicit brewing of, 67, 110, 135, 140; municipal hall, 109–110, 125, 147
Benares, 178
Benedict, Burton, 6n
Benedict, Ruth, 243
Bhagavad Gita, 39, 172, 175
Bilharzia, 136
Blood donations, 178–179
Boer Republics, 248
Boers (see also Afrikaners), use of term, 215
Boer War, see Anglo-Boer War
Bourgeoisie, petty, 173–175

Boy, use of term, 212, 227, 230–231
Boycotts, 108, 233
Brahmin, 32, 172
Brazil, 6n
"Bread and circuses" device, 87–92
Bushmen, 188

Cambridge, 162
Cane, see Planters, Sugar
Cane cutters, 18, 54, 89, 97, 106, 108, 125–126, 139
Caneville:
climate of, 24; as company town, 6, 65, 123; heterogeneity of, 7, 10, 31, 54–55, 100, 153, 193–194; hinterland of, 25, 29; location of, 15; map of, 26; population of, 15; relation to South Africa, 4–6; topography of, 24–28
Caneville Centre, 27
Caneville Experiment, 66, 69, 71–73, 77, 93, 99, 100, 121, 122, 197, 248
Caneville River, 21, 198
Caneville Sugar Company (CSC) ix, 9, 10, 85, 144, 155, 205, 256; assets of, 123–124, 130; attitudes towards, 114–117, 121, 215, 218; connection with Town Council, 68, 69, 77, 80–81, 86, 115–116; employees of, 72, 75, 76, 78–79, 88–91, 108, 123–124, 127, 129, 139–143, 158, 160–161, 205, 225; hierarchy of, 78–79, 139–143; history of, 20–22; policies of, 10, 69–77, 85–100, 147–149, 155–156, 198–199, 201, 204, 207–208, 215–217, 239; position in industry, 19–20, 126, 146; power of, 19, 86, 91, 95, 98, 126–127, 180, 257; relations with central government, 69–72, 101–102n; shareholders of, 124; structure of, 78–79, 161
Cape of Good Hope, 3
Cape Town, 79n

Capital (*see also* Property) 17, 65, 89, 123–124, 128, 186, 247
Capitialism, 88
Cars, *see* Motorcars
Caste:
among Hindus, 38, 39, 40, 43, 45, 152, 191, 192–193, 245, 247, 257; racial, 43, 151–152, 154–155, 189, 192–194, 196, 245, 247, 255, 258
Cattle, 182
Central African Federation, *see* Rhodesia
Cetewayo, 32
Change, 6, 119, 158–159, 165, 179–180, 189, 241–253; cultural, 32, 63–64, 179, 241–245; economic, 21–23; in population, 28, 247; political, 104, 248
Chicken pox, 136
Chiefs, African, 51, 62, 67, 183, 192
Child labour, 140
Christ, 44, 167, 243
Christians, *see* Churches, Christian
Christmas, 155, 163, 167
Churches, Christian, 30, 33, 40, 43, 49, 51, 54, 56, 59, 60, 76, 98–99, 131, 167, 188, 195, 206, 242, 255; Anglican, 162, 185, 206; Catholic, 27, 32, 33, 35, 59, 99, 156, 164, 185, 206–207, 227; Dutch Reformed, 34, 164; Methodist, 164, 185, 206; Presbyterian 185; Protestant, 27, 30, 33; Separatist, 52, 60; Zionist, 49, 53, 59, 185
Cinema, 90, 201–202, 236
Civil Servants, 34, 133, 160, 234–235, 258
Class, social, 27, 42, 44, 49, 50, 54, 58, 151–152, 155–165, 173–192; of informants, 11–12
Climate, 15, 24, 37, 54
Clubs, *see* Voluntary organizations
Colby, B. N., 6n
Collins, M. E., 198n
Colonialism, 194, 245
Coloureds, 4, 28, 29, 33, 35, 45, 47, 53, 56, 60, 128, 152, 153, 156, 165, 187–189, 195, 204, 209, 221
Colour-bar, *see* Segregation
Commensality, 166, 171, 223–224
Commerce, 25, 128–219, 203–204
Commonwealth of Nations, 4, 22–23
Commonwealth Sugar Agreement, 23
Communication, rupture of, 107, 209, 225–226, 237, 258
Communism, 73, 99, 213, 225n, 251
Competition, racial, 122
Complaints, 107–109, 113–116
Concubinage, 40, 47, 166, 183, 221–223
Congo (Léopoldville), 122, 249
Congress Alliance, 101n
Congress of Democrats, 225n
Consciousness, political, 106, 110–112, 116, 175, 180, 250
Consensus, 152–153, 161, 243-246
Conservatism (*see also* Traditionalism), 110, 111, 117, 162, 174, 176, 183, 218, 242
Consultation, government by, 79, 93, 119, 208, 225, 251
Consumption, conspicuous, 177–178
Contact:
between racial groups, 47, 48, 155, 157, 196, 197, 200–202, 206–207, 217, 220, 221–239; between religious groups, 166–167; law of, 237
"Control of potential opposition" device, 87, 96–99
Conversion, religious, 39, 40, 43, 47, 166, 167
Cook, S. W., 198n
Cooking (*see also* Diet), 42, 45
Coolie, use of term, 86, 139, 210, 211, 227, 235
Co-optation, 87, 94–96, 119
Courtesy titles, *see* Titles
Cox, O. C., 152
Craftsmen, *see* Artisans
Creoles, *see* Mauritians
Cultural pride, 45–46, 52, 58, 255

Cultural shame, 52–53, 58, 59, 182, 183, 255

Culture, 32, 50; African, 31, 32, 46–56, 57, 61–62; European, 31, 32–35, 43, 44, 48, 50, 52, 53, 57, 59, 60, 61; Indian, 31, 35–46, 50, 51, 57

Dancing, 12, 89–90, 179–180, 202, 212, 223, 243

Davis, A. W., 5n

Deception, use of, 232–233

Democracy, 73–74, 100–101, 104–105, 113, 122, 213, 245, 256

Despotism, benevolent, 85–86, 88, 98, 119–122, 194, 204

Detribalization, see Acculturation

Deutsch, M., 198n

Diet, 36, 38, 46, 49, 53, 88, 89, 134, 136, 166, 205, 224

Discrimination:
  racial, 8, 12, 35, 41, 49, 56, 59, 60, 69, 83, 86, 96, 97, 107, 112, 115, 116, 120, 136–149, 153–157, 165, 190–192, 197–209, 237–240, 255–259; sexual, 41, 42

Diseases (see also Health), 136

Disequilibrium, 252–253, 258

Dishonesty, 216–217, 226

Divide et impera, 100

Divine Life Society, 39, 43, 118, 171, 172, 243

Diwali, 38

Dogs, use of, 161

Dollard, John, 5n, 151, 193

Donations, 178–179

Dress, style of, 31, 37, 42, 48, 49, 50, 53, 54, 177–178, 184–186

Drinking, 36, 38–39, 48, 67, 70, 109–110, 155, 159–160, 204–205

Dual standard, racial, 86, 106, 157

Dube Village, 27, 47, 48, 55, 56, 67, 70, 76, 83, 84, 98, 108, 109, 128, 133, 182–185, 187, 198–201, 203, 206–207, 217

Du Plessis, Dr. Peter, 72, 85, 165

Durban, 10, 15, 20, 29, 55, 68, 107, 112, 117, 127, 146, 156, 158, 162, 189, 197n, 207, 210, 219

Durkheim, Emile, 63

Dutch (see also Afrikaners), use of term, 215

Dynamics, social, see Change

Easter, 163

Eastern Cape, 53

Economics, 65, 76, 77, 123–150

Education (see also Schools), 40–42, 49, 54, 58, 61, 70, 90, 112, 138, 144–146, 158, 162, 173, 176, 184–185, 188–192, 195–196, 219, 230, 247

Elections, see Franchise

Elizabeth, Queen, 77

Emergency, state of, 106n

Employment, see Occupations

Endogamy, 38, 40, 151, 168, 170, 172, 177, 221

English, 3, 33, 35, 58, 63, 65, 68, 69, 73, 78, 79, 124, 154, 156, 158, 160, 161, 165, 256; attitudes of, 69, 154; attitudes towards, 69, 215, 219; use of language, 9, 11, 30, 32, 39, 41, 42, 45, 48, 49, 50, 54, 56, 69, 81, 173, 175, 177, 179, 184–185, 227, 229, 243

Entertainment (see also Sports), 89–92, 155, 159, 164, 201–202

Equilibrium, 252–253, 258

Ethnocentrism, 210

Etiquette, 163; racial, 6, 9, 83, 84, 88, 91, 107, 109, 116, 155, 197, 208, 223, 226–234; table, 45, 223

Europe, 162

Europeans, see Whites

Exports, sugar, 23

Extended family, see Family, Kinship

Factory, sugar, 17, 20–21, 78, 125, 140, 204

Fairwind, 28, 71–72, 113, 117, 199

Family, 7, 64, 193; African, 133–135, 182–183, 187; extended, 64, 135, 183; Indian, 29, 42–43,

135, 174, 187; nuclear, 64, 183; patrilineal, 183; patriolocal, 135, 183; polygyny, 182–183; White, 29, 155
"Family affair" device, 87, 92–94
Fanagalo, 46, 215, 229, 236
Farmers, 16–17, 97, 123, 126, 129, 132, 155, 174–175
Fear, role of, 219, 225, 236
Feudalism, 115, 122
Field notes, 11
Field sections, 21, 25, 89, 198
Field workers, see Cane cutters
Fiji, 6n
Fires, cane, 23
Fluctuations, economic, 22–23, 24, 124–126
Franchise, 34n, 66, 74, 76, 80, 83, 84, 101, 105, 109, 208, 216
Freedom: restrictions on, 66–67; struggle for, 220, 242
French (see also Mauritians), 21, 30, 33, 34, 35, 62, 73, 156
Friendly Women's Guild, 179, 206
Functionalism, 244
Funerals, 38, 166
Furniture, 162–164, 174–177, 187, 205

Gandhi, Mahatma, 21, 57, 96, 108, 178, 242, 255
Gardner, B. B. and M. R., 5n
"Gentlemen's agreement," 18, 127, 140
German, 34
Gonorrhea, 136
Goshalia, B. L., 81, 102n, 112, 117, 126, 130, 133, 235
Government: central, see South African Government; municipal, see Township; provincial, see Natal, Province of
Great Britain, 3–4, 16, 34n, 47, 63, 124, 162
Great Trek, 165
Greeks, 126

Grievances, see Complaints
Group Areas, 70, 71, 72, 112, 114, 191, 198, 199
Guilt, feelings of, 157, 239
Gujarati, 30, 37, 39, 40, 44, 128, 168–170

Habsburg, 77
Hadj, 176–177
Hadji, 177
Hancock, Roger, 69, 78, 81, 82, 95, 116, 229, 235
Happy Girls Club, 179–180
Health, 18, 20–22, 67, 81, 85, 88, 116, 135, 136, 143, 187
Health Clinic, 27, 205
Health Committee, 80
"Herrenvolk egalitarianism," 159–160
Heterogeneity of Caneville, 7, 10, 31, 35, 45, 54–55, 100, 153, 193–194
Hierarchy, see Stratification
High School, see Schools
Hindi, 30, 39, 47, 128, 168, 170–171
Hindus and Hinduism, 9, 30, 31, 32, 33, 36–46, 47, 51, 57, 58, 59, 75, 76, 81, 111, 118, 128, 130–131, 152, 165–177, 179, 191, 222, 242–243, 245, 255
Hindustani, see Hindi
Holleman, J. F., ix
Horrell, Muriel, 51n, 61n, 145n
Hospital, 28, 85, 143, 205
Hotels, 27, 128, 204
Hottentots, 188
Housing, 10, 21, 22, 27, 85, 89, 114, 127, 133, 134, 140, 142, 155, 161–164, 174–177, 183; racial inequalities in, 18, 86, 143; segregation in, 71–72, 75–76, 108, 112–113, 198–201
Huguenots, 34
Humour, 38, 212, 231–233
Hurley, Archbishop, 207
Hurwitz, N., 17n
Hygiene, see Health
Hypergamy, 168

Illegitimacy, 186
Illiteracy, *see* Literacy
Imam, 32, 36, 118, 169
Immorality Act, 221–223
Income (*see also* Wages), 18, 133–142
Indenture of Indians, 18, 20, 21, 33, 173
India, Republic of, 45, 46, 170, 171, 211
Indian Ocean, 15
Indian Taxpayers' Association, 99, 101–104, 117
Indians, 4, 9, 25, 193; arrival of, 20, 33, 227; attitudes of, 81, 111–117, 154, 167, 209, 218–221, 225, 236; attitudes towards, 73, 142, 143, 157, 210–212, 216–217; caste and *varna* among, 171–172, 177, 191; cultural tradition of, 31, 35–46; disabilities of, 107, 112, 130, 136–137, 157, 190–192, 220; economic position of, 126, 128–132, 134–136, 140–143, 169–170, 174–178, 190, 192, 246–247; family among, 42–43, 174; leadership among, 116–119, 225; linguistic distinctions among, 30, 168–171; occupations of, 16–17, 20–21, 27, 41, 79, 84, 90, 96, 128, 129, 133, 135, 170, 175, 190, 216; on Town Council, 80–82, 248; population figures, 28–29; religion among, 30, 38–40, 44, 52, 166–168, 206; residential segregation of, 25, 27, 71–72, 75–76, 100, 198–201; riots against, 22, 163n, 216, 219–220; social class among, 27, 44, 58, 95, 96, 107, 165, 168, 169–170, 173–180, 189–192; status of, 154, 165; Westernization of, 6, 33, 40–46, 142, 152, 165, 167, 173–175, 179–180, 194, 242–246
Induna, 139
Industry, 4, 6, 15, 59, 96, 126–128, 146, 247, 249–250
Inequality, racial, 59, 73–74, 86–87, 130–143, 197–209, 240; economic, 17–18, 49, 86–87, 130–138, 139–143, 148, 246; in distribution of power, 19, 80–83, 121; in education, 144–146
"Influx control," 125, 246
Informants, 10–12
Intelligentsia, *see* Professionals, Teachers
Interaction, racial, *see* Contact
Intermarriage, *see* Marriage
Interviews, 9, 10, 11, 12, 210, 226, 233
Irrigation, 17
Islam, *see* Muslims

Jargon, use of, 13
Jews, 211, 216, 220
Jonesville, 153

Kaffir, use of term, 46, 86, 91, 106, 139, 143, 156, 210, 212–213, 227
Kaffir beer, *see* Beer
Kaffirboetie, 8
Kassim, Mohammed, 81, 95, 117
Khan, A. B., 95, 117
Khan, Dr. O. B., 81, 82, 95, 112, 117
Kinship (*see also* Family):
among Africans, 183; among Indians, 42, 167, 168
Kluckhohn, Clyde, 243
Kluckhohn, Florence, 243
Koran, *see* Qur'an
Krishna, 44, 243
Kshatriya, 172
Kuper, Hilda, ix, 6n, 50, 171n
Kuper, Leo, ix, 237

Labour inefficiency, 137–138, 147–148, 246, 257
Labour unions, *see* Trade unions
Land (*see also* Group Areas):
communal tenure of, 62; cultivation of, 16–17, 20–22; distribution of, 130–132; expropriation of, 117, 191; ownership of, 16–17, 92, 102–103, 113, 123, 130–132, 191; use of, 25, 71, 123, 130; value of, 113, 123
Langa, 22

Latin, 32
Leadership (*see also* Power), 99, 110–111, 116–119, 225
Liberal Party, 75, 216, 225
Liberalism, 8, 75, 80, 81, 105, 144, 206, 207, 223, 225, 227, 229, 248, 253
Liquor raids, *see* Drinking
Literacy, 11, 49, 50, 106, 173–174, 177, 179, 185, 188, 243
Lobola, 49, 62, 243
Local Government Ordinance, 68
"Location," *see* Dube Village
Loco Village, 28
London, 162
Lumpenbourgeoisie, 188

MacCrone, I. D., 6n, 210n
Machiavelli, 66, 87, 94, 250, 251, 256
Madras, 170
Madrasa, 36, 37
Madrassi, 170
Mahatma's Hill, 27
Mahatma Village, 27, 103
Maistry, 171
Malaria, 22, 85
Malfunctions, social, 146–149, 244–245, 251–253
Malnutrition, 136, 137
Margaret, Princess, 77
Marriage (*see also* Endogamy), 37, 38, 39, 47, 49, 66, 167, 169, 177, 186; between castes, 172; between language groups, 39, 168; between *varnas*, 172; cross-cousin, 168; inter-faith, 36, 40, 166; interracial, 221; parallel-cousin, 168
Marx, Karl, 65, 119, 138, 151, 251
Master-servant relationship, 226–228, 230–231, 233–234, 249
Mauritians, 6n, 21, 33, 34, 35, 56, 58, 78, 128, 155–158, 160, 189, 195, 198, 206–207, 221, 227, 232, 239
Mayer, A. C., 6n
Mayer, Philip, 53
Measles, 136
Mecca, 45

Memon, 30, 37, 128, 168–169
Merchants, 23, 44, 102n, 111, 116, 128–129, 133, 135, 166, 170, 173, 175–180, 190, 211, 217, 218, 220, 226, 236, 256
Messianism, 59
Methodology, 9–12
Mexico, 6n
Migrant workers, 9, 11–12, 18, 21, 29, 30, 48, 89, 125, 137, 139–140, 148, 183–184, 246
Mill, *see* Factory
Miller, Edna, ix, 8, 10, 36n, 166n
Miller, Richard, 81, 83, 86
Miscegenation, 157, 188, 189, 221–223
Mobility:
   geographic, 183; social, 158, 189–191
Mohammed, 168
Mohammedans, use of term, 228
Monoculture, 30, 126, 150
Morality, standards of, 180, 186, 196
Mortality, infant, 135, 187
Mosca, G., 151
Moslems, *see* Muslims
Mosques (*see also* Muslims), 27, 36, 118, 168, 169
Motorcars, 163, 164, 174, 175, 177, 187
Moving pictures, *see* Cinema
Mozambique, 30, 55, 181
Multi-racial societies, 6, 30
Municipality, *see* Township
Muslims, 30, 31, 33, 36–46, 47, 51, 56, 58, 75, 81, 111, 117, 118, 128, 130–131, 165–170, 173, 176, 177, 191, 193, 206, 221, 242–243, 255
Mvusi, Rev. Ambrose, 82, 84, 98, 107, 227
Myrdal, G., 151, 193

Names, use of, 163–164, 172, 227
Nao, 171
Natal:
   Colony of, 20, 227; Province of, 5, 15, 18, 21, 22, 29, 30, 32, 33,

41, 46, 66–68, 79, 144, 161, 165, 179, 219; University of, 196
Natal and Zululand Bantu Cane Growers' Association, 19
Natal Indian Cane Growers' Association, 19
Natal Indian Congress, 81, 99, 111, 117, 165, 178
Natal Indian Organization, 111, 165
Natal Sugar Millers' Association, 19
Nationalism, African, 53, 59, 214, 220
Nationalist Party, 4, 34, 53, 61, 63, 69, 70, 72, 75, 101–102n, 106, 113, 121, 147, 164, 165, 194, 204, 215, 218, 219, 247–248
"Native Administration," 62
"Native Law," 62
"Native location," *see* Dube Village
"Native Reserves," 125
Natives, use of term, 28, 55, 82, 88, 125, 162, 212–213, 228, 230–231, 234, 236, 237, 245, 250
Ndebele, 55, 181
Negroes, American, 53, 54, 152, 188, 196, 198n
New Year, 164, 179
Ngoma, 89
Ngubane, Julius, 82, 84, 98, 110
Nguni, 55
Nietzsche, 66
Nigger, use of term, 213, 227
Nkosi, 227
Non-Europeans, *see* Africans, Coloureds, Indians
Non-European Sugar Advisory Board, 19
Non-European Unity Movement, 111
Non-Whites, *see* Africans, Coloureds, Indians
Nuclear family, *see* Family, Kinship
Nyanja, 30
Nyasa, 55
Nyasaland, 181

Objectivity, problem of, 7–8
Observation, 12, 210
Occupations:
of Africans, 11, 16–17, 20, 21, 49, 79, 84, 90, 96, 129, 133, 135–136, 139–143, 164; of Indians, 16–17, 20–21, 27, 41, 79, 84, 90, 96, 128, 129, 133, 135, 164; of informants, 11; of Whites, 16–18, 34, 78–79, 129, 133, 155, 163; racial distribution of, 17–18, 27
Oligopoly, 17
Opposition, political, 22, 48, 59, 60, 66, 71, 92–96, 99–118, 120, 213, 218, 233, 258
Output restriction, 16, 125
Overproduction, 16, 23, 247
Over-reaction, 220
Oxford, 162, 196

Pagans, 185–186
Pakistan, 45, 46
Pan-African Congress, 110
Panchayat, 171
Parsons, Talcott, 152, 243
Pass laws, 56, 67, 107
"Passenger" Indians, 173
"Passing," 151, 154, 156, 189
Passive resistance, 21, 57
Paternalism, 6, 10, 66, 85, 88, 119–122, 209, 212, 213, 216, 230–231, 249–251, 255; attitudes towards, 106, 119–122, 231; implementation of, 94, 105, 204; limitations of, 121–122, 249
Paton, Alan, 222
Patrilocal family, *see* Family
Pensions, 87, 134, 136
Pettigrew, T. F., 6n, 210
Pietermaritzburg, 29
Pigmentation, *see* Skin colour
Planters, cane, 16–17, 97, 123, 126, 132, 155
Pluralism, 63, 64, 153, 194, 202, 242–245
Police, 10, 22, 27, 34, 66, 67, 70, 107, 110, 160, 202, 224, 234
Politics, *see* Opposition
Polygyny, *see* Family

Pondo, 18, 30, 31, 55, 88, 89, 108, 109, 110, 140, 142, 181–184, 233
Population:
 of Caneville, 15, 28–29, 130, 247, 254; of Natal, 29; of South Africa, 4, 29, 152, 225n
Portuguese, 62
Post Office, 27, 34, 66, 116, 133, 137, 160, 202, 208, 229, 235
Poverty, 133–136, 146, 173–174, 186–188, 224
Power, 65–122; centralization of, 19, 77–79; and leadership, 118–119; legitimation of, 66, 87, 119; monopoly of, 87; structure of CSC, 78–79; use of, 4, 6, 19, 87, 120; view of, 65–66, 87; and wealth, 65, 123
Prejudice, 237–240; class, 168, 170; ethnic, 182; racial, 12, 106–108, 153, 157–158, 194–195, 199, 209–221, 224, 257–259; religious, 167, 185–186
Presbyterians, see Churches
Prestige, see Status
Production, 15–16, 20–22, 23, 137, 246
Professionals, 116, 135, 173, 175–180, 190, 219, 220, 224, 236
Progressive Party, 34, 68, 75, 154, 162, 216, 225
Prohibition of Mixed Marriages Act, 221–222
Proletariat, see Workers
Property, 93; racial distribution of, 130–132; real estate, 22, 67, 92
Prostitution, 222
Protestants, see Churches
"Protestant Ethic," 177
Public opinion, 100–101, 104–105
Public Safety Act, 106n
Punctuality, 221
Punishment, corporal, 21, 139

Questionnaires, 10, 210
Qur'an, 36, 37

Race, 5, 29, 73–74, 76, 106, 152, 224; of Caneville population, 29; of informants, 11

Race relations, see Attitudes, Competition, racial, Contact, Discrimination, Etiquette, Prejudice, Segregation, Stereotypes
Racialism (see also Apartheid, Discrimination, Prejudice, Segregation, Stereotypes), 4, 5, 9, 12, 34, 43, 45, 53, 60, 62, 73–74, 76, 83, 86–87, 96, 99, 106, 127, 143–144, 153, 154, 162, 195, 202, 209–221, 238, 253, 255
Railways, 15, 20, 24, 27, 34, 66, 116, 129, 130, 137, 146, 160, 205
Rainfall, see Climate
Ramadan, 36, 37
Ramakrishna, 43–44, 243
Rambiritch, B., 44n, 166n, 171n
Recreation, 85, 107
"Red" Africans, 53
"Red King," 68n
Reference book, 107
Reference group, 35
Reinterpretation, 64
Religion (see also Churches, Hindus, Muslims), among Africans, 30, 49–52, 54, 59, 110, 185–186, 195, 206–207, 224; among Indians, 30, 36, 38–40, 44, 52, 166–168, 206, 224; among Whites, 30, 33, 52, 162–163, 195, 206–207; and acculturation, 44; conversion, 39, 40, 43, 47, 166, 167
Representation, 93, 98, 99, 109, 111, 114, 115, 117, 119, 225; sectional, 79–82, 95, 100
Respectability, 184–186, 195–196
Revivalism, 59, 62
Revolution, 104, 234, 239, 253, 258; French, 249, 255
Rhodesia, 16, 55, 124, 181
Rice mill, 126, 136
Riots, 22, 163n, 216, 219
Roads, 15, 25, 27, 28, 67, 113, 115, 116
Royal terminology, use of, 68n, 77

Saivists, 39
Sanathanists, 39

Sanitation, *see* Health
Sanskrit, 32
Scabies, 136
Scapegoating, 69, 216, 219, 258
"School" Africans, 53
School Committees, 84, 98, 117
Schools, 242; African, 27, 47, 49, 56, 67, 84, 90, 98, 102n, 138, 145–146, 191; Catholic, 27, 145; Indian, 27, 28, 37, 39, 40–41, 47, 72, 90, 102n, 113–114, 116, 117, 118, 134, 138, 144–145, 166, 176, 180, 190, 191, 221; White, 138, 144, 156
Secularization, 38, 60, 175
Segregation:
attitudes towards, 112–113, 143, 212; racial, 5, 25–28, 34n, 41, 45, 66, 69, 70–72, 75–76, 91, 99, 100, 109–110, 112, 115, 138, 143–146, 153, 155–156, 190–192, 197–209, 212, 217, 219, 221, 224, 237–240, 255–259; sexual, 37, 43; "voluntary," 71, 76, 113, 203, 207–208, 240
Servants, 76, 133, 142, 161, 164, 175, 198–199, 222, 227, 237
Sex ratio, 29
Sexual behaviour, 40, 47, 66, 157, 166, 180, 183, 186, 221–223
Shakespeare, 175
Sham, L. S., 99, 103, 111, 117, 227
Shangaan, 30, 55, 181, 183
Shares, sugar, 19, 22, 124
Sharpeville, 22
Sherwood, Donald, 66, 68, 69, 72–79, 85, 87, 101, 120, 124, 161, 163n, 205
Sherwood, Reginald, 68, 69, 77, 78, 81, 85, 88, 92, 96, 124, 138, 162, 164, 227, 229, 235
Sherwood, Ronald, 20, 85, 205
Sherwood, William, 20
Shops, 27, 102n, 128–129, 179, 203–204, 216, 226, 236
Sirdar, 44
Skin colour, 31, 45, 56, 107, 112, 138, 155, 169–170, 188, 195, 210, 218
Slums, *see* Housing

Smuts, Jan C., 68
Social class, *see* Class
Solidarity:
in-group, 58; of Muslims, 38; organic, 63
Sotho, 55, 181
South Africa, 5, 6, 120, 124, 133, 146, 151, 171, 191, 197, 202, 207, 211, 237, 249; loyalty to, 218; population of, 29; Republic of, 4, 15, 66, 100, 101–102n, 107, 108, 113; Union of, 3, 4, 15, 34, 66, 181
South Africa Act, 3
South African Cane Growers' Association, 19
South African Government, 22, 53, 61, 62, 63, 66, 67, 69–72, 96, 98, 106n, 144, 145, 147, 160, 173, 183, 192, 198, 215, 218, 233, 247, 257
South African Institute of Race Relations, 7
South African Sugar Association, 19
South African Sugar Yearbook, 16, 24
South West Africa, 4
Spanish, 62
Special Branch, *see* Police
Sports, 89–92, 97, 111, 161, 178, 216–217, 220; organizations, 97, 216; racial segregation in, 27–28, 72, 91–92, 143, 156, 198, 200–201
Standards of living, *see* Capital, Health, Inequality, economic, Malnutrition, Property, Poverty, Unemployment, Wealth
Stanger, 79n
Status, 150, 151–196; and acculturation, 44; and age, 193; ascription of, 6, 154, 180; criteria of, 38, 160–165, 173, 182, 184, 186, 193, 247; symbols of, 159, 162, 163, 194; of women, 37, 64
Stereotypes (*see also* Attitudes), 157, 237; ethnic, 182; racial, 142, 199, 210–218
Stock, *see* Shares

Stratification, social, 6, 12, 27, 37, 39, 42, 44, 46, 63–64, 73, 95, 96, 105, 132, 151–196, 202, 208–209, 247, 252, 257
Streets, see Roads
Strikes, 18, 21, 96, 101–102n, 108, 138, 246
Sucrose, 24
Sudra, 172, 191
Sugar barons, 20
Sugar belt, 15
Sugar cane, 15–17, 24
Sugar industry, 15–19, 146, 247
Sugar Industry Central Board, 19
Sugar production, 15–16, 20–22
Sugartown, 21, 27, 28, 137, 155, 156, 163, 198, 223–224
Sundkler, B. G. M., 49n, 52n
Sunni, 36
Surplus value, 138
Suppression of Communism Act, 106n
Swanepoel, Jan, 70, 83, 84, 91, 199, 205, 217, 229, 235
Swazi, 55
Swimming pool, 200–201

Tamil, 30, 39, 168, 170–171
Taxation, 48, 67, 80, 92, 99, 102–104, 109–110, 113, 130, 146
Teachers, 38, 49, 110–112, 116–117, 118, 121, 144–146, 170, 175, 180n, 187, 190, 191, 224, 233, 235
Technology, 57
Telephone, segregation in, 204
Telugu, 30, 39, 168, 170–171
Temperature, see Climate
Temples, Hindu (see also Hindus), 27, 28, 36, 39, 171
Titles, use of, 227–229
Toilets, segregation in, 203
Tonga, 55
Topography, 24–28
Town Council, ix, 67–68, 98; actions of, 103–104; attitudes towards, 93, 102, 104, 111, 113–116; establishment of, 79; meetings of, 82–83, 94; officials of, 86, 102n, 115, 129, 201, 225, 232; policies of, 69; powers of, 67–68, 85, 92; property of, 130; relations to central government, 68–72; relations to provincial administration, 68; representation on, 79–82, 93, 95, 110–112, 117, 248
Town Hall, 27, 102, 125, 203
Town Secretary, see Swanepoel
Township, 27; boundaries of, 24; government of, see Town Council; population of, 15, 28–29
Trade licences, 128, 129
Trade unions, 96–97, 149
Traditionalism, 58; among Africans, 53, 182, 183; among Indians, 37, 38, 41; among Whites, 61
Transkei, 30, 53, 55
Transportation, 15, 25, 146, 205
Travel, 162, 164, 177
Trekboer, 61
Tumin, Melvin, 5n

"Uncle Tom," 154
Unemployment, 23, 125, 134, 136
United Kingdom, see Great Britain
United Party, 34, 68, 69, 81, 106n, 112–113, 121, 162, 164, 215, 218
United States, 24, 31, 53, 54, 151–153, 187, 193, 195, 196, 198n, 237
Urbanization, 4, 6, 49, 64, 121, 182–184, 251
Urdu, 30, 36, 37, 39, 168–170

Vaisya, 172
Values, 48, 51, 60, 152, 243–246, 254, 258
Van den Berge, Pierre L., 6n, 36n, 44n, 121n, 166n, 171n, 197n, 210n, 248n
Varna, 39, 172
Verwoerd, H. F., 23, 233
Vicious circle, 237–240
Virilocal family, see Patrilocal family
Voluntary associations, 98, 106,

118, 143, 166, 171, 174, 178, 205–206
Voting, *see* Franchise

Wages (*see also* Income), 19, 20, 21, 97, 112, 114, 121, 126, 127, 133–142, 147–148, 175, 186–187, 246–247; minimum, 18, 139–140; racial differences in, 19, 106, 107, 133–142
Wagley, Charles, 6n
Walkley, R. P., 198n
Warner, W. Lloyd, 151, 153, 158, 193
Washington, Booker T., 82
Water supply, 23, 67, 115
Wealth, 123–150, 186, 190; distribution of, 130–132; relation to power, 65, 123
Weather, *see* Climate
Weber, Max, 65, 119, 123
Weltanschauung, see Values
Westernization, *see* Acculturation
West, James, 195
Whitehead, Thomas, 69, 72, 75, 76, 77–82, 84, 85, 86, 88, 92, 93, 95, 98, 103, 116, 118, 163n, 201, 223, 225, 227, 229, 235, 248
Whitehead Stadium, 92, 95, 97, 114, 178
Whites, 4, 9, 20, 188, 193; attitudes of, 9, 35, 45, 54, 61, 62, 69, 73–77, 86–87, 90–91, 105–106, 120, 127, 143–144, 154, 156–157, 188, 194–195, 199, 202, 206, 209–214, 219, 222–225, 229, 238, 250, 259; attitudes towards, 60, 108, 115, 116, 154, 209, 214–216, 218; cultural tradition of, 31, 32–35, 213, 242–245, 254; domination of, 33, 34n, 48, 52, 53, 58, 59, 60, 69, 80–81, 106, 116, 119, 121, 152, 154, 155, 181, 200, 218, 219, 234–

235, 247–248, 254, 256; economic position of, 130, 137–138, 140–143, 246–247, 256; linguistic distinctions among, 30, 52; occupations of, 16–18, 34, 78–79, 129, 133, 155, 163, 234–235; population figures, 28–29; privileges of, 4, 5, 18, 19, 46, 86, 91, 96, 106, 120, 138, 140–144, 147, 201, 209, 246; religion among, 30, 52, 162–163, 195, 206–207; residential segregation of, 27, 71–72; social class among, 96, 105, 155–165, 189, 227–228; status of, 154; on Town Council, 80–83
Whooping cough, 136
Wilner, D. M., 198n
Women:
as workers, 140; education of, 175–177, 243; emancipation of, 223, 243; role of, 106, 112, 179–180, 243; status of, 193
Woods, C. A., 18n
Woods, Dr. L., 81
Workers (*see also* Migrant workers), 17, 23, 29, 54, 134, 139–142, 158, 170, 173–174, 190, 220, 228, 232, 250
World War II, 246

Xhosa, 9, 30, 46, 54, 80, 181

Yankee City, 153

Zanzibaree, 47, 49, 56, 206, 221
Zionist sects, *see* Churches
Zoning, 67, 75
Zulu, 9, 11, 18, 22, 30, 32, 46, 47, 54, 55, 56, 62, 68, 80, 90, 181–182, 206, 215, 219, 221, 227, 229–230
Zululand, 15, 53
Zululand Railway, 15, 20, 24